"This elegant and timely, even prophetic word to the end time church is a book on spiritual renewal. Yet it is more than that. Mahler writes brilliantly on the need to be a true disciple of Jesus. Taking illustrations from history, the Bible and modern life Mahler outlines a case for spiritual disciplines that will mark a revived church in a secular age. Jesus said in Mathew 6:18, 'seek first the Kingdom of God and all these things will be added to you'. For Mahler this seeking of the Kingdom is to be found in knowing, following, and obeying Jesus Christ. May God use this book to renew His bride in these challenging times."

Dr. Willem Fietje
President of the Associated Gospel Churches of Canada

Drawing on his personal and pastoral experience, Ron Mahler, in *The Necessary Christian* gives an urgent appeal for the need for authentic spiritual renewal. The reader will be reminded that such a need exists not just "out there", i.e. in the world, but especially "in here", i.e. in the church, if the church is going to be the church and regain its voice to a world and culture that has lost its way. Ron writes, "...in order for true revival and spiritual renewal to take place, in the church, the need for it must first, be realized; secondly, the need must also become a full-blown desire." May the Spirit of God use the message of this book to create an unquenchable thirst in His people and His church that impacts our world for God's glory.

Dan Degeer
President, Kawartha Lakes Bible College

Bev,
Thank you for your support.

Revive & Renew

2016

THE NECESSARY
Christian

An End-Time World is Dying for a Resuscitated Church

RON MAHLER

THE NECESSARY CHRISTIAN
Copyright © 2013 by Ron Mahler

All rights reserved. Neither this publication nor any part of this publication may be reproduced or transmitted in any form or by any means, electronic or mechanical, including photocopying, recording or any information storage and retrieval system, without permission in writing from the author.

All Scriptures unless otherwise indicated is taken from the Holy Bible, New International Version®, NIV®. Copyright © 1973, 1978, 1984, 2011 by Biblica, Inc.™ Used by permission of Zondervan. All rights reserved worldwide. www.zondervan.com. The "NIV" and "New International Version" are trademarks registered in the United States Patent and Trademark Office by Biblica, Inc.™ • Scripture quotations marked (NKJV) or "New King James Version" are taken from the New King James Version / Thomas nelson Publishers, Nashville: Thomas Nelson Publishers, Copyright ©1982. Used by permission. All rights reserved. • Scripture quotations marked (NLT) are taken from the Holy Bible, New Living Translation, copyright © 1996, 2004, 2007 by Tyndale House Foundation. Used by permission of Tyndale House Publishers, Inc., Carol Stream, Illinois 60188. All rights reserved. • Scripture quotations marked (MSG) are taken from The Message. Copyright © 1993, 1994, 1995, 1996, 2000, 2001, 2002. Used by permission of NavPress Publishing Group.

ISBN: 978-1-77069-808-6

Printed in Canada

Word Alive Press
131 Cordite Road, Winnipeg, MB R3W 1S1
www.wordalivepress.ca

Cataloguing in Publication information may be obtained through Library and Archives Canada

To John G. Thank you for caring.

The United Nations' Population Fund estimates that there are now **seven billion** people living on this earth.

Roughly 5 billion of them do not know Jesus Christ as their Saviour.

Many of the 2.1 billion professing Christians in the world no longer identify with Jesus' Kingdom values and redemptive agenda.

"The society or culture which has lost its spiritual roots is a dying culture, however prosperous it may appear externally."
Christopher Dawson, 1933

"revive (v): come or bring back to consciousness, life, or strength; come or to bring back to existence."

"renew (v): make new again; restore to the original state; reinforce; resupply; replace; resume after an interruption"

The Oxford Dictionary of Current English (Oxford University Press, 1992), 779, 767.

Contents

O Church, Where Art Thou? (A Poem) — x
Acknowledgements — xi
Introduction: Is Revival in the Church Necessary? — xiii

1: It's a Mad, Bad, Sad World After All — 1
2: Between the Coffee Counter and the Old Church Doors — 11
3: Of Wayward, Waffling, and Wishy-Washy Saints — 21
4: Grossly Gaunt Believers and the Famine of the Word — 33
5: The Stained Glass Scandal of the City on the Hill — 45
6: Deceived and Ornery Sheep Begin to Divide the Fold — 53
7: Just Give Me 2 Chronicles 7:14 or Bust! — 61
8: Be Afraid, Be Very Afraid; It's God We're Talking About! — 73
9: Moving Mountains and Erecting Monuments in Their Secret Place — 85
10: Brokenness Looked in the Mirror and Saw Authenticity — 99
11: I Believe in the Merits of Dead-Again Christianity — 109
12: Biblical Arguments for the Consumption of Humble Pie — 123
13: When Heaven's Runaways Return Home: Malachi's Message — 137
14: Christians Open the Gospels Only to Find "Help" Wanted — 149
15: Everybody Wants to Rule the World, But Only One Can Change It — 165
16: Why Don't They Want My Jesus or My Christianity? — 175
17: Ode to the Task of Shiny, Happy "Good News" People — 185
18: Muted Disciples and the Screaming Social Menagerie — 199
19: Tiny Seeds Are All We Need: Becoming Beacons of Ministry — 215
20: Catching the Church Acting Like They're Already in Heaven — 229
21: Finishing the Devil's Powerful Sermon on Suffering: The Ballad of Job — 241
22: Terminal Lifers and Those on the Edge of Eternity — 255

Endnotes — 267
Also by Ron Mahler — 273
About the Author — 275

O Church, Where Art Thou?
Ron Mahler

O Church, Where Art Thou?
When darkness presses down like a cement canopy,
The devil's black umbrella bullying our necessary light

When worldly hope has slipped into a cloak of invisibility,
Blinded to its welcome and power to achieve

When weighty, sinking hearts beat as with a limp,
Their plummet, slick, and with much momentum

When trials buy shares in the company of souls,
Profiting from their weakness, projecting maladies

When no answer is worthy of its desperate breath,
Ears remain in want without pronouncements of grace

When creation prances about in feathery, proud indifference
Fearless and carefree believing in many more tomorrows
O Church, Where Art Thou?

Acknowledgements

I'd be remiss if I didn't mention how my wife, Elaine, and our kids had to endure seeing me in a catatonic-like state in front of my laptop for hours that became days, then weeks, months, and eventually an entire year while I worked on this book. Thank you for not only allowing me to pursue my dreams but for your patience and cheerleading!

I couldn't love you more!

Thanks and love to my mom and to each of my supportive siblings as well.

INTRODUCTION

Is Revival in the Church Necessary?

Revival in the Church! Has the overused yet underappreciated term rendered the actual event of revival overrated? Have we reached the point where we are beyond the hope of seeing revivals and spiritual renewal sweep through churches across the globe? Have we become too spiritually acclimatized in the Church to a mediocre faith and a low expectation of the power of God? *Good questions,* you say? I'm just getting started!

The very mention of the word *revival* can stir up a tornado's worth of emotions and prejudices, not only within the Church but outside its walls as well. Mention the word *revival* to your closest religious skeptic, and you may very well pay for it in coins of ridicule, for months!

Not every Christian, for that matter, does a "happy dance" when the topics of revivalism and renewal movements are being discussed. There are those amongst God's people today who feel revival is not even a specific biblical idea; we don't need it, should quit talking about it, and should cease from praying for it! In fact, many genuine and well-intentioned Christians believe the only thing we as Christians can count on happening is a great turning away from the faith amongst those who claim to be in the Church camp. I can certainly see how the Bible points to that reality. Still, how should we, as Bible-believing people, today, interpret the supernatural occurrences that have come upon God's people, not only in history but in the present day, as they've prayed for what we call *revival* and its spiritual first cousin, *renewal?* I find this reality too interesting to ignore.

How should we understand this controversial topic of revival? Should we see the event of revival as a periodic experience in the life of the Church? Or is revival something that can be experienced individually (as well as corporately) and on an ongoing basis? Are revival and renewal two different spiritual animals? Can we even scrum together a proper biblical interpretation of what it means to be revived, not to mention renewed in our faith, as Christians in the Body of Christ? How can we, as individual Christians and the Church as a whole, even know if we have been revived? Are we going to witness an unprecedented outpouring of the Spirit on earth in the form of a spiritually restorative revival as we get closer to the Rapture of the Church?

The subject of revival has been argued from many different theological spectrums and biblical perspectives throughout the history of the Church. What is absolutely clear is that everyone seems to have their own opinions on the matter. I am one of them! From my vantage point, history has shown us two things about God's people, one being that we are capable of exhibiting the most incredible kinds of good known to the human race, the other that we're capable of exhibiting the most incredible kinds of wicked behaviour known to the human race.

Throughout the history of the world, more wars than we can count have been started and much bloodshed justified in the Name of God. Cracking the pages of any book on the history of Christianity and reading through it can be quite a depressing exercise. It's not hard to see how often the Church has failed to live up to its glorious calling and commission, choosing instead to embrace division and scandal, while kidnapping the Name of Jesus and dragging it into ill-repute. How many times, for that matter, did a privileged and blessed Israel fall away from the Lord, only to bow to and serve pagan gods of nonexistence?

It is not my intention in the pages ahead to provide biblical proof that we need revival in the Church today. Though God invites His people (indeed the world) to turn to Him in order for their lives to be revived and spiritually renewed, the fallen nature of humanity provides ample enough evidence that we *need* to be constantly resuscitated in the vitality of our faith. Even as a redeemed people, we Christians remain creatures of our bad spiritual habits. We are not learning as well as we could be from the history of our ethical shortcomings and moral failures.

Various people upon returning from visiting Christian churches all over the world have shared some jarring observations. Their findings uncover and expose a glaring deficiency within God's people. Though the gospel is reaching more people than ever before, the common spiritual denominator many esteemed church leaders, especially, have come to agree on is how lacking the worldwide Christian Church is in spiritual maturity. The seemingly mercurial spirituality in the Church of Jesus Christ that still exists today was described by the late Christian statesman John Stott as "sixteen million miles wide, and about a sixteenth of an inch thick."[1]

In light of such findings, it's interesting that there are those in the Church today who are adamant that "revivalism" isn't as biblical an idea as we might think, and neither are its spiritual merits necessary in the Church. The next paragraph shares that exact perspective.

> Do we need revival? No! We need transformation. And this transformation cannot be achieved by "weeping and wailing" before God (as the revivalists would have us do), brought on by some "unusual" outpouring of the Spirit. The transformation that the Bible talks about is the *continual* sanctification through the Word and the power of the Spirit (Rom. 12:1, 2; Phil. 1:6; 2:12, 13; 3:20, 21). Transformation is the product of our prayers for the courage and the grace of the Holy Spirit; standing fast with the Word in battle; not wavering, not compromising, not being overcome with fear, but steadfast in the cause of the truth— TRUTH—a word foreign to most of the revival movement, both past and present.[2]

Let me state first that I am in absolute agreement with this view, in terms of how it cites the need each Christian has to be continuously transformed by the truth of God's Word and by the power of the Holy Spirit. However, I am resolute in my belief that God's people *can* benefit from the periodic outpourings and "unusual" workings of the Holy Spirit as He manifests His power through us. By this I do not mean some heightened form of spiritual ecstasy as a singular momentary "experience," though I have seen this sort of event happen and have talked to believers who've felt "blessed" by such an encounter with the Spirit of God.

That said, what I refer to as revival and spiritual renewal is something so spiritually practical in the life of a Christian that it should be sought after as a *way of life*. Who amongst God's people could deny their constant need of being enabled anew in the spiritual disciplines and in the fervency of their faith? What Bible-believing Christian could argue against praying for God to arrest their depleted zeal to mourn for the souls of the spiritually lost, for Him to recharge their burden to pursue the Great Commission more consistently? Such desires can be revived, even if it takes a season of earnestly seeking God in prayer for it to happen. Prayers of longing that have been stewing in the fire of God's empowering Spirit can result in the most amazing amounts of spiritual fruit in the lives of God's people. This is what revival and renewal is all about!

If revivalism in one form or another is unbiblical, as some say, how do we explain the Spirit of God powerfully moving through the burdened prayers of Christians throughout the world, causing mass conversions and spiritual renewal within churches and denominations? In such cases, has God not revived or renewed something or someone?

In 1936 the fires of a revival spread throughout the campus of Wheaton College, just west of Chicago. A senior student named Don Hillis rose up in a chapel to voice a plea for revival. The students present promptly responded with an all-day prayer meeting. As a result, faculty and students confessed sins and reconciled with one another.

The Wheaton campus was once again touched by the Spirit of God some seven years later. On the heels of a message on confession of sin, the captain of the cross-country team stood up and openly confessed that he had violated college policy by leading his team in a Sunday race. Furthermore, such vices as pride, criticism, and cheating were confessed by other students present.[3]

God is a practical God, and so why shouldn't revival and spiritual renewal in the lives of Christians be practical as well? We don't have to see "revival" in terms of the traditional tent-meeting-like spectacle where the rising sound of old-time hymns carries through the muggy summer-night air, where sweaty preachers holler and convicted people slobber!

God does, however, respond in powerfully reviving ways whenever His people *are* in the position of being wholly surrendered to Him. Throughout history, it was when the Church had sunk low in the depths of its disobedience and fading and shrivelled up congregations were close to folding that desperate Christians cried out for God's mercy and grace and for the outpourings of the Spirit to revive and renew them.

Again, I certainly do not confuse true revivalism with so-called "outward manifestations" of the Holy Spirit that seem to come upon God's people to the point where they get caught up in all sorts of disorderly and audibly bizarre behaviour. Though God does work at times outside the limiting "box" of our spiritual conceptions and understandings, some of what people associate with revivals is without a doubt *biblically* suspect. Furthermore, I certainly do not prescribe to the belief that "revivalist preachers" are always needed to bring Christians closer to the brink of revival and unbelievers to the point of salvation.

Though there are people whom God specifically gifts to minister in certain situations, "everyday" believers themselves can seek to be revived and renewed in their own lives as often as necessary (as a way of living the Christian life). This happens through the persistent reading of God's Word, humble, transparent prayer, and an unmovable resolve to live a more scripturally attuned and godly life.

The problem is that we have a sinful nature that can drain the reserve of our spiritual gas tanks. There are corridors of time when we feel we have suddenly entered a "dry" zone in our spirituality. A season of doubt has set in around us; an unmovable crisis of faith has parked itself beside us and won't move; a squeezing discouragement seems to be shrink-wrapped around us. There are just times when we feel we're losing steam in our service to God and when the joy of our faith and salvation have been rudely hijacked.

Just as repentance is to be a constant feature of our redeemed lives, so too, as a people who are being made into the likeness of Christ, we need to continuously ask God to revive and renew our battered, worn-down faith and underfed spiritual lives. There are cobwebs in the *house* of God and dusting that needs to be done on the devotional lives of the *people* of God!

As you read along, it is my prayer that you will be challenged to seek an ongoing personal revival in your own life as a Christian. Or, if you doubt where you stand with God or can't say with certainty that you are a follower of Christ, my prayer is that you'll be moved to explore more deeply who Jesus is and discover the extent to which He went in order to demonstrate His love for you, a love that speaks of the great plan He has for your life and mine, both now and in eternity!

God loves His Church, and despite our periodic (for some, frequent) feelings of spiritual aridness and emptiness, He wills to revive us as often as necessary, for Christians and the Church of Jesus Christ are very necessary! This is great news for us in light of the world we live in and are called to redeem, a world that's getting more mad, bad, and sad by the minute. As we continue to journey through these end-times and last days, and as we prepare for Jesus' coming again to this earth, revivals and renewals of our faith (not the implementation of the latest mega-church sanctioned curriculum or the newest and hottest outreach angle) will be priority *numero uno* in the Church!

CHAPTER 1

IT'S A MAD, BAD, SAD WORLD AFTER ALL

According to the scientific community, physicists are a step closer to finding the Higgs boson, which they hope will explain the existence of mass in the universe. Nobel Prize–winning physicist Leon Lederman nicknamed it "The God Particle," because it is "so central to the state of physics today, so crucial to our final understanding of the structure of matter, yet so elusive."[4]

Those who have been working on smashing atoms in laboratories have found that the planet we live on is based on the science of electromagnetism. Items such as iPads, cameras, and televisions depend on electromagnetism as well, and by extension so does our society. Scientists are trying to break down matter to the point where they can pinpoint one specific subatomic particle, to see if it can explain why most elementary particles in the universe have mass.

I don't know about you, but I find such news to be thoroughly fascinating, on both a personal and spiritual level. What should such endeavours on the part of scientists tell us about our quest as a human race in general? I believe that, above anything else, when we peel away surface layers of human challenge and achievement, underneath we will find a deep yearning to pursue our Creator. We want to find out if our planet and the human race were, indeed, set in motion by some intelligent, determinative, creative force. In short, *does God really exist?*

Despite the fact that there's been a great turning away from the *idea* of God, the world unconsciously seeks Him out. This is where the Church of Jesus Christ must stand up and be counted upon to not only affirm the existence of God, but reflect back *to* the world something of His divine will and eternal purposes.

Some would say that it's tragic and not the least bit ironic, that as many in the world are looking for God, a great percentage of us who are Christians are missing in action when it comes to our faithfulness to evangelize. Just like the prophet Jonah, who lay sleeping in a boat of resistance to God's call on his life, we curl up in our own bunks of indifference, hiding from our calling.

Sometimes it's a case of the Church being too caught up in its traditions, divisions, and complacency to realize its need to wake up and put its hands back on the mission plow, the life-and-death commission Jesus handed over to us in the Gospels (see Matthew 28:18–20).

As Christians we are in a very real spiritual battle for the eternal souls of mankind. It's a battlefield, swelling by the hour with the potential of millions of added casualties. When will God announce, "Enough is enough" and put an end to this present age? In the meantime we are called to be spiritually armed and ready soldiers of the faith, willing to engage our enemy (Satan) in the "good fight" (2 Timothy 4:7).

As Jesus' return to this world draws nigh, our evil opponent isn't letting up on any spiritual front. As the clock of our present age ticks closer to the commensuration and fruition of Armageddon, the devil will only intensify his attack against Christians. The souls of billions of people whom God created for Himself remain in a position of rebellion towards Him, and the gospel bids us to march into the spiritual war of our world. Our objective as an army of God is clear: spread Kingdom truth and rescue the spiritually lost, just as Jesus did.

On this note, convicting questions confront Bible-believing Christians. As individual disciples, are we even aligned with Jesus' Kingdom values? Are we as the Church of Jesus Christ really identifying with our Lord's redemptive agenda? Are we pursuing the spiritually lost as much as we should? Or have we settled for a Christianity free of the expectations of basic training (discipleship), participation in spiritual warfare and strategic operations (missions)?

Each of us must seek the renewal of our own "Private Christian." We need to be awakened, to rise and shine for Jesus with our spiritual battle armour in place. We need to hunker down in resolve and be willing to count the cost of wearing Heaven's uniform in a realm where our enemy deceives those we need to free.

Sadly, there is still too much superficial religiosity in God's house today. We need to dig deep and make tough but necessary inquiries of ourselves, inquiries that ask, for instance, Where is the attracting quality and visible effectiveness of our faith and spirituality today? Do we believe that the commission Jesus Christ gave us is so great that we allow it to regulate our daily priorities? Our goal as

Christians should be to consistently live as Jesus' shining stars so our glow of righteousness will be unstoppable in its spread into the darkening and dangerous world we inhabit. In this late hour of our existence as a fallen human race, the Church should be turning on its spiritual afterburners and with blazing intent be impacting and penetrating its sin-thickened culture much more than what it is.

We know *where* to find most Christians on a given Sunday morning. Church services all over the world are loaded with multimillions of people who claim to be followers of Jesus Christ. The Christian Church, as a religious institution, has the largest membership of any organization around in the world today.

The reality, however, is that the number of people who belong to a certain movement shouldn't count as a reliable litmus test for how effective that movement actually is. Churches lose an estimated 2,765,000 people each year to nominalism and secularism.[5] Though millions of people (Protestants and Roman Catholics) on a global scale are said to be a part of the universal Church of Jesus Christ, many of them are not living as cost-counting disciples or identifying with the Lord's priorities and values of spiritual transformation, mission, and service. With more and more congregations rapidly aging, shrinking, and even closing, one wonders where the voices of righteousness and faith are going to come from in the next few decades.

There is a difference between Christians merely being *in* church, or *belonging* to a certain church, and actually *being* the Church, a difference between verbalizing that you are "Christian" and actually living *as* Christ would have you live.

Like many other believers, I am often tempted to be critical of the very family of God I am a part of. In due fairness to all Bible-believing Christians, living in this gloomy, morally spiralling, spiritually decaying time can be terribly difficult. In fact, living in an ever-changing and increasingly secularized society makes it all the more daunting for God's people to take a stand for biblical truth, even though it is as important as ever that we do.

As I collected research and resources for this book, its theme and direction became clear. God has put within my heart a prayerful and reflective concern for where I am as an individual Christ follower on the spiritual track of the race that is the Christian life. Like many Christians, I am also burdened for where the Body of Christ is today in the viability of its testimony and spiritual influence in the world.

As a redeemed people we are called on by Christ to be flaming bright torches of eternal hope that soar like spears penetrating a world dying for our redemptive light. All Christians, no matter where they live on this earth, have a unique context for living out their faith. Each believer must periodically assess how he or she is doing on that front, a spiritual physical, we might call it, that checks how effectively he or she is impacting his or her specific context for the glory of God.

A politician, not too long ago, claimed that the twenty-first century will be one of human prosperity and peace, that somehow we will rise above our mistakes of the past and realize our potential as people. I wouldn't bet on that! The Bible says that the trend in our spiritual and moral standards in the last days will be on a *downward* slope, not an upward one.

Let's consider again the current state of the world and why it's dictating the public mood the way it is. We are living in a time of unprecedented social upheaval on a global scale, where very little seems certain, pure, or sacred anymore. Peace and harmony within society, around the world, is swiftly ebbing away from us, appearing now to be altogether unsustainable. We are a hurting and anxious human race, as reflected by cascading news headlines that dump more and more troubling and depressing realities of life on our front doorsteps and "home pages" of the Internet each day. The winds of stark change are constantly whipping around us, leaving us chilled by their damp implications.

The continued slipping of global economic stability, coupled with the extreme lack of confidence in the world markets, has many experts baffled and scurrying to search out viable long-term financial solutions for the future. Unemployment rates in countries around the world are ever-climbing; in some nations they're skyrocketing! A wobbly housing market and foreclosures on mortgages seem all the rage now, while the less wealthy feel like the money they do have is slowly turning into the "Monopoly" kind.

That's just one aspect of a long list of social heartaches and headaches challenging the world today. The tearing of the traditional family fabric, with its ensuing social repercussions, along with the fading hopes and dreams of ordinary working people over the past thirty years is changing the already unpredictable and chameleon-like complexion of our societal landscape. Our impressionable youth continue to see illicit sex glamourized in the movies, even as pornography goes right on destroying the homes, marriages, and reputations of many people. There are mounting civil uprisings and disobedience in many cities across the world. So-called "peaceful" street demonstrations against lawmakers and authority are turning more violent and are leading to increased criminal activity. Events like the massacre of innocent children at a Connecticut elementary school especially confirm and expose the degree of wickedness within humanity, growing unconscionably and increasingly out of control.

There's an unsettled political and social landscape taking root and creeping across the map of nations. Calloused anti-church, anti-Christian sentiment, coming from lobbyists, legislators, and dictators alike, is slowly handcuffing our religious freedoms. The Bible is clear that the demonically driven cannons of persecution that the antichrist will eventually point squarely at God's people will indeed produce a blast heard around the world.

There's a new kind of awareness of the desperate condition in which we, the human race, find ourselves in. What was once an occasional "mood swing" where one gets "down" about life has become the new normal for a lot of people. In fact, the Center for Disease Control (CDC) recently noted that antidepressants are now the number one prescribed drug in North America. A survey conducted by Ipsos Reid for *Reuters* found that overall, around the world, 14 percent of people believe they will witness the end of the world, in their lifetime![6]

Consider some of the newsworthy items from the recent past that support the biblical prophecy that our present world is edging closer and closer towards ruin and a coming global crisis. A church leader in the deep south of the United States burns a Quran, inciting more hate propaganda towards Western civilization and the Christian Church; an armed American soldier leaves his army barrack, opening fire on seventeen Afghani civilians, killing them all; a Norwegian gunman goes on a racially ideological induced shooting spree in Oslo, randomly killing seventy-seven people; a retired man in Greece, distraught over being relegated to scrounging for food and unable to pay his bills, chooses to commit suicide in a populated marketplace; terrible persecution is being suffered by Iraqi Christians at the hands of extremists; as well as all the never-ending sabre rattling going on in the volatile region of the Middle East, where Israel remains surrounded by its scheming enemies.

There are other clouds hanging over the world, carrying their own fair share of darkness as well. The earth's natural resources are running thin and could soon be tapped out, while necessary commodities such as electricity and gas are getting ridiculously and frighteningly expensive. The countenances of many stressed-out and hyper-anxious people today make it seem like we're all doing our best human impression of an "Angry Bird"! We're a mad, bad, and sad human race, who often feel helpless and overpowered and who seem to be always shouting, "We're not going to take it anymore!"

Suddenly, the prophetic events described in the book of Revelation are not looking so indecipherable and far off after all. If we try to stretch out the possible future scenarios building within our society, why shouldn't the horrific images and realities of the Bible's last book seem closer than ever before?

Recently I came across a cartoon artist's rendering of two prophets, one holding a sign that warns "Global austerity is near," while the other totes a warning that "*The end is even nearer!*" The rising end-time storms presently seeping up and over the levees of our world's stage ought to motivate the human race to reach out to Jesus Christ.

The United States, for example, has an ever-expanding mission field. There is "an unprecedented reshuffling of Americans' spiritual identity," a *Washington Post* writer noted, citing a recent Pew Research Study. The poll showed that one in five adults in the U.S. now holds no religious affiliation or specific belief system. That is roughly 20 percent of people in one of the world's most populated nations, increased from 8 percent back in 1990.[7]

Such news concerning the spiritual climate of our age ought to embolden the Church to make Jesus Christ known all the more. What is killing and eating away at our planet is not global warming; it is not the loss of the rainforests; it's not even the wearing out of our natural resources (though they are all important). What's really killing us is our disregard for God and His will for our lives, not to mention the exaltation of everything that is anti-God and our desire, as the human race, to be gods for ourselves.

When times are grim and becoming grimmer by the hour, and when a spooked world yearns for the sustenance of hope, peace, and a better life, the Church absolutely must emerge as focused and relevant, revived and renewed, to meet that need.

All too often, however, God's people fall short in their efforts to rise to such a vaulted status in the world. Oftentimes, instead of impressing the world by our witness, the Church causes the world's eyes to roll when we act in ways utterly contrary to the character of our Saviour. Spiritual complacency and periodic corruption and hypocrisy within the Church knock the legs out from under its intended identity and purpose as a Christlike redemptive force in the world, suggesting that anything we do for the glory of God is like a message written in the sand: easily blown away by the slightest of hostile winds. Too often, the Body of Christ is defined by its differences and disunity, when it should be identified by its mutual love and unified witness.

Why are so many studies and polls showing that there's very little evidential difference between a Christian life and one that has not been redeemed? Unfortunately, God's people often blend in with the moral mishmash of the fallen world, to the point where they become indistinguishable from the spiritually lost of the world.

It's a terribly difficult spiritual exercise to set some serious evangelistic fire to a world dampened by sin and soaked in its own indifference to God, even more difficult when so many Christians appear to be stuck in the ruts of their own challenged testimonies. The truth is, God's people often spend more time laying blame on the world for its treatment of us than being the kind of disciples Christ calls us to be as a witness *to* the world. Such realities break God's heart.

Jesus had a lot to say about religious people who presumed to be the kind of righteous exemplary leaders the first century world needed. The last time I checked the Gospels, the Lord's assessment of such people still wasn't glowing. One of the terms Jesus used to scathingly describe the so-called righteousness of the religious elite in His day was "blind guides" (Matthew 23:16, 24). He pronounced the Pharisees and other religious leaders who were supposed to be spiritually enabled and visionary to be, in fact, *failing* the Jewish nation.

Today, our twenty-first century world still needs God-fearing, scripturally savvy and wise Christian leaders to lead the spiritual way. More than it needs another kind of strategy for growth, the Church needs a renewed dependence on the power of God and a faith that strives to see Him mightily move through their prayers and ministries. If we in the Church are to be the spiritual compasses Jesus commands us to be, ready to meet the spiritual challenges of this new millennium, we will need the ripple effects from heavenly waves of revival and spiritual renewal to come barging into our lives.

The Bible tells us that Christians are to know the signs of the times and to be able to see clearly enough through them to interpret what they are leading us into (Jesus' coming again, and the end of the present evil age). As we draw nearer to those events, the Church is to bring about with greater force the spreading of the hope that is the gospel of Christ.

For me, it's not so much a question as to whether the Church *can* be a formidable redemptive powerhouse for God in a darkening world. It's rather a question of what it will take to see more and more pockets of God's people engaged in mission and God's Spirit bringing restoration and salvation wherever the Church may tread.

How badly do we as the Church of Jesus Christ want to experience Heaven's outpourings of empowerment and blessing upon us? How much do we crave God's vision for His Church to be revived in our hearts and our desire to individually live out the Great Commandment and Great Commission to be renewed? How badly do we want this, and are we willing to count the hours in prayer it may take?

The Scriptures remind us of our great spiritual heritage as God's people. Jesus gave His Church a trust before He ascended into Heaven; it's the same one our believing ancestors passed on to us, *a ministry torch*. The saints of yesteryear who left their sacrificial thumbprints of ministry on the surface of this needy planet were ones who were *faithful* in the ministry handed down to them by Christ. It is ours now to humbly hold, to keep lit, and to carry on with till our Lord returns.

Their spirits live on to fuel and inspire our struggle as Christ followers in the Church today. They are the "great cloud of witnesses" (Hebrews 12:1), who exist as more than just words of a biblical passage. They are actual visitors to our congregations, cheering us on as we worship. They, along with the Holy Spirit, hold us accountable today. Until God sends His angels from the four corners of the earth to harvest His people from a world primed for His victorious reappearance, our presence and evangelistic work in it is not finished.

The international perception of the Church is unfavourable at best. Consequently, God's people face a steep uphill climb if they are to once again have the world not only look upon them in the light of integrity but also look to them for the spiritual guidance and hope it's so desperately in need of. Though we didn't set down the spiritual standards and parameters of our missional presence in this world, if we claim Christ as our Lord and Saviour we must live, and even *die,* by them.

As a generation of Christians alive on the earth today, we are a desperate people. As a result of our having dropped the "ball" of our testimony, we need humility and our Saviour's forgiveness. We need God's mercy and grace to rekindle our passion for evangelism, to reignite our fervency to serve Him, and to recharge our voices for biblical truth. It really is a mad, bad, and sad world we live in, and yet a world God so loves that He chose to send His Son to it in order to die for its redemption (John 3:16).

While many Christian believers are actively serving God and testifying about Him in their neighbourhoods and workplaces, it can still strangely appear as though God's people have fallen silent. Is it just me, or does the Church in general seem to be incognito, when it really ought to be in the face and in the place of culture?

We're in the eleventh hour of our world's allotted time, and our Saviour's call to His disciples is that we fully immerse our lives in His commission to us. Eternity is ahead of us, and there we can enjoy the fruit of our labours for our Lord. But that is then. For now, Jesus desires that we remain spiritually teachable and pliable as Christians. One day the Church will be gone, millions and millions of light-bearing believers snatched from our earth's premises. On that day the Holy Spirit's presence in each and every Christian, which is influencing the world and holding back chaos and all-out moral darkness, will no longer be here. But we are not gone as yet! Until that day, we must shake the world with our spiritual salt and light it by the life of Jesus Christ alive within us!

Ultimately, Christians must be found faithfully serving Jesus Christ whenever He returns or He calls us to our heavenly home. And if our Saviour taught us anything, it's that we serve Him best whenever we are willing to rub our shoulders with those who are lost and dying spiritually somewhere out in our mad, bad, and sad world.

CHAPTER 2

BETWEEN THE COFFEE COUNTER AND THE OLD CHURCH DOORS

A Revived View of What It Means to Experience God

I've always been a closet fan of the church building steeple. Like tall needle-nose structures that help us identify a particular city (as the Empire State Building does for New York City), church steeples point to our attachment to the ultimate spiritual reality, *the heavens and the realm of God Almighty!* Steeples, by making us crank our necks in order to peruse their northward-pointing height, have us do something in a physical manner that each of us as human beings are to do in a spiritual way: look up!

Though it's believed that the idea of the religious obelisk (steeple) probably had its origin in the phallic symbols used in pagan worship, since the time of Constantine's conversion to Christianity they have sat atop structures housing God's people as they've gathered for public worship.

You have probably heard the cute little children's rhyme "Here's the church, and here's the steeple; open the doors and see all the people!" Whoever coined that verse no doubt would tweak a few things today if he or she could see how many people, on average, are *actually* inside churches these days, not to mention how spiritually dilapidated, underperforming, and ineffective for God we have become. In fact, avid and committed Bible-believing Christian churchgoers today might be more apt to describe their church experience by quoting another familiar saying, "To live above with saints we love, oh, that will be glory; to live below with saints we know, now that's a different story!" Sadly, for most Christians when they think about church life, this probably hits home with greater relevance than the children's rhyme.

When it comes to sketching a definition for how the Church sometimes comes across, we might use the more modern quip "The lights are on, but nobody's home!" We know people *go* to God's house every day and can be seen as being at "home" on any given Sunday, but why does it seem in the Church as though someone hasn't changed a light bulb or two? Why does the spiritual power current running through the Church as a whole seem to be flickering off and on so often? Shouldn't the collective presence of God's people on a darkened sphere be so heavenly iridescent that it can't help but illumine the towns, cities, and communities it's situated in with the righteousness of Christ?

Surely there hasn't been a full-scale power outage within the witness and ministry of the Church. Yet why does it often appear to be so dimly lit when Jesus said His Church was to be the *"light"* of the world? After all, Jesus didn't give us His light so that we could turn around and make it resemble a poorly functioning "Bic" lighter with a puny flame. In all seriousness, a less than fully lit Holy-Spirit-ignited Church can only hope to make faint spiritual projections on the darkened canvas of our God-averse world.

While there is said to be roughly two billion people professing to *believe* in Jesus Christ and follow Him, in the United States alone, 3,500 to 4,000 churches close their doors each year, with signs giving every indication that the trend is continuing.[8] Common sense tells us that there are either fewer Christians to support these churches or more believers deciding to check out of the Church. Though Jesus and the Church are not identical, they are *inseparable*. Sadly, however, many Christians claim to cling to the one while discarding the other!

A troubling recent poll points to the fact that one-fifth of believers under the age of thirty feel that God is absent from their church experience.[9] This makes me wonder what Christians are looking for today when they go to church and what for them constitutes community and a meaningful worship experience.

In *The Gospel According to Starbucks,* Leonard Sweet explains that the coffee company's success can be attributed to how the think tank at Starbucks Inc. has mastered how to present what they want the consumer to buy. The marketing people at the company's offices dreamed up an intimately enveloping atmosphere in their outlets to complement their simple product: coffee. It's worked! According to Leonard Sweet, when we head into our local Starbucks store, we're not really choosing to do so in order to stand in line for a cup of coffee. Rather, we stop to take in the experience *surrounding* that coffee.

Sweet goes on to draw the difference between how one might process their Starbucks experience while waiting to get to the counter and how a good number of Christians tend to approach going to church. "Too many Christians line up to follow God out of duty or guilt, or even hoping to win a ticket to heaven. They completely miss the warmth and richness of the experience of living with God."[10]

Though they spent a great deal of time with the Lord and got a bird's-eye view of supernatural things others would give every tooth in their mouth to see, I've always wondered if the original twelve disciples ever felt they were missing something in their association with Jesus. Did they ever feel things with Him were getting too mechanical? Were they ever bored and desperate enough to ask, "Master, are You finished with us now? Can we go back home?"

After Jesus called the twelve to follow Him, they kept going along with Him all the way to His ascension, eventually putting down the foundational structures we operate by even today as the Church. The spiritual lessons, the hard teachings, and even the ghastly exorcisms they were privy to gaze upon all worked out and made sense in the end for Jesus' disciples. His post-resurrection appearances put to rest any thoughts in their minds that they had been had or that they'd wasted their time hanging with their paranormal, radical rabbi friend Jesus. However, their journey to faith with the Lord came with spiritual ups and downs, and even gross misunderstandings.

Even though God Almighty (in Jesus) was up close and personal with the disciples, so much so that their very shadows could even blend together, the Gospels do indicate that the disciples were left unsatisfied at certain times by their relationship with Jesus. It's as if the Lord was challenging them to search for more in their understanding of God and not depend on being spiritually spoon-fed by Him.

It's possible that the disciples' experience of God incarnated quite frequently became abstract. They stood next to the Truth, but often the Gospel accounts show us that they didn't comprehend that Truth, and neither did they always understand their experience of the Son of God in their midst. Jesus was splashing new spiritual colours, patterns, and designs on the mental artwork of how His disciples had pictured God to be. The original twelve followers often failed to get the fact that Jesus was transcendent and that His presence and eternal majesty couldn't be encapsulated in one particular way or captured at any given ministry stop.

The disciple Peter found that to be true, and then some! One hard lesson in particular stands out. We know it better as the account of the Lord's Transfiguration.

In the Luke 9 passage we catch Peter (the admirably enterprising and sometimes petulant disciple) totally mesmerized by the supernatural goings-on up on Mount Hermon. Though Peter couldn't possibly wrap his mind around all he saw that day, his heart was on his tunic's sleeve for all to see! If we're hearing Peter's heart correctly in the Gospel account, he simply wanted to remain imbedded in a moment that had left him out-and-out gob-smacked. Between the lines of the Scripture we can almost hear Peter saying, "Why can't we just stay and live here on the mountain? This is awesome, Lord! I knew following You would lead to something like this! Woohoo!"

However, the Bible says that Peter "did not know what he was saying" (Luke 9:33). Operating on a tiny thread of spiritual understanding, Peter innocently wanted to somehow freeze-frame the heavenly lightshow and love-in he observed on the mountain that day. The well-meaning disciple no doubt thought that it probably couldn't get much better spiritually than hanging with the iconic twosome of Moses and Elijah, let alone with Jesus in the mix as well! While others could only experience the great patriarchs and prophets of Israel through the words of an unfurled Torah, he was suddenly a time traveller, blessed enough to see Moses and Elijah jump off the scrolls and onto the same mountain his feet were so unworthy of touching.

It's like you and me meeting a celebrity we like and admire. The last thing we would want is to move on from his or her presence too quickly! Who could blame Peter for choosing what was most appealing to him? If left to pick between the daily rigmarole of having to compete with adoring crowds for Jesus' attention and pitching a tent to cohabit with the heroes of the faith, it's no wonder Peter relished the idea of kissing off the waiting world and putting down permanent stakes up on the mountain. Peter (a fisherman turned lucky duck) figured that Jesus, being a master carpenter, could lend a hand in building some huts so that the two Old Testament legends could just *veg* awhile.

Jesus, however, knew He was going to have to play the role of killjoy and disappoint His scheming disciple by pricking his ballooning plans. Despite the enormous spiritual privilege given to Peter and the two other disciples (James and John) to see the person of Jesus in powerfully blinding fashion being affirmed and magnified as God in all His glory, there were no "we've arrived" attitudes and statements permitted from the followers on the mountain that day. They hadn't reached the pinnacle in terms of the purpose of their association with, and experience of, Jesus Christ. The disciples would still have to dot all the *i*'s and cross all the *t*'s of their faith. Their ministry work wasn't finished yet; in fact, it had only just begun.

Although Peter had initial hopes for all of them to become resident mountain men, the Father meant the event of the Transfiguration to show Peter and the other disciples something of great spiritual worth. What the three disciples got to eyeball on the mountain was intended to cause a momentary jolt of spiritual clarity for them. The Transfiguration of their friend and Master teacher was designed to encourage the "inner three" followers that they were on the right spiritual track in terms of following Jesus. In other words, He was who He said He was! "This is my Son…listen to him" (Luke 9:35). Jesus is the One who the Bible testifies is the exact fulfillment of the promise that came through the patriarchs and prophets of Israel (thus the presence of Moses and Elijah).

Though the Transfiguration was spiritually exhilarating, physically breathtaking, and even provided a touch of Heaven on earth, it was *not* the disciples' final destination; nor did it mean that they had cornered all that it entails to experience God. Jesus' Kingdom had not yet fully come; there were people to be ministered to and souls to be won. The great light the three disciples had witnessed around Jesus would only make Him that much larger spiritually in their hearts and minds. Nowhere would that be more obvious than when the disciples would again encounter the darkness of their world, down off the suddenly sacred terrain of the mountain.

The lesson here is that the poignant spiritual moments and divine detours God draws us away to that allow us to intimately experience Him are meant to strengthen the infrastructure of our faith and motivate our mission; they are not the be-all and end-all of our Christian experience. In fact, any given church service could arguably seem something like the "mountaintop" experience Peter and the other disciples had, where we might connect with the living God on a new spiritual level. Like you, I have experienced some incredible worship services where the presence of God, the glorification of Jesus, and the power of Holy Spirit have left me wanting the experience to never end.

Peter, James, and John saw and heard things they'd never been exposed to prior to their trek up the mountain with Jesus; they wanted to bask in the afterglow long after the world's best ever stage show had subsided. The disciples saw Jesus on a heaven-like runway and in the company of two great Israelite leaders whom they'd learned of in Hebrew school. To make things even more meaningful, the spotlight was set upon Jesus, *not* the spiritual giant Moses or the revered Elijah.

The disciples with Jesus that fateful day, like many others during the Lord's ministry years, wanted to experience all He had to give. Who would have wanted to miss out on some fantastic show of divine power at the Lord's miraculous disposal? Who really wanted to be absent when some controversial comment fell from His lips, having instead to depend on hearing about it second-hand from another disciple or from someone in the marketplace the next day? Wherever Jesus blazed a trail, His followers eagerly went along too. They wanted to get an apprentice's view of something spectacular and otherworldly, something supernatural He might end up doing, and to perhaps predict the fallout!

Many of us go to worship every Sunday because it's what we've grown accustomed to doing on the Lord's Day. We're spiritually programmed to experience part of our faith in the context of God's house and with His people. Our pastor and friends will be there, and our favourite worship songs will be played—and so we go there. But sometimes we go to church hoping we'll see and feel something *(anything)* of what took place at Jesus' Transfiguration, something other than what's *supposed* to happen according to the bulletin or a PowerPoint slide, something aside from the expected and usual menu.

However, perhaps unconsciously, some Christians have bought into an idealistic one-stop-shop version of Christianity that believes they can receive everything God has to offer them simply by showing up at church. They want to come away with a great experience of worship, with all needs and expectations met—no other assembly required! They'll just suck in the blessings like a spiritual Slurpee till they're bloated by how much "experience" they take in from the overflowing bucket of entitlement.

The spiritual life wasn't meant to work like that!

For those who prefer a more casual turn-it-on-and-off-when-convenient flavour of Christianity, Sundays are where it's at. One day of the week they put their time in, hoping that God will bless their sacrifice and that it transfers into some sort of heavenly favour or blessing for them (they scratch God's back, He'll scratch theirs). They end up limiting their potential for experiencing God's work in their lives to one day a week.

Jesus wants to be Lord of our lives, not just Lord of an exclusive twenty-four-hour period of them! A nominal Christian once told me that although he went to church, he didn't feel he had to "bring it home" with him. God wants more from us than what some genuine Christians or quasi-Christians are willing to give Him one day a week.

Contrary to what some "Christians" believe, God wants us to take Him home with us. He wants to plunge into our circumstances of life and work in our families, in our marriages, and in our relationships with our children, and not just in our Sunday congregational gatherings. Imagine us telling our own kids that we'll love them and do good things for them while we're in the home together, but away from it we don't know them! I'm not in the minority in believing that God's much more active *outside* the church service than He is in it.

Sunday mornings in church can seem like a parallel experience of entering our favourite coffee shop (Starbucks or otherwise). We take our place in the lineup (enter the building), wait to come to the counter (sit in the seats) in order to receive the product we came for (the music and the sermon), and in that we're satisfied in our Christian experience.

If our worship experience happens to be grand, something like that of Peter's on the mountain (though far less thrilling, I'm sure), we too may emphatically respond, "I could just stay here forever!" Like sitting down with our tasty lattes and close friends in the coffee shop, where we can experience "community," we can look for the total package of what it means to authentically experience God solely within the comfort and familiarity of our weekend services.

For certain, we need to find a church where we can experience meaningful and substantial fellowship. We shouldn't at all feel reticent to want to experience God in such a way that we see Him powerfully infiltrating our corporate worship services. We *should* crave intimately experiencing God at our church gatherings; after all, the Bible does say that God inhabits the praises of His people (Psalm 22:3).

What happens though when we don't "feel" the all-inspiring, all-encompassing presence of the Holy Spirit when we're in the pew? What about when we don't feel like we're "getting" or "seeing" all that we long for or when the product coming from the platform a lot of Sundays seems unworthy of our effort to line up at the spiritual consumers' counter of God's house? What about the seasons when almost every sermon the pastor preaches begins to sound like one we've heard before and we can't wait to leave? Oftentimes what goes on in our hearts is what really needs to change, not what we're getting from the front of the sanctuary.

The point is that on any given Sunday we're *not* meant to experience all we would like to out of our weekend worship services. Are we being presumptuous by thinking that we *should* be experiencing the whole divine program in our church building atmosphere? I think many believers expect that of God and of His ministering people on a continual basis. It could be a case of spiritual laxness, feeling it takes too much personal time and effort to apprehend a more well-rounded Christian experience outside of Sunday morning, when someone isn't serving up something for *us*.

Be honest: how many church services have left you feeling like you'd rather stay in the sanctuary than exit the building? A meaningful, life-altering spirituality cannot come about as a result of our skyrocketing demands upon God's servants. An on-fire-for-God kind of Christian life experience cannot be awarded to the believer who thinks that God's rich and endless spiritual supply should be amply poured out for them every time they take their place in our worship centres and sanctuaries. Our spiritual transformation as Christians comes from a transcendent deity, from a God who cannot be locked, stocked, and preserved to perform to our expectations every time we take Him out of our church-setting box, like some kind of goods we've purchased.

Yes, as Leonard Sweet accurately purports, Starbucks does give us an experience that complements the product it sells, right where we are; no need to go anywhere else. Companies like Starbucks market an experiential product, and they do it rather well. When you walk into a Starbucks coffee shop you're walking into more than just a cafe; you're bound to experience more than just a cup of coffee. It's a store, a library, a social network, a mini mall—take your pick. It's all there for us. Just walk in, order, sit down, and get ready to *experience!* We could siphon a cathedral of knowledge while we worship at the throne of the coffee bean. Cultures, life stories, and a global network are all known to converge at local coffee shops like Starbucks.

For some of us Christians, that's the problem with our perspective on Sunday mornings: we'd rather do church at a place like Starbucks and break off from the stagnant coil that is the traditional church worship setting. Perhaps we are getting spoiled and conditioned by the conveniences (even harmless ones) that the world at our doorstep has to offer us. Various influences within our culture affect our view of how we should experience Sunday worship, perhaps more than we'd readily admit.

Could it be that an underlying source of the ants-in-our-pants restlessness we tend to feel as we do our time on Sunday mornings is something subliminally planted in us from our observations and experiences of the worthwhile things our culture has going for it? We can be so taken by the creativity of our society that it can make our church experience seem a little inferior.

Certainly, the purpose for entering a church service, in the purest sense, can't be compared to the reason why people flock to cafes. However, perhaps we Christians have no idea how much we've been impressed and inspired by our society's valuing of certain cultural surroundings. Many newer church buildings are constructed with a warm and contented Starbucks-like atmosphere, even theatre-like ambiance, in mind. The goal is to duplicate and deliver a culturally relevant model and experience to the masses, within the context of a "worship" environment.

As the Church, we need to accept that the world's way of doing things doesn't necessarily have to be the Church's way, even in these modern times. Or maybe the Church *should* alter some aspects of its public worship gatherings in order to redeem what our culture today views as important and indispensable but is so often devoid of God.

No matter what environment we prefer to worship God in on Sunday morning, the realities of what it means to be a disciple cannot be packaged, consumed, or even enjoyed in the same manner we seize upon the altar (the counter) of our local cafe fellowship. We definitely cannot experience all that God wants us to experience as His people at our church services. We can't even possibly realize in our entire time of living all that God has for us! Our weekly worship encounters are bit parts of the greater sum of our Christian spiritual life. They're mere celebrations of what God is doing in our lives, in our ministries, and in the world. Gathering to fellowship with others as we worship at church amounts to no more than a dollop of spirituality on our worship plate, only a drop in the great bucket of what it means to enjoy the living waters of our faith.

In our church worship experiences, we praise, we give, we read, we listen, we share, we serve, and we pray. But if we want to be blessed in addition to our Sunday services and our predictable, orderly Christian activities and meetings, we need to keep something else in mind. We must never lose sight of the fact that we can always experience our Lord just as much the minute we step a toe outside the front door of our church buildings or living rooms and away from our comfortable clusters of safe Christianity.

God may be "in the house" where two or three of His people are gathered, but He owns the big, wide world too, and He is there as well! To quote Leonard Sweet once more, we as God's people need to "learn to pay attention...to identify where God is already in business right in your neighborhood."[11]

So if you're looking to drink a great cup of coffee in an atmosphere that enables and completes a great experience–nothing else needed but a good book, a laptop, or a conversation—then you should go to Starbucks (or to some other public cafe). If you want to experience a relationship with a great God, observe something of His glorious being, and benefit spiritually from how multifaceted His love and resources are, by all means, go to church. But remember that you will need to look outside of there as well to find and experience even more of

God. In fact, we might just run into Jesus working at the local mall, at the always busy community centre, at the pub uptown, at a school, and yes, He may even show up at a Starbucks and turn some coffee into living water!

We can experience God just as powerfully in the undesirable gutters and resistible crevices of everyday life. We're guaranteed to find a great worship experience, as well as a sermon application, tucked into the messy nooks and crannies of our world, if we'd only get out more! It may take a personal revival and the fruit that comes from a time of spiritual renewal in our lives to clear the way for us to see that and to experience it.

CHAPTER 3

OF WAYWARD, WAFFLING, AND WISHY-WASHY SAINTS

A Revived Submissiveness to the Will of God

"This is love for God: to obey his commands" (1 John 5:3).

While I was in Bible college, a group of students belonging to the evangelism committee would meet every Friday to do outreach ministry in downtown Toronto. The students would deliver bagged lunches to the homeless and offer hot beverages to prostitutes in the so-called "red light" areas of the city. Being very "green" in ministry skills at the time, I finally worked up enough gumption to join the committee members one Friday evening on one of their evangelistic outings. Though the winter night air was bone-chilling, my apprehensive spirit was burning with anticipation of the unknown, of an experience that I was certain I'd never forget.

What I observed during the three hours we were on the streets was deeply heart-probing and conscience-scraping, to say the very least. The ministry outing indeed ended up translating into an unforgettably faith-stretching and spiritually shaping experience for me. As Bible college students, we were the *steeple people* worshipping God by our service to the "street people"; we were the gospel in full throttle! The homeless we served and we who were willing extensions and instruments of Jesus' hands and feet were mutual absorbers of the resultant blessings.

Prior to the ministry outing there were no faces or names for me to attach to the label of "street people." Afterwards, God wouldn't allow any of the faces or the names of the people I encountered that night to fade from my memory. I took away with me many a mental photocopy of the homeless.

While I found numerous people on the street to be very pleasant to converse with, there were others who seemed noticeably bitter, edgy, and even hardened and angry. There were also those who appeared lifeless, their eyes blank and their minds spacey from whatever drug or drink they ingested or had been ingesting for some years.

The greatest discovery I made that night was that most of the homeless, though appearing to be social misfits, were once "normal," functioning people, who just happened to have made a "few wrong moves" in their lives. Incredibly, a lot of them were actually on the run from loving homes and good things. Some of them just wanted to feel like they belonged again, as if their lives really mattered to someone. Some of them longed to feel "alive" again; others yearned for healing, even forgiveness.

After our Friday night trip to the needy downtown regions of the city was over, it appeared as if things remained the same for both us students and those who made their living rooms and bedrooms on the often less-than-kind streets. As we ducked into our warm cars to head home, perhaps not much would change for the street people. They were left sitting on the same cold slabs of concrete we found them on. Many, I was sure, would continue to nurse a victim mentality, if not a martyr's complex of sorts. It seemed to me that too few were hungry enough (though many were certainly desperate enough) to seek a personal turnaround and a more meaningful and secure position in life.

During the ride home, the other students and I found we had mixed emotions about the whole experience. Strangely, though the homeless were supposedly the ones in need of a touch of God, it was us, as His ministering people, who felt ministered to that night. We expected to provide some mercy in the midst of the collective messes of lives gone astray, yet it was us, who already knew of the love and grace of Heaven poured out in Christ, who ended up seeing our own human frailties and spiritual insecurities written all over the misgivings of the street dwellers.

I didn't count on being so personally impacted by what I'd seen and heard. I felt totally unworthy to possess the gift of eternal life and the forgiveness of God while others (the homeless), whom I was no better than, were living without such hope and peace. That the spiritual laboratory in which this all took place was far from the confines of any church building, spiritual book, or religious institution still speaks to me today.

There, on the overcrowded and unfriendly city streets, surrounded by its bright lights and urban offerings and out from under the protective Christian bubble of our school, I felt closer to Jesus that singular night than I ever had before. Among the "hungry" and the "thirsty," among the "stranger" and the "sick," as well as the emotionally imprisoned, "the least of these," I felt like I had really met and worshipped my Saviour (see Matthew 25:35–40).

As I conversed with people I had never seen before or had very much in common with, judging them was the furthest temptation from my mind. Actually, the experience caused me to think hard about how fortunate *I was* to have what *they didn't*.

The totality of my experience out on the main streets and back streets of Toronto that were occupied by beguiling drifters and the mentally and physically vulnerable, as well as the purely mysterious, reminded me of the single most important thing that secures my life, the hope I have and the belonging I feel from being a child of God, and that no matter what happens to me in my life, God will always have a special place preserved for me.

However, even though God's eternal acceptance of me as His own is scriptural fact and therefore should cause me to be daily grateful, that is not always how I act as a disciple of Christ. There are moments in my Christian life and in my relationship with Jesus when, if I didn't know any better, I'd think I'd departed from Him in some way, something that's as painful to admit as it is strange to write. Many believers have found themselves in a world of spiritual hurt in a real hurry simply because they neglected the owner and occupier of the home of their hearts.

I know that in making a few wrong moves of my own (spiritually) I could easily find myself, like the people I met on the street, running from love and a good thing (the security of my relationship with God). It is illogical to think that a child of God could ever want to break free from the perfect, safe, and loving arms of our Heavenly Father; our sin and inherited (fallen) human nature, however, make such a notion rather *logical*. Rebellion towards our infinitely good and Holy Creator remains attractive to us, offering a spiritual freedom that on the one hand is exciting and tantalizing and yet on the other is dangerous and harmfully conditioning to us spiritually.

When waffling in our obedience to God becomes a habit, it's like we've gotten used to turning our backs on Him, which ultimately means we've grown too fond of turning towards sin. If such a spiritual stance becomes commonplace in our lives, we'll become contrary and counterproductive vessels, redeemed lives that paradoxically shortchange the amazing potential they have not only to be immensely blessed by God but to be an enormous blessing to others.

In our Lord's time, portions of salt would often get mixed up with sand, thus nullifying its quality as a preservative. Jesus would have the wayward, waffling, and wishy-washy disciple consider, then, what temporal *or* eternal good could ever come from a witness so handicapped that it forfeits its spiritual effectiveness to influence the unsaved. "But if the salt loses its saltiness, how can it be made salty again? It is no longer good for anything, except to be thrown out and trampled by men" (Matthew 5:13). The reality that backsliding Christians are grieving and quenching God's power source (the Holy Spirit) in their lives will become evident, sooner or later, in some convicting and consequential form or other. "Be sure that your sin will find you out" (Numbers 32:23).

Could this be one of the main reasons why there is such discontentedness in the spiritual lives of so many Christians today? Could this be the reason why the efficacious light of Christ in His Church so often fails to shine forth as bright and powerfully as it should? Could the fact that young Christian singles today are as sexually active as their unsaved friends be a direct result of a generation that has already walked away from any notion of living righteously before God? Why have they chosen instead to wander upon the dead-end streets of spiritual independence and defiance? The cold, hard truth about so many of us who claim to be God's people is that we tend to *depart* from Him, some for longer and more spiritually intense periods of time than others.

Although God's Word tells us that He has blessed His people "with every spiritual blessing" (Ephesians 1:3) and that "His divine power has given us everything we need for life and godliness through our knowledge of him who called us" (2 Peter 1:3), we yet possess the propensity, as sin-addicted beings, to turn a "blind eye" to God's goodness to us, leaving us with only one alternative: to hitch ourselves to the fleeting, spiritually overrated leg-room of disobedience and the empty promises that come from gratifying our sinful desires.

A movement away from God doesn't begin with a singular disobedient activity as much as it incubates over time through a radical shift in the heart, a shift that if left unchallenged leads in one direction only: spiritually downward. Once the heart of an individual believer, or even a group of believers, has spiritually shifted, a departure from the priorities of God usually follows suit. I'm not suggesting that someone who is authentically saved can subsequently "lose" their salvation; it's a consequential loss, rather, of one's motivation to live in the light of that salvation that results from a wayward spiritual life. Inevitably, when the focus of a Christian's heart moves off Christ, it produces a domino-like effect in the life of the child of God. It's when the believer begins to arbitrarily hurdle over biblical commands by means of a hardened and darkened sinful resolve.

Have you ever wondered what the life of a Christian who's in need of revival and spiritual renewal looks like? Maybe we see that kind of person reflected back to us in the mirror each morning we awake! Have you ever wondered what any given church congregation resembles spiritually when its ministry is in need of being recharged by the power of God's Holy Spirit? Perhaps we could exclaim here, "Yeah, I'm a part of one!"

As God's redeemed and yet sin-marred people, we should know how plausible it is for any one of us at any time to throw our sinful natures a bone. There are moments when we are fooled into thinking we have a handle on certain situations and issues, only to discover that we are not as strong and anchored in those areas as we thought we were!

Being choosy and sloppy with obeying biblical commands is a spiritual gamble not worth the roll of its dice; at its very core, it's the art of demonic deception. We've all heard the snaky, reasonably sounding breath of the devil come calling in our hour of spiritual weakness and vulnerability, "Go ahead and do it. God's got bigger sins to deal with; besides, other Christians are doing it too."

However, the Christian who's been walking with God long enough and who's thoroughly acquainted with His Word knows that to go *against* that Word (in any way, to any degree) is a really bad idea; after all, we know how that worked out for the paradise-dwellers of Eden named Adam and Eve!

Don't believe the darkened, bogus yammer within our society that claims, "God doesn't care what you do in your bedroom or with whom you do it with." I wonder if David (Israel's king) *and* Bathsheba would agree with such a statement! I've been astounded at hearing Christians spout with indifference similar sentiments about what they do in private; it's their business, they say, and therefore not even *God's,* one's left to assume!

Any talk of spiritually wayward Christians and biblically wishy-washy churches might sound a bit clichéd, even passé; we've seen it so much that, sadly, we're now desensitized to it. Unfortunately, though, many professing Christians and even Christian denominations today have done the unthinkable and either have entirely lost touch with their Christlike identity and biblical mission or are on the slick brink of it. It's when the spiritual vertebrae of believers and churches begin to soften until they bend or even break to whatever tsunami of corrupt ideology (under the guise of theology) pounces their way and sucks them in.

Is there a sadder occurrence in our world than that of a once "on fire" Christian or church that no longer appears to be a light-infused, spiritually salty alternative for the world to consider, who gives us the impression that they've made a few wrong spiritual turns and are now on the run from the love of their heavenly home and a profoundly good God? Whenever the spiritual firmament in the house of God is conflicted, those out on the streets of unbelief (the unsaved) are the ones who unknowingly feel the spiritual effects the most. When God's people get caught in the spiritually divisive and destructive vise-grip of discord, it almost always equals the squelching and even death of their missional consciousness. The tightening effect of unresolved and ongoing quarrels amongst God's people can strangle the evangelistic air out of them. Sadly, many churches around us are in this very position. I know of a few at present; perhaps you do too.

Consider an alarming piece of data compiled by the Barna research people, reflecting that 25 percent of 440 people polled in the United States couldn't think of a single positive contribution the Church makes.[12] As well, when solid theological teaching is shelved in favour of religiously sprinkled yet spiritually superficial pep talks, it's no wonder Christians have become less impactful in their culture. It's the uncompromising Word of God that both saves and changes lives!

Pastor and author Dr. David Jeremiah writes, "Unfortunately, biblical Christianity is no longer preached from every pulpit in the land…the church has lost her way. I believe with all my heart: As goes the church, so goes the nation."[13] It's possible for any church whose doctrinal beliefs and faith statements profess Jesus as the Christ and Saviour of the world to get to the place where its heart ceases to beat for the very gospel truth it purports to believe in and follow. This doesn't happen overnight, but the lead-up to it is elementary on a spiritual level. When wayward and waffling Christians allow themselves to be influenced by a biblically incorrect worldview, they tend to make choices that supersede the place, purpose, and redemptive thrust of God's Word for their lives. In the Bible there is great precedent for this reality. In fact, the existence of wayward, waffling, and spiritually wishy-washy people of God goes way back to the first nation to ever know and follow the Lord (the one true God).

When Moses addressed Israel on the terms of the covenant the Lord made with them, the patriarch warned, "But if your heart turns away and you are not obedient, and if you are drawn away to bow down to other gods and worship them, I declare to you this day that you will certainly be destroyed" (Deuteronomy

30:17–20). Moses' portentous address to God's chosen people well over three thousand years ago is long-reaching and just as spiritually piercing from its BC distance!

God may not strike us down because our hearts have dipped in their allegiance to Him, but playing the foolish and dangerous game of spiritual roulette puts God's patience to the test. Absolutely no disciple of Jesus is above falling into sin by any spiritual qualification or classification. Even some of the most godly and well-respected Christian leaders have been deceived and caused great damage to the reputation and ministry of the Church.

When this happens, it's not always on a grand moral scale. Though as God's people we get involved in doing "Christian" things and practice expected spiritual disciplines, somewhere along the way we may avail ourselves of faulty and careless Christian living and spiritual thinking. I've seen this happen too often in the lives of sincere believers who inexplicably feel it's suddenly permissive to mangle the Scriptures in order to justify a certain change in their lifestyle or alteration in their worldview.

We can't expect something out of our relationship with God and out of our spiritual life experience that's not there for the having. God is not made of clay so that we can sculpt Him; He's not a deity that can be turned into our "yes man" or our "good buddy." Neither can God be bribed or made to twist the righteous standards and commands in His Word. God will always act according to His Word and character; His creation is asked to respond in kind by honouring Him and worshipping Him accordingly. Genuine Bible-believing Christians may not be easily talked out of obeying God, but they most certainly can be *disappointed* out of living obedient lives. The attitude is "God didn't come through for me, so why should I try so hard to obey?"

In the previous chapter, I discussed how some of God's people are taking the Church hostage, as it were, by holding out for an instantly satisfying all-sufficient (Starbucks-like) church experience before they'll hang their hat in any given body of Christ. Their "ideal" church setting may be elusive, yet their mindset remains rock-hard: "Please me, or I'm gone."

As people who take in weekly sermons (sometimes more than one), certainly there are times when we'd like a little dash of something more than a three-point acronym-laced message. Perhaps it's quite natural for us from time to time to desire a little extra spice and dressing to go along with the expository meat-and-potatoes preaching we're used to getting. However, if we've grown bored and disillusioned with the church life scene overall, where does that leave us as

Christians? If we no longer desire to keep the spiritual disciplines of the faith and we foster a take-it-or-leave it attitude towards all that comes with fellowship and biblical accountability, something's spiritually out of whack with *us*, not with the purpose of the Church and certainly not with the Bible's inerrant directives.

Though a healthy and vibrant spiritual life cannot be acquired by what we do liturgically or via a specific worship style, it doesn't make those preferences and practices any less worthwhile and important for shaping and building up the faith of a Christian. It's all about where our heart is as we engage in the spiritual disciplines and what our purpose for doing so is. Merely fostering a "going through the motions" style of religiosity can never lead to internal transformation (the goal of our redemption); to the contrary, it leads only to a pretentious and shallow spiritual existence and experience of God.

As we sit in a worship service or participate in some spiritual activity (prayer group, Bible study), we should periodically ask ourselves, "Why am I really here?" In the Middle Ages, most Christians, it would seem, attended church with the sole intention to worship the Name and Person (the worth-ship) of God in Christ. (It didn't hurt to have images of hell-fire suffering glaring at you from the stained glass windows on the periphery, either!) There was a time in the Church when worshippers going off to mass or to a service adopted a steeple-pointing perspective. That is, they were there with a spiritually vertical preoccupation: to bless God.

Sometime after that point in history, however, a heart-shift occurred in how believers came to view their activity and presence in the house of God. Our aim moved from spiritually vertical to one that's horizontal in nature. Now we go to church for what *we* can get out of it: *we* want to be blessed by God (the pastor's sermon, the worship music, the programs, the fellowship). It's a view that seems to be inverted from the original.

At the risk of sounding prudish I can't help but conclude that the spirit of our day, one of a predominant selfishness rather than selflessness, has grown deep roots within the Church. Many Christians I've known have visited churches as if they were religious stores, shopping around for one yet rarely getting to the point of actually buying what's going on in any of them!

Too many of Christians are consistently inconsistent in their worship attendance and in the use of their spiritual gifts. They say they can serve outside of the church building just as easily as they can in one and can hear a sermon anytime they want. The averages, however, point to the fact that they *don't* actually make time for such activities and disciplines outside the context of the Body of Christ. The danger is that Christians can become indifferent to their required place and importance in the Church, even nomadic and difficult to pin down. Like butterflies fluttering around, they never land anywhere or stay anywhere for long. As a result, some of God's wayward people have become problematic in terms of their testimony and usefulness in the advancement of the Kingdom of God on earth.

The Lord is not looking for disillusioned, protesting disciples to withdraw from the rest of His people just because they're wavering in their faith or waffling in their submission to Him and His will for their lives. Some Christians within the earliest monastic communities stepped away from the established Roman Catholic Church out of a disgust for the hierarchal corruption, deplorable morality, and abuses of power amongst its clergy. If we're a Bible-believing Christian today, we can hardly claim to have a worthy enough reason for pulling away from the Body of Christ.

It's uncanny how we as twenty-first century believers can act so similarly to our spiritual ancestors of Israel by reliving their mistakes. It wasn't enough for the Lord's chosen people to know Him so definitively as the one true God. It wasn't enough for them to be specifically summoned out of the pagan world to be a people and nation for Him; it wasn't enough either for Israel to be taken under the Lord's divine wing and to be blessed as human beings beyond any previous group of people on earth.

The Israelites experienced all the supernatural special effects that Yahweh could throw their way: heavenly generated pillars of fire, air-delivered provisions of food (manna), the miraculously mind-tripping manipulations of nature (the parting of the Red Sea), and the like. Wasn't the show of love and benevolence on God's part towards His people that featured encore after encore of sovereign deliverance convincing enough for the people of Israel to realize that He alone was worthy to be worshipped?

Why wasn't a God who had no qualms about showering His people with faith-building installments of His grace good enough for His people? Why did they so often drop back and even drastically drop off in the intensity of their obedience to the Lord? Why were the Israelites often a restless, bored, and disenchanted people who could turn away from their God without so much as a spiritual blink, to the point where they sought out the futile pleasures of a darkened, godless culture? How could people who were adequately informed of who the Lord is and who were loved and treasured by their God have fallen so blindly and badly for counterfeit deities, only to end up with a kind of spiritual currency that could buy them nothing but the judgment of their Creator?

Could it be that Israel was guilty of holding unrealistic expectations of the Lord? Could we as Christians and as the Church today be just as "stiff-necked" and "stubborn" as Israel was described as being in Scripture? If we didn't know any better we might think as God's people today that we are spiritual carbon-copies of the Israelites; like them we too seem willing to settle for so much less than all the love and goodness the Lord wills to lavish on us.

I imagine a cartoonish scenario in Heaven where the Father, by the prayer-phone and looking over the tawdry shape of His people, says to an already nodding Jesus, with the Holy Spirit concurring alongside Him, "Those foolish people of ours! They should be calling the revival hotline already; we've only been nudging them towards it for thousands and thousands of earth-time years!"

We can only pray (but we *must* pray) for that to happen in our churches around the world today. However, we must first see revival and spiritual renewal as being wholly necessary, a burden we can no longer bear but rather unload in prayer and want to see come to fruition. The more those who profess to be Bible-believing Christians tune out Jesus' redemptive agenda in this world, before they eventually drop out of the Church altogether, the more we should grieve. What potential spiritual shape will the witness of God's people take on in the not-so-distant future?

As biblically prophesied there's been a great turning away from God in our world; in the Church, however, even a hint of such an action is as utterly confounding as it is tragic. One doesn't arrive at a wayward Christian life by staying focused upon the "main things" of the faith. Obedience to the Word of God is essential for the child of God if for no other reason than keeping our relationship with Him, as well as with other believers, a close one.

Too many Christians are acting like they're homeless street people; though they're *God's* people and therefore belong to His family (the Church), they still choose to run from a loving home and a good thing. God desires more for us as His people than to solely experience His loving arms wrapped around us; He wants us to wrap our arms around each other as well, to be with each other. The Bible says that the people of God (regardless of their hurts and histories) are not to "give up meeting together, as some are in the habit of doing, but let us encourage one another—and all the more as you see the Day approaching" (Hebrews 10:25).

Of Wayward, Waffling, and Wishy-Washy Saints

The Church and individual Christians are in great need of getting closer to where they should be spiritually, especially as the number of days before Christ returns grow ever so fewer. What better place from which to begin that process as a people of God than in the *Word* of God!

CHAPTER 4

GROSSLY GAUNT CHRISTIANS AND THE FAMINE OF THE WORD

A Revived Hunger to Know God through His Word

Whenever I watch a television program featuring a host of young actors, it doesn't take very long to notice that most, if not all, of them have two things in common: they all have glistening white teeth, and they're all as thin as the spindles on the front porch of my house. Thin has been "in" for quite some time now. Culturally, one is thought to look more hip and cool and have a better chance at fitting in with the (th)in crowd if one is, well, thin!

During my high school years, being thin was considered an embarrassment to a young person. Most teenagers I knew wished that they could gain some muscle mass overnight so as to not be singled out and ridiculed for their wiry physical frames! I was often called a "bone rack" as a reward for my gangly looking appearance as a teen. This was particularly exasperating when I let my aspirations of joining our school's football team (as a wide receiver) out of the bag. Not only did other kids mock me, but the coach couldn't hold in his amusement either, bursting out in laughter! I could run fast, but I also had visions of needing to put my body back together if I was ever hit or tackled. So did everyone else, I presume!

Yet thin is *in* today, and more than just in terms of one's physical appearance. We like our technology thin, for instance. Can iPads get any thinner or cellphones any more sleek than they are?

Thin seems to be in as well when it comes to how we as people receive and process information today, which comes at us with lightning speed. We are now living in the "information" age. With so many people of different learning capacities and educational backgrounds surfing the net and library banks for research, the complexities involved with knowledge intake have introduced the world to the "dumbing down" era. It's a term that concerns the hiding of natural thought processing and intellectual abilities, a trend that involves the lowering (thinning out) of intelligent content within literature and news.

According to John Algeo, the former editor of *American Speech*, the neologism *dumb down* means "to revise so as to appeal to those of little education or intelligence."[14] A prime example of this is how gifted children often do not excel in classrooms that are geared more towards students with lower reading levels and capacities for retaining and recalling information. The same can be said of certain news publications in which it is obvious by the quality of journalism that the people who read it are of the general public who have an average grade 10 reading level. On any given topic experts are usually brought onto television programs to "dumb down" the layers of information for the layman viewership. This is done in order to communicate a more scaled down and basic "Coles Notes" version of the subject material.

Dumbing down is a cultural trend that I believe has spread beyond the secular realm of society. There's also been a dumbing down in the culture of the Church (particularly in the West) in terms of the delivery and intake of God's Word.

Ask members of your small group which they'd prefer, to take in bite-sized video teaching on biblical precepts and fill in a blank or two or to read an entire Bible book, break down and apply the precepts themselves, and then come to the group ready for a discussion. Do we even have to guess at which option would be preferable to most members of the group?

Christians in the present-day Western Church especially are thoroughly advantaged. We have a plethora of scholarly resources available to us that can assist us in our understanding and application of God's Word. All we need to have is the desire to tap into them; all the hard, studious work has been done for us. Like with TV dinners, all we need to do is dive in! We should be the most educated and useful believers in all of the world for the Kingdom of God. But we *could* be some of the most gaunt believers to ever exist in the entire history of Christianity when it comes to our reading and knowledge of the Bible.

We have great excess in our society, and Christians are guilty of filling up on things of their culture at the gross expense of ingesting the Word of God. If Jesus could not "live on bread alone" (Matthew 4:4), what makes so many of God's people today think they can? It's an endeavour in spiritual drifting for any Christian to try to navigate through the high-sea waters of deception in this life without the anchoring wisdom God gives us in His Word for our journey of faith.

The Lord often rebuked Israel for their neglect *and* ignorance of His righteous commands and precepts, a reality within the nation that frequently led to them being judged. "My people are destroyed from lack of knowledge" (Hosea 4:6).

Many people in the Church today who claim to be born-again apparently are not well-schooled in the Word of God either, so much so that a good number of believers don't even possess a basic grasp of Christian doctrine. Gordon MacDonald, chancellor of Dallas Seminary, asks, "Why are too many [of God's people] ignorant of the core Bible stories?…Why does it seem as if many Christians are more passionate about their politics than their knowledge of scriptural foundations?"[15]

In my travels as a pastor I have often noticed a stark deficiency in some believers' knowledge of Scripture. Even more disconcerting has been the cavalier attitude some Christians have displayed towards *attaining* it!

It doesn't help one iota either that God's people are often influenced by their culture's preoccupation with sensationalism and entertainment. As a result we have become somewhat obsessed with creating "moving" weekly worship services, which tend to reinforce short attention spans. This can leave worshippers preferring to take in a continuous display of visual stimuli rather than to listen awhile to the hearty depth of God's Word being expounded.

However, our seemingly thin knowledge of the Bible on average today stems from beyond what happens in church on Sundays. It can be argued that Christians of varying ages and generations simply do not have the kind of conviction about the Scriptures that's required for them to mature spiritually. In addition, many young believers seem to have an aversion to taking the time to learn and study God's Word.

A 2009 survey on biblical illiteracy in the United States revealed some startling results. It appears from the information gathered that professing believers (particularly those of a younger generation) do not hold to a strict biblical worldview; nor are the Scriptures central to their daily life as Christians.

There is "less engagement" with God's Word.

> While many young adults are active users of the Bible, the pattern shows a clear generational drop-off—the younger the person, the less likely they are to read the Bible. In particular, Busters and Mosaics are less

likely than average to have spent time alone in the last week praying and reading the Bible for at least 15 minutes. Interestingly, none of the four generations were particularly likely to say they aspired to read the Bible more as a means of improving their spiritual lives.[16]

People are also viewing God's Word as "less sacred." "While most Americans of all ages identify the Bible as sacred, the drop-off among the youngest adults is striking: 9 out of 10 Boomers and Elders described the Bible as sacred, which compares to 8 out of 10 Busters (81%) and just 2 out of 3 Mosaics (67%)."[17]

There are those who believe God's Word to be "less accurate." "Young adults are significantly less likely than older adults to strongly agree that the Bible is totally accurate in all of the principles it teaches. Just 30% of Mosaics and 39% of Busters firmly embraced this view, compared with 46% of Boomers and 58% of Elders."[18]

Interestingly, God's Word is being viewed in the same light as other religious writings: "more universalism." "Among Mosaics, a majority (56%) believes the Bible teaches the same spiritual truths as other sacred texts, which compares with 4 out of 10 Busters and Boomers, and one-third of Elders."[19]

Such revelatory data should have all of us in the Church prayerfully concerned about the biblical backbone of the future generation of the Church. The reality of a thinning biblical literacy amongst Christians today (some who could be up and coming leaders in the Church) is not only pushing the Church of Jesus Christ further towards the edge of a crisis of perceived irrelevancy within our society; it's also exposing the growing ranks of biblical immaturity within its own walls.

Without a doubt, the emaciated face of biblical literacy amongst young Christians today, along with their lack of conviction that the Bible is uniquely God's authoritative speech to us, has led to a Church (at least in the Western world) that resembles grossly gaunt and famished believers. This is particularly dangerous for the child of God for one main reason: it leaves them open to being duped by the cornucopia of "spiritual" ideas and teachings being batted around in our culture today. We are in dire need of the life-giving and spiritually filling meat-and-potatoes ingredients of Scripture!

Possessing a readily retrievable knowledge of God's Word is central to our understanding of what it means to be Christians who are on a journey of spiritual sanctification and maturation. During His ministry on earth, Jesus demonstrated how vitally important Scripture recall is for those who are following Him on a path of discipleship. In the Gospels, the Lord periodically pointed out to the religious elite of His day that the main reason they failed to comprehend His teachings and live righteously before God was their sieve-like knowledge of the Scriptures. The ability to know God's general will for all occasions of life so that we won't be easily taken in by the honey-dripping fibs of the devil is something Christ modelled for us to *live out,* not admire!

A growing biblical illiteracy amongst Christians today only confirms the urgent need for God's people to seek a personal revival in that area of their lives. Though our hearts must be open to what God has to say to us, first the Bibles in our churches must also be opened and taught in depth. To quote pastor and author David Jeremiah once again,

> Genuine revival is rooted in solid biblical teaching. A revival that doesn't rest on the Word of God will either fade out or will turn into an ostentatious display of emotionalism and sensationalism…Nothing except a return to Scripture can arouse a nation, a church, or an individual back to God…We must have the power and authority of God's truth.[20]

To possess a decent grasp of the Bible is to arm ourselves with the ability to tell the difference between what is true and what is false on a spiritual level. A healthy knowledge of God's Word is a gift that keeps on giving, in that it assists us whenever we dialogue with the spiritually lost about the Scriptures. No other text, when read and internalized by faith, can affect the moral and spiritual fibre of society like the Bible can; it's a Word we can depend on and can rest our eternal souls and security on with absolute certainty.

Whenever we receive news pertaining to a world event or, on a more personal note, hear some revelation about a close friend that causes us concern, we hope the information we're getting is accurate. The bottom line is that we hope what we're being fed is *the truth and nothing but the truth*. However, second-hand information, "grapevine" types of scoops, and even news reports in general are not always the most dependable sources in terms of accuracy. How can we know with certainty that what we are being told isn't what we *need* to hear but rather what we're told we *should* hear? When it comes to spiritual things especially, we want to be sure that what we're being fed is the absolute truth beyond a doubt.

The Bible is reliable for giving us the truth about the human predicament: *we're sinners and we need a Saviour.* Scripture also provides a holistic timeline of God's involvement in world history and explains His redemptive plans for it (past, present, and future). What makes the Bible so profoundly different from the religious texts of other faiths isn't how warm and fuzzy it leaves us after we've read it. What separates the Bible from any other religious document is its fulfilled prophecies!

Skeptics from many walks of life, some of them iron-willed atheists, have come to faith in Christ, even while earnestly and sincerely trying to disprove the Bible's content. No wonder the Bible says God's Word is "living and active" and "sharper than any double-edged sword" (Hebrews 4:12). So if one is going to take on Scripture, one should be prepared at the same time for it to fight back and for the possibility of having one's disbelief slain!

Biblical unbelief is totally indefensible and thoroughly irrational. One cannot outsmart the sovereign, infinite wisdom of Almighty God, no matter how determined one is or how much of the "alphabet" appears after one's name. It is the darkened, foolish mind that refuses to believe this. One must take God at His Word, not only because it's *true,* but because one's eternal welfare depends on it.

For the Christian, believing in the Word of God is just the starting point of faith, not the finish line; the in-between should be filled by a pursuit of *knowledge* of it. There are atheists and agnostics who can articulate their disbelief in the Bible as absolute truth far more effectively than some Christians can apologetically *justify* their belief! Why is the consistent critique of the Church that many Christians are ignorant of basic biblical content, not to mention its interpretation and application? If God's Word is powerful, trustworthy, and life-altering, as we know it to be, why are such a great number of believers acting like they're *so not into* reading more of it?

We need to pray for a revived fascination with what our Creator and Redeemer is saying to each one of us about the people He wills us to be; we need to rediscover with spiritually newborn eyes and hearts the promises our Heavenly Father has made us and longs to bring to a realization in our lives.

During the sixth century BC when Judah was in a spiritually vandalized condition and in need of national revival, King Josiah became the catalyst for godly and righteous reformation. In the eighteenth year of Josiah's reign, he launched a project to do some repairs on the temple. While the labourers were at work, Hilkiah, the high priest, stumbled upon scrolls containing the Book of the Law (most likely the Pentateuch). Hilkiah then handed the scroll to Josiah's secretary, Shaphan, to read, who then relayed it to the king, reading some of it in his presence. Faced with a fresh revelation of God's Word and the importance of maintaining a monotheistic faith, the wunderkind monarch Josiah sought to rid the nation of all its idolatry and the things that provoked the Lord's anger. Josiah's reaction to the hearing of God's Word began a process of spiritual awakening and restoration (we'll call it revival) in the land of Judah (see 2 Kings 22:8–13).

Given that many Christians today are in terrible need of their very own "Josiah moment," should we be surprised when some express fear and hesitancy to share Scripture with the spiritually lost? As a pastor I have had contact with a number of believers over the years who told me they would serve needs, pray for people, and volunteer if asked but would not share their faith or dialogue with non-believers about the Bible. This is a difficult topic to broach for any Christian who is underfed and malnourished in his or her intake of Scripture.

Putting intelligent thought and words behind the face of our faith and learning to stand on the promises of God (to borrow the hymn's line) under the heat of non-believing inquisition is a worthy task, one that requires more than a cocksure and overly simplified theological answer on our part. It's not the best response to emphatically claim, "I just choose to believe!" It goes without saying that we *must* believe. But our faith shouldn't come across to people as a dart-in-the-dark kind of exercise. We may never know when we'll encounter someone who might be looking for a reason to believe, almost as much as they are seeking to justify their doubts, in how we respond to their inquiries.

Whenever we engage in a spiritual conversation with a non-believing person, we must guard against giving off a form of faux faith where we can't define our beliefs very well by the Word of God. Consequently, we can end up looking and sounding like a plastic "religious" person, the kind many unbelievers see as being a dime a dozen.

That said, we should never feel like we have to stand on our heads theologically when we're called upon to "give the reason for the hope that [we] have" as Christians (1 Peter 3:15); the Spirit of God must first *open* the hearts of non-believers if they're to receive and be convicted by *anything* we share with them on a spiritual level. Realistically, though, being able to effectively communicate our belief in the Bible is a spiritual balancing act on the scales of fact *and* faith. Christians must communicate to the unsaved that mere cognitive ascent is overrated when it comes to a belief in God's Word. There must also be a leap of faith to accompany intelligent thought! My son Dakota could hear all day that his father will catch him if he jumps off a tall rock near our home, but at some point he still has to put his faith in me by leaping into my arms.

Trusting in God and putting our faith in His "love letter" to us (the Bible) works similarly. In order to answer the question of the Bible's validity as God's authoritative Word to us, we must give a balanced explanation that makes room for both God's involvement and the human element in the forming of the canon of Scripture. In one sense the Bible is a *human* document because its authors were as fallen spiritually as you and I are. The authors of the Bible each wrote using their unique personalities, perspectives, and creative writing skills. It's similar to the same spiritual transaction that takes place whenever the Word of God is expounded by human teachers.

By the same token, because the Bible is about God's involvement in human history since the creation of the world, it is also a spiritual document. Even though Jesus is the central person in God's address to us, threaded through both the Old and New Testaments, God chose to communicate His message of redemption in Christ through the *critical thinking* of human vessels. Some of the Bible's authors were writing from first-hand accounts, while others wrote from the memories of the apostles' teachings in the early Church (known as the "apostolic circle"). The authors of the Scriptures, then, were responsible for the recording, preserving, and the passing on of the accounts and events of Jesus' earthly ministry as they understood it—through the presence of the Holy Spirit in their lives.

Therefore, the writings in the Bible are not *merely* human ideas; neither are they the product of a recklessly sovereign "dictating" God who overrode and even determined the pens of the apostles. Rather, its writers (who were accepted and respected by the very first Christian communities) had reliable authority. This comes closer to the meaning of the biblical term *inspiration* that the apostle Paul speaks of in his second epistle to Timothy: "All Scripture is given by inspiration of God, and is profitable for doctrine, for reproof, for correction, for instruction in righteousness, that the man of God may be complete, thoroughly equipped for every good work (2 Timothy 3:16–17 NKJV).

If we grasp that God desires to make us whole and to round out our lives spiritually by the administration of His Word to our hearts, why then as "sheep" are we not eating more from it? Knowing and accepting God's Word is absolutely indispensable for revival and spiritual renewal to impact the lives of stagnant, biblically starved Christians. "J. H. Merle D'Aubigné, noted Reformation historian, writes, 'The only true reformation is that which emanates from the Word of God.'"[21] The Protestant reformers knew that only a fresh discovery of the life-changing power of God's Word could lead to the spiritual health of Christians.

In the book of Ezekiel we see this truth communicated in a profoundly symbolic way. The prophet Ezekiel in a vision was instructed by God to "prophesy" the "word of the LORD" to the "dry bones" in the valley (Ezekiel 37:4). As a result of Ezekiel's prophesying to the field containing an arid humanity (which symbolized Israel's seemingly hopeless position while exiled in Babylon), the clanking skeletons rattled together until they were fully restored to bodily form, even becoming "a vast army" (Ezekiel 37:10). Israel, as a nation for God's glory, would be made whole again! They would be granted renewed strength through the purifying and spiritually clothing power of God's Word.

Jesus, when He was tempted in the desert at the apex of His ministry, told the devil straight out (and us, from a distance) that godly living makes no provision for taking shortcuts with one's spirituality. With Satan whirling around Him and spinning the best of his seductive webs, the Lord got some desert dust flying the devil's way when He threw down the gauntlet on this matter. "It is written: 'Man does not live on bread alone, but on every word that comes from the mouth of God'" (Matthew 4:4).

In other words, there can be no substitutes to our discipleship and spiritual growth as God's people. We are both sustained and matured in our faith by what proceeds from God's mouth (His Word) and not from any spiritual discount deals devoid of a required obedience and trust. If we ourselves are weak in the Word, how can we encourage and build up *others* in the faith? Like the saying goes, "If we stop learning today, we stop teaching tomorrow."

It raises the question, how do we hope to mobilize and commission another generation of effective teachers in the Church if we're so apathetic about knowing the Word of God today? Even more disconcerting, how are we going to defend the faith we hold to if we cannot explain from the Scriptures why it is essential for everyday living? The Word of God isn't just one aspect of our faith; as Christians, *it informs our very faith!*

We seem too contented as the Church with being spiritually skinny. Yet "thin" is never "in" when it comes to the amount of God's Word we are feeding ourselves with. Some of us need to put on a little "meat" in that area so that the clothes of our faith will fit us better and we can be more spiritually useful to God.

Chuck Swindoll, in his book *Hand Me Another Brick,* touches on the importance of Christians being well-fed by God's Word in order for the Church to experience a revived sense of purpose and ministry. "Like smelling salts, a revival can restore believers whose love for the Lord has grown faint. After weakened Christians have been revived through the proclamation of God's Word, they exhibit a new passion for the things of God and often begin to share the gospel with others."[22]

The Church of Jesus Christ today needs more modern-day Ezras who are efficient and fearless in pronouncing and interpreting the Word of God to the people of God, just as the scribe Ezra did for Israel on the cusp of their return from exile to their homeland of Jerusalem. Oh how we as Christians living in these last days need to uncover and rediscover the heart-cutting, ash-applying, tunic-tearing voice of God in His Word!

We need the fattening spiritual calories of Scripture from not only a pabulum version of its doctrine but also its theological solid food. We need this from our own devotional life "quiet times" and small group ministries and from those who occupy the offices of pastor and teacher in the Church. If we're ever going to see and experience a spiritual awakening in God's house, the precepts of Scripture must be served up with vigour and a "take no prisoners" urgency from biblical expounders.

Pastor and author Steven J. Lawson notes,

> With *sola Scriptura* as their battle cry, a new generation of biblical preachers restored the pulpit to its former glory and revived apostolic Christianity...A heaven-sent revival will only come when Scripture is enthroned once again in the pulpit. There must be the clarion declaration of the Bible, the kind of preaching that gives a clear explanation of a biblical text with compelling application, exhortation, and appeal.[23]

Charles Haddon Spurgeon concurred in recognizing the correlation between revival in the Church and a recovered priority of Bible-centred preaching. "I would rather speak five words out of this book than 50,000 words of the philosophers. If we want revivals, we must revive our reverence for the Word of God. If we want conversions, we must put more of God's Word into our sermons."[24]

Whether we hear God's Word spoken or taught or go before the Word on our own, we are confronted with a spiritual examination. Yet when we read the Bible we are to see the mirror image of Christ in us on its pages as well. As Christians we don't have to fear being ultimately condemned by God when we go before Him. However, we most certainly encounter times at present when Scripture reflects back to us a conviction that we have not been spending time in it and because of that are not living a spiritually sound life. When Christians look into the mirror of God's Word, they need to see more than a grossly gaunt believer who neglects the very spiritual food needed for the life-journey that is the Christian walk. The unsaved need to see believers as people of spiritual sensitivity who balance biblical literacy and conviction with intelligent, relevant faith. If only *thin* wasn't "in" in the Church!

CHAPTER 5

THE STAINED GLASS SCANDAL OF THE CITY ON THE HILL

A Revived Godly Sorrow for Sin

Jesus' teaching in the Gospel accounts show us how much He utilized powerful word images and pictures to drive home spiritual applications for His listeners. One of the word pictures the Lord used to describe the effect that His disciples were to have on the world was "a city on a hill." What that city is to emanate, of course, is the righteous glow of God's "light" to the "world" through His people (Matthew 5:14–15).

In that particular portion of the Sermon on the Mount, Jesus was asking His disciples to read between the spiritual lines of His teaching. The Lord appealed to the common sense of His students when He stated the obvious about a city on a hill: it's one that "cannot be hidden." Further to that point the Lord reasoned that neither would anyone in their right mind "light a lamp and put it under a bowl," which would result in the lamp's flame being snuffed out.

Each of the Lord's word pictures underscore an all-important spiritual reality for Christian witness in the world during these last days: *be seen, and be seen as righteous*. The Church must be as unavoidably visible as a "city on a hill" and function as a "light" in a dark world. Imagine, Jesus was asking Christians to actually *live* like they're Christians!

Truly, for a disciple of Christ to act in any way contrary to their true identity and purpose amounts to spiritually scandalous activity, a prospect that not only grieves the heart of God but inevitably invites a reviled response from the very world the Church hopes to impact for His glory.

By now we are unfortunately all too familiar with the reams of reports concerning numerous allegations of sexual abuse by priests in the Roman Catholic Church. One report notes that at least eight dioceses entered bankruptcy reorganization due to the massive liability they face from sex abuse settlements. Most cases centred around the Church's cover-up of abuse and the retention of offending clergy.[25]

Such revelations have infuriated the public and given Christianity-bashers even more ammo to add to the vigorous hate they already possess for the Church. To be sure other cases of sexual abuse have been reported within other branches of the Christian Church. However, much has been made of the Roman Catholic Church's shoddy attempt at cleaning up the moral and spiritual mess resulting from the tragic scandals. The situation was captured in Linden MacIntyre's raw and riveting *The Bishop's Man*. The gritty book explores the dark secrets and sorrowful tribulations of one Father Duncan MacAskill, a Roman Catholic priest in Nova Scotia. MacAskill is sent to do the Church's dirty work in shuffling off clergy accused of abuse while preventing scandals from becoming public knowledge.

The reality of scandals within the Christian Church (Roman Catholic or otherwise) has only emboldened an already hostile anti-church culture that watches the latest news headlines, waiting to pounce on anything that resembles a controversy. People who have no use for the Church are always looking for the chance to feel good about shouting "Hypocrite!" Any perceived scandal in the Church (especially those that directly involve the clergy) make the Christian witness in the world seem invariably suspect. As a result, trust in the institution of the Church is waning more than ever, and respect for its leaders and their authority in the community seems to be draining faster than water in a newly plumbed sink. Clearly, what has been sown in terms of scandal within the Church has reaped its inevitable consequence: more mud being thrown on its already dirt-caked reputation throughout the world.

Let's face it, the perception of the Church as a powder keg of the worst kinds of hypocrisy and opportunism is a reality in our religiously pessimistic culture. As Christians we shouldn't stop at just wincing whenever we see our world sneering at the Church or the media gloating over the failures of God's people. We should be deeply upset for harming God's reputation and for breaking His heart.

It's particularly painful when the famous and influential in popular culture take the Church to task for talking one way and doing another. When the mucky laundry of God's people is hung up for greater public consumption, the embarrassment that ensues can be a difficult pill to swallow; it goes down our throats like a boulder.

It's like the point that U2 singer Bono makes in a not so subtle lyrical rebuke of the Church in the band's 1995 song "Please." The vocalist seems to genuinely despair that Christians often act like they're one thing (holy) but can't hide the fact that they're really another (scandalous). Bono has enough common-man clout as well as spiritual grounding (despite his eccentricities) to gain the ear and the respect of prominent evangelicals. He's a cerebral songbird who doubles as urban preacher expounding an altruistic doctrine, and his congregation (U2 fans) likes the sound of his sermons.

In some ways I can appreciate how Bono exposes religious superficiality, just enough to air out hypocrisy, challenging those who *should* know better (God's people/the Church) to *do* better. Christians can never advance the Kingdom of God even one spiritual millimetre when righteousness is confused with entitlement and outward ritual outshines inward transformation.

Christians who have a good grasp of the Church's development through the ages (a history that includes both incredibly high and low spiritual points) fully realize why scholarly historians have not always been very kind to it. The Church hasn't always produced rainbows in terms of its witness; that we must accept. However, it's unfair to compare any institution in the present with its scandalous "black eyes" of yesteryear, though it seems to be a popular thing to do in anti-church polemics. Everything from the witch hunts to the Crusades to papal corruption and hierarchal nepotism in the Church has been used as reasons why people don't trust the established Church and don't want to be a part of it.

It doesn't take ugly baggage within the history of Christianity for some to hold an eternal grudge against Christians. We who advocate righteous living are doing a great job ourselves at giving the watching world reason to question whether Jesus has actually changed our lives for the better. The witness of the Church of Jesus Christ suffers when all sense of godliness is ditched in the lives of Christians in favour of sinful behaviour that even leads to *criminal* activity.

A disturbing and bizarre event recently happened in a Baptist church in the deep south of the United States. During an intense conflict between leaders, one pastor tased another, while another leader stabbed the mother of the pastor who used the taser! Do not adjust your eyes; you read those words correctly. This did happen in a church!

As a leader who's been in the Church a long time and is thoroughly aware of the emotional capabilities packed within heated conflict, I wasn't at all that shocked to hear about this happening amongst God's people, even amongst God's shepherds. However, those of us who believe in a Saviour who suffered to free us from such deeply sinful behaviour should be saddened by these unfortunate stories coming out of the Church. Something is spiritually way out of whack whenever the place of God's house and the sanctity of its testimony and ministry affords people punch lines such as "I went to a church service, and the Jerry Springer show broke out!"

Someone once told me that if I showed him "a reason to believe" he would believe. Truth is, although Jesus *is* reason enough for anyone to believe in God and trust in His Son for their salvation, it's the *individual Christian* that most unsaved people are judging the merit of His message by, something I find altogether terrifying. The incredible spiritual responsibility that the follower of Christ bears to represent Him in this world as a part of the "city on a hill" is quite sobering.

The Church is called to be a magnetic passageway for the unsaved to consider the faith. However, the fact that Christians sometimes make better stumbling blocks and barricades than attractive streamlines of spiritual guidance should be the catalyst that puts legs to our prayers for revival and spiritual renewal in the Church. Given that God's people tend to act in ways that reinforce religious stereotypes and slow down those who need to come to Christ, how can we not crave standing under frequent showers and even downpours of revival today? If we are going to be spiritually believable guides who point people to the Saviour, we must cast aside our umbrellas of indifference and get Holy Spirit wet!

As Christians we are all spiritual role models for a lost world. Our society is aimlessly groping around in the dark, trying to feel its way to a door that will open the way to real hope. The problem is, it can't find it without the assistance of God's people. The Church, then, must come alive and realize its "city on a hill" potential to function as a much needed spiritual map of the road leading people to the promises of God and a better day ahead.

Though I've yet to personally use a GPS while driving my vehicle, I've been a passenger in cars when a GPS either malfunctioned or couldn't read certain regions or streets. The reaction of the driver can be hilarious, if not dangerous. I've seen cars come close to veering off the road because the driver was too occupied with the contrarian device that sat atop the dashboard.

That's the reality of living in a technological age. We've become reliant upon computerized technology (the BlackBerry blackout, anyone?) to get us by. As a consequence we find ourselves totally lost and even sidelined when the gadget we're dependent upon stops working the way it's supposed to!

Our spiritual lives in a sense function like a spiritual GPS. The unsaved are more dependent upon our Christian lives operating properly (righteously) as a means of Godward guidance for them than we'd like to think. Therefore when the Church falters or fails in some way, it's almost like we're taking the world along with us off God's intended road for them.

Again, this was something that occurred all too often within the nation of Israel. In Isaiah 42 the Israelites had their mission laid out for them quite plainly. God's people were to be "a light for the Gentiles" (Isaiah 42:6). The Lord was clear in that Israel was intended to be a blessing to the nations around them in Canaan (Genesis 22:18). The Israelites were the schooled ones, the enlightened ones on the things of Yahweh. Consequently, it was their task to reflect the knowledge they had of their holy God to the hordes of religiously ignorant people surrounding them.

Their mission path seemed straightforward enough, yet the nation had no problem getting themselves off the beaten spiritual track at various intervals! Unfortunately, even the leaders of Israel failed miserably to maintain righteous living and brought shame and consequences upon themselves and the nation as a whole.

One of those leaders was King David. Though he wasn't the only king in Israel to "blow it" and incur God's judgment, his dramatic fall from prominence and honour shows how low the mighty have to sink sometimes before they realize how spiritually scandalous their lives have become. After David went off course morally and spiritually as a result of his affair with Bathsheba and by his subsequent plotting of her husband's (Uriah's) death, he awakened to the fact that not only did he need God's pardoning for his sin but he was in dire need of having his passion for living for the Lord revived and renewed.

In the psalms we read many heart-and-soul passages where David cries out for that exact reality to come upon him. One of those passages was even used as a lyric in a popular Christian chorus: "Create in me a pure heart, O God, and renew a steadfast spirit within me. Do not cast me from your presence or take your Holy Spirit from me. Restore to me the joy of your salvation and grant me a willing spirit, to sustain me" (Psalm 51:10–12).

If Christians are not continuously seeking to be orientated spiritually on a vertical plane (towards God), then people without Christ will quite naturally keep orientating themselves on a horizontal plane (comparing the quality of their righteousness to human standards). The easiest spiritual hurdle for the unsaved to jump over is the one that resolves that their righteousness is no less than that of those who claim to *be* righteous!

When I was a youngster my favourite book to read at bedtime was Leonard Kessler's *Mr. Pine's Mixed-Up Signs*. Mr. Pine is a sign-painter in a place called Little Town whose mayor asks him to replace all the sun-faded and aged signs around the town. A comical series of events ensues. Everything would have worked out fine if Mr. Pine hadn't misplaced his all-important spectacles and ended up installing all the newly painted signs in the most inappropriate of places. For instance, the sign Mr. Pine put on the mayor's door read "This Way to the Zoo!" The sign over the bank said "Bread!" Oops!

Sadly, a similar book could be written about the Church, couldn't it? Throughout the history of Christendom God's people have posted the wrong moral signs and given erroneous spiritual directions to an already misguided world. Like Mr. Pine, the Church has often operated as if it were missing its spiritual lenses as signposts for God.

The spiritual aftershocks stemming from the Church's failures and shortcomings throughout its history pose a formidable challenge for the reputation of God's people, especially in the arena of evangelism. It's a reality that's led many people within the Church to wonder how a lost world will find its way to the Saviour when we as His own people are blocking His redemptive avenues on earth.

How *can* we as Christians in Christ's Church ever hope to powerfully minister for Him if we're tripping our own selves up while entangling the unsaved along with us? How can we be that shining and exemplary "city on a hill" for the world Jesus calls us to be when our lights are always going out via the conflicting spiritual signals we too often give the world as a testimony?

Some in the Church see the predominant characteristic of God as judgment-oriented: "He's angry, and there's Hell to pay!" Other Christians see God primarily in a more gracious light as One who lovingly understands our weaknesses and promises to be faithful in forgiving us. We understand why God can be displeased and even become angry at His people sometimes. However, we are thankful that He is also a God of great mercy and the God of fresh starts and new chances.

God certainly knows our penchant for wicked behaviour as His *finite* people; He also knows our potential to be powerful lights for Him as His *redeemed* people. Church, we've got to repent where we have failed to be the kind of righteous and visible "city on a hill" people the Sermon on the Mount tells us we should be; it's one of Jesus' convicting word pictures that's adhered strongly to the collective conscience of all His disciples throughout the history of the Church.

We need God's forgiveness for those times when we've allowed scandal within the Church to be the "bowl" that hides and extinguishes the flame of what's supposed to be an alluring Christlike testimony for the world. In our confessions, may we seek to have the wick of our witness relit so that God's Name may be hallowed once again, not only in the halls of His house on earth, but also in the world.

CHAPTER 6

DECEIVED AND ORNERY SHEEP BEGIN TO DIVIDE THE FOLD

A Revived Concern for the Unity and Mission of Christ's Body

If there is a greater paradox that exists in this world than that of the spiritual journey of a disciple of Christ, I have yet to hear of it. There are times in my Christian life when I'm absolutely on fire for God; it's evident in how I pray *faithfully*, in how I act *righteously*, in how I think *biblically*, and in how I serve *consistently*. By contrast, there are the times in my life when I am not praying faithfully; times when I'm not acting righteously, when I'm not thinking biblically; as well as times when I am not serving consistently. Simply, we who the Bible refers to as "sheep" are quite often a contradiction unto ourselves!

As Christians we shouldn't be ignorant of the fact that our hearts for God do indeed seem to skip a beat or two at times and even beat irregularly in certain seasons of our spiritual lives. An occasional lapse into spiritual arrhythmia arises when our will to live out the unique quality of our redeemed lives gets arm-wrestled by our sinful nature, letting it overpower our minds and dominate the desires of our hearts.

During these sin-infused arid valley seasons of the spiritual life, we'll most likely find that the spiritual vision of our lives has blurred. When we're not keeping our eyes on the road marked for discipleship, spiritual accidents of many kinds await us. The signs that we may be stuck in such a condition or headed towards it are obvious; in other words, we should be able to spot the warning signs along the path of our spiritual journey!

It's when our adherence to biblical values begins to slip and we subsequently begin to compromise more with God's commands. It's when our intent to live like the person Jesus saved us to be seems to idle in a spiritual never-never land. It's when we become a little too carefree about decisions we make, when prayerfully consulting God becomes an afterthought, if there's any thought of doing so at all! It's when we're easily drawn away from our commitments in attending public worship and serving God, towards trivial distractions and priorities.

Perhaps the main evidence that the spiritual alignment of our lives is in sorry shape is when our longing for intimacy with God has recessed to the point where we feel less burdened to be in His presence or before His Word on a continual basis. There are brothers and sisters in Christ all around us who step into these spiritual potholes and who foolishly wander as God's sheep into darkened spiritual forests. *You* could be that brother or sister in Christ!

With the plethora of resources at our disposal these days to aid us in living the spiritual life, in addition to the privileged and varied access we have to God's Word, it's hard to fathom why we continue to struggle with holding up our end of the love-relationship we have with the Saviour. It's even more difficult to accept that current contingents of Jesus' Church either have already left or will leave the authority and coverage of God's Word in exchange for something spiritually odious and downright deceptive.

Paul's prophetic words to Timothy speak to this present reality. The apostle alerted the young pastor at Ephesus that a time would come when people would no longer "put up with sound doctrine" but rather move out from the Church and embrace the folly of "myths" and other false teachings (2 Timothy 4:3–4).

I remember being at a general denominational conference when a pastor stood up and announced that his view of homosexuality had changed and that he could no longer stand with and support the denomination's biblical understanding of and stance on the issue (being sinful behaviour). This minister then proceeded to verbally relinquish his credentials right on the spot. This was not an isolated occurrence within this denomination on this subject either! With trends in the mainline Protestant churches pointing towards leaders either straying from or full out departing from the orthodox teaching of the Scriptures on various social issues, we ought to be more concerned with what Jesus would have to say about such a reality within the Body of Christ.

Today, if each of our churches were to actually receive report cards from the Lord, I wonder how anxious we'd be when opening them. Even more spiritually hairy a thought is what Jesus might state in the reports if He addressed each individual believer as well! Quite possibly the Lord would use words similar to the ones He addressed to the church of Laodicea in Revelation 3. The spiritually wandering Laodicean church received a righteous reproof (more like a shellacking!) in the congregational assessment and subsequent correction Jesus laid on them.

Though we may not know a whole lot about the church, what's obvious is that the Christians in Laodicea struggled in their allegiance to the Saviour. "I know your deeds, that you are neither cold nor hot. I wish you were either one or the other! So, because you are lukewarm—neither hot nor cold—I am about to spit you out of my mouth" (Revelation 3:15–16). Talk about crystallized indifference on the part of Christians getting its due divine comeuppance! Another church, in Ephesus, received a letter from Jesus recorded in Revelation 2. The quality of the love they had for the Lord and for each other prompted a warning from Jesus that if things didn't turn around, they'd have their "lampstand" taken from them (Revelation 2:5). Sure enough, the ancient city of Ephesus eventually came to ruin (including the ancient church there)!

Jesus clearly stated to the Ephesian church that it was possible for a body of believers (as a judgment upon them) to lose their claim as being stations of light, "lampstands," for Him. How altogether odd it is to think that a group of Christians could gather as a church yet no longer have Christ's missional blessing amongst them or His stamp of spiritual approval upon them. Imagine being told by the One we think we're worshipping and serving that our overall spirituality isn't cutting it in Heaven. Imagine today having some of our fancy-faced buildings and vaunted ministries shut down by our heavenly denomination on account of them being spiritually weighed and found wanting.

The overarching spiritual message of Jesus to the Revelation churches couldn't have been more pointed: *it's a privilege for anyone to be a part of representing Almighty God on this earth, not a right;* no pretenders or part-timers may apply! The aforementioned address of Jesus to the church in Ephesus especially should serve as a caveat to any church today whose very heart and core either are teetering on wandering or have already fully wandered away from God. Given that reality, it's encouraging to know (and it must delight the heart of God) that there are some evangelically based "renewal" movements taking place within some mainline Protestant denominations in Canada at the present time.

I believe we could all admit with certainty that, whether we have a burden to see it happen or not, the universal Church of Jesus Christ is gravely in need of revival and spiritual renewal today. One could fairly argue, "Hasn't it always?" The answer of course is an emphatic "Yes!" Yet we appear to require transformational revivals in frequent measure today as a rapidly expanding pervasive spiritual darkness seeps further into the heart of humanity. However, if even pockets of churches all over the earth could be awakened and restored in their biblical focus and spiritual fervency, there could be great spiritual momentum for the Kingdom of God. We must remember that our morally porous and socially mangy world remains Satan's region of "authority" (Luke 4:6). No wonder we're in such a colossal pickle spiritually!

It's plain to see that the world is now on an unprecedented and slick path of change, some things for the better but many things for far worse. The reality is that the cause and effects of change in the world ultimately challenge the Church of Jesus Christ to respond in kind.

Certainly, the Church *has* been walking its own road of change since its existence. Change (whether it be in culture or in operations) within the Body of Christ can be an opportunity for God's people to not only study where they're at in the faith but also to grow. In many respects, the way we "do" church now has been forever altered. From multi-media and PowerPoint presentations to coffee shops and stores in church foyers to Christian branding and adoption of spiritual consumerism, change in the Church is here to stay. It's not our grandparents' (or even our parents', perhaps) Church anymore!

Though our hearts must be focused upward as we serve and worship God, we must also keep looking outward to see what makes the society we are called to redeem go 'round. Christians need to be constantly evaluating and adjusting how they relate to their post-Christian postmodern culture as a part of gauging how they can effectively minister to it.

However, our ministries must never become cultural mirror images of what our society wants the Church to be. Though we must listen to what our culture desires from the Church, we must always filter its counsel through the Word of God. Christians must keep biblical principles as their chief motivation for whatever they change in their ministry. Churches, for instance, must steer away from pressures to turn its ministry mandate of evangelizing the world into nominal neighbourhood programs and initiatives that merely offer help and social assistance; they must steer clear of replacing the components of discipleship and the preaching of deep biblical precepts with non-offensive, spiritually scaled-back "pointers" that call for no commitment to Christ or life change.

As much as disciples of Jesus are to be countercultural, the challenge of our missional assignment exists in that we must still *encounter* our culture! Though Christians are "aliens and strangers" in the world (1 Peter 2:11), the world doesn't have to view God's people as a sort of "holier-than-thou" species or as spiritual extraterrestrials who congregate in their church spaceships and who possess an other-worldly dialect to match it! We can get too far from the world as the Church (become too heavenly minded), yet we can get too close to it as well (and become no earthly good).

Our ever-changing world not only provides the context and opportunity for Christian mission, it also presents (and tempts) God's people with any and all diversions and distractions, many of which become pre-emptive tools and traps the devil uses to undercut the spiritual zeal and evangelistic efforts of God's people. Despite the "good ideas" our culture possesses and can influence Christians by, the Church must be *the Church*. It must remain distinct in what its purpose and presence mean to its world and not dissolve into a veritable Xerox of the local Lion's Club or YMCA. Though this may sound too academic, when attendance and financial figures in the church plummet, God's people can get awfully desperate as well as deceived. When other organizations are attracting more people to their functions and events than we are as the Church, we can jump too quickly (and without much prayerful consideration) in trying to copy what we perceive as "working" and "successful" in society.

Sometimes God's people act like they've forgotten that the Saviour of the Church is still *Jesus* and not a singular program or some attracting gimmick. In its answer to what's "trending" within its culture, the Church must be careful not to misplace or replace Jesus at the centre of all it does. People still need the Saviour today, and it's the tough and yet equally rewarding task of the Church to communicate this truth to its world.

Differing views within the Church as to our identity (what makes us "Christian") and purpose (what we should be doing as the Body of Christ) can lead to interpersonal conflicts and head-on collisions of agendas, to God's people forming "sides" against one another. The reality of change within the Church (as is the case within any organization) tends to present challenges that inevitably test and affect corporate unity. Do we really need to discuss here how unnecessary quarrelling and division has weakened and undermined the ministries of many a church? It has throughout the history of Christendom! As Christians we need to get straight who our real adversary is, who the real competition is (the devil)! I've known churches that entered into prolonged seasons of ministry-exile as a result of congregational fragmentation. Dissension in the Body of Christ is the oil that makes the engine of indifference to testimony and mission run!

Is it any wonder why Jesus' prayer for His disciples before He left them was a revival-esque petition for unity? Jesus was well aware of the fact that His Church would need to keep all the spiritual essentials close to their heart and in constant sight. "My prayer is not that you take them out of the world but that you protect them from the evil one...Sanctify them by the truth; your word is truth...May they be brought to complete unity to let the world know that you sent me" (see John 17:15–23).

"Rolling" with our ever-changing culture and bringing about operational change and new mission strategies in the Church should *never* come about at the expense of unity. Rather, it's by the unifying presence of God's people (by their love) that the world will know that they are Jesus' disciples, not by some freshly forged and polished vision. Without love we're just annoyingly noisy Christians, "resounding gong[s]" (1 Corinthians 13:1). The Church of Jesus Christ must be on its spiritual toes and keep its collective heart glued to what Jesus was praying for in John 17 in terms of His disciples' future ministry.

Consequently, because the Church identifies with a suffering Saviour (whose enemy is now *their* enemy), it behooves us as believers in Christ to see ourselves as being in constant need of revival and spiritual renewal.

Revival has often been understood as a "spiritual" event that produces "outbursts of mass religious fervour" brought about by "intensive preaching and prayer" on the part of Christian believers.[26] Martyn Lloyd-Jones, a Welsh minister of the twentieth century, was an ardent proponent of revival. He defined revival as "an *experience* in the life of the church when the Holy Spirit does an unusual work."[27] Even if the Spirit of God does at times move in inordinate ways during the event of revivals, we can rest assured that great spiritual good can come about.

Revivalism is linked to social reform movements in the United States within the nineteenth century. Christians impacted by the "Great Awakenings" were instrumental in bringing Christian education to the fore and in improving treatment for prisoners and the mentally ill. The fact is, a revived and spiritually renewed Church can affect righteous change in its culture, even if there continues to be a great turning away from the Lord within every facet of it.

As often as I have heard missionaries share about their experiences in advancing the gospel, there always seems to be an underlying asterisk of regret that not enough regions (and consequently not enough people) are being reached for Christ. To this present day, even after all the missions that have been undertaken by the Church throughout its history, millions of people remain eternally lost spiritually for lack of a saving knowledge of Jesus Christ. Many don't even know where to begin connecting the spiritual dots that lead to Him.

This can be vastly true of our own everyday turf as well. Heartbreakingly, I've come to know many young people who don't have even a pittance of knowledge of who Jesus is or why an event like Christmas is celebrated.

Consider statistics showing that half of the marriages in the United States end in divorce. The number of teens who have taken their own lives has increased 300 percent in North America since 1940. There've been roughly 33.5 million abortions in North America over the past twenty-five to thirty years. Like God, we as His people should be weeping over a sin-crusted spiritually dying world. But are we? Or are we too focused on putting up our "dukes" with our fellow Christian brothers and sisters over change or theological differences and issues? What are we doing to shore up any disunity in our individual churches? What are we doing individually to contribute to Jesus' purpose for His Church?

With so much mission left to be accomplished in our world for Jesus, unity in the Body of Christ and oneness of purpose and commission is an absolute essential. Given the Church's propensity for being divided as well as fatigued and disengaged in the faith, a verse like 2 Chronicles 7:14 becomes that internal alarm clock within believers that sounds a spiritual wake-up call. It's a call to the urgency of revival and renewal amongst an often deceived, ornery, and conflicted people of God. It is to that pivotal yet timelessly applicable Old Testament verse and spiritual harbinger I now turn.

CHAPTER 7

JUST GIVE ME 2 CHRONICLES 7:14 OR BUST!

A Revived Hope for Healing and Renewal

"If my people, who are called by my name, will humble themselves and pray and seek my face and turn from their wicked ways, then I will hear from heaven and will forgive their sin and will heal their land" (2 Chronicles 7:14).

God is a big God. I mean, He's a really, really *big* God! Do you know that if a rocket shot through the air at a speed of five miles per second, it would take 37,200 years for it to go just one light year? God thinks big because He's infinite! God created a massive universe that spans the heavens so far beyond our ability to wrap our puny minds around that we can't possibly grasp on this side of eternity how great and mighty He really is.

Remember the words the Lord used to challenge Job when His servant thought he could be Almighty God's critic: "Where were you when I laid the foundations of the earth?...Do you know how its dimensions were determined and who did the surveying?" (Job 38:4–5 NLT). King Solomon realized he was dedicating the newly built temple to a God whom "even the highest heaven, cannot contain" (1 Kings 8:27).

A God who is infinite (and infinitely wise), not to mention uncontainable and therefore indescribable, beyond full human comprehension, is a God who's worthy of our faith and trust. In fact, God, in and through the ministry of Jesus Christ is so enormously benevolent that He wills to bless this world and each one of our lives beyond our pea-sized capacity as finite people to measure (Ephesians 3:20–21). We could live for well over a hundred years, and even if we've been walking with the Lord since we were "knee-high to a grasshopper," we'd never get a full handle on just how good and faithful our Heavenly Father really is.

I doubt whether there's any other single verse from Scripture that stands out as much as 2 Chronicles 7:14 does as a bellwether for the promise and hope of revival whenever we find ourselves huffing and puffing in our faith. In 2 Chronicles 7:14 we have a heavenly waterfall of counsel to carry us back towards the spiritual current of God's Kingdom-operating dimensions that He's established for our lives.

No amount of increase in technology, no amount of political correctness or hopes for social advancement and economic prosperity has been able to solve age-old problems and the bondages of sin. The human problem is an innately and uniquely spiritual one. The only hope our world has for healing (and ultimately for redemption) is to humbly turn to its Creator and to throw itself upon His mercy. When revival and renewal flood through the spiritual arteries of God's people, the "land" becomes the beneficiary of the overflow of blessings. Waves of spiritually righted, mobilized, and vision-filled Christians and churches in these last days can only bode well for the land (the world) at large. This isn't rocket science, as they say, yet there's a required calculation in the spiritual equation for how revival can become a reality: *we must take a verse like 2 Chronicles 7:14 seriously!*

Talk of revival amongst some of God's people may indeed be mere lip service, while others in the Church may treat the term as a nebulous idiom (they've never seen it happen or don't get what it's all about). Within some theologically conservative circles the very mention of the word *revival* is promptly dismissed as a possible tipping point for all that is charismatically controversial, scripturally wonky, and questionably "fleshy" on a spiritual level.

I remember being at a Vineyard church service during the mid '90s, at the height of the so-called "Toronto blessing." The goings-on at this particular Vineyard church were at times as much bizarre and jaw-dropping as they were at times God-honouring. I happened to be sitting next to someone who received a jolt of the Holy Spirit from a person on the platform, who apparently was sending out the Spirit's power to whoever desired it. The person beside me suddenly began to shake with such gyrating intensity, I thought I was sitting next to the resurrected hips of "Elvis the Pelvis" in his heyday!

The unusual happenings at the Toronto chapter of the Vineyard "blessing" were often referred to as a revival. I couldn't help but feel, however, that some of what was going on around me could have equally been dubbed "The Toronto

Contortion." It's no mystery, then, why so many Christians cite some of the more bizarre occurrences associated with "revivals" to pour water on any talk about the subject in the Church. This is an unfortunate and short-sighted attitude to have towards biblical revival.

Thankfully, there are many believers who see clearly through the heightened suspicions surrounding the event of revival and grasp the potential that an authentic revival has for producing spiritual fruit and bringing about Kingdom gain.

I knew of an older pastor who used to pray for revival in his neighbourhood. He did this by going out on his balcony every day and praying over a piece of vacant land across the street from his building. The pastor's sustained prayer was that one day a Bible-believing, soul-winning church would inhabit that spot and reach its community for Jesus. Amazingly, his prayer was answered!

Praying for revival may seem like a marathon endeavour, even a hopeless spiritual venture. Despite the arduous effort that fruitful prayer can demand of us, Scripture bears witness to the fact that God wills to revive us again and again! The onus is on His people to will it themselves, enough to keep praying for it.

Just as Christian parents are burdened for the spiritual quality of their own children's lives, God's people belong to Him, and so He cares about the spiritual condition of *His* children. In 2 Chronicles 7:14 the Lord reminded Solomon of that very truth; His people (Israel) *belonged* to Him and thus were "called" by His *name*.

AS GOD'S PEOPLE, WE *BELONG* TO HIM AND ARE CALLED BY HIS *NAME*

As God's people in the Church, we have been *called out* of the world by God in Christ. The original New Testament Greek word for this is *ecclesia*, meaning that Christians are a people who are set apart for God and for His purposes in the world. This means that we, in the same sense as Israel, now belong to God.

And just as we desire to give our own children good things, so God desires to bless the socks off His children. If we want God to move in powerful ways in our midst as Israel experienced, if we want to see our churches and individual ministries spiritually fortified and empowered to bear fruit, we need to closely examine what God was saying to Solomon in 2 Chronicles 7.

Just what did the Lord require of His covenant people of Israel in order for them to be revived, and what might He be asking of us as His Church today so that we can see the revival and spiritual renewal we so long for?

When Israel was called out of the world and made into a great nation with the promise of descendants as numerous as "the stars," they were *called to be God's people.* From that point on, God put His Name on them; He *owned* them. It's like what we sometimes do with our children's possessions when they take them to school. Elaine and I are forever using a Sharpie to mark our kids' names on their shoes, caps, and other paraphernalia so that the other children will know that these items belong to our kids. We do this because other kids could have the exact same items, and the name identifies what item belongs to whom. Even though another boy may have the same backpack as my son Dakota, my son's name makes his backpack distinct from the other boy's backpack.

In a similar sense, the numerous pagan people of Canaan (indeed the known world) were to recognize that the Lord's Name was upon Israel as belonging to Him. The pagan people claimed to have many gods, but the one true God of the Hebrews claimed the ownership of but *one* people: Israel. The idea was that whenever the Canaanites looked at the people of Israel, their distinct spirituality as a covenant people under God's righteous laws would display the name of Yahweh written all over them. God, the Author and Lord of all creation, chose a ragtag band of people (Israel) to be His "treasured possession" (Deuteronomy 7:6). They were now *His* people, and He was *their* God.

Likewise, each believer in the family of God is treasured by Him as His own possession. We Christians take that truth for granted at times. We can end up taking back our lives in a sense by living contrary to the reality that we've been "bought at a price" (redeemed by Jesus' blood) (1 Corinthians 7:23). We who are Christians no longer have ownership of our lives (we've denied ourselves). Even our ministries don't really belong to us (they're entrusted to us for the purpose of God's glory). Too often as believers we can go through an entire day carrying ill-advised attitudes, speaking careless words, and generally conducting ourselves like we've contracted a form of spiritual amnesia: we've failed to remember whom it is we belong to and whose Name it is we are bearing!

The grassroots problem with the Church isn't whether we are singing the right songs, have an appropriate building, or are crafting the right mission statement. The problem isn't a question of whether we are keeping up with the "Joneses" in terms of integrating the latest ministry ideas either.

Our fundamental problem spiritually is that even as we belong to God and have Jesus reigning in our hearts, we *still* have sin residing in our lives, and we struggle to break free from personal iniquity. It's a spiritual monkey on our believing backs we cannot rid ourselves of completely in this earthly realm. Our sin is a detriment to the work of God in our lives. Sinful behaviour will always pull the rug out from under our best intentions and ministry plans and can eradicate any hope we have for true spiritual revival to take root in our lives and churches.

An additional problem is that we tend to have short memories as people in general. The context of 2 Chronicles 7:14 suggests that Israel throughout their history forgot who plucked them out from the salad bar of paganism in their world and made them into a great and feared people. *They forgot who they belonged to!* It was out of a love for Israel that God purposed to call a man named Abram (and later changed his name to Abraham, which means "the father of many").

God called Abraham out from the obscure land of Ur of the Chaldean people and promised to make a great nation through his offspring. The Lord put His plan of redemption into action at that point, a plan to bless all the people of the earth through His designated servant and representative Abraham (see Genesis 12:2–3).

God desired to make a covenant (a pact) with the people He redeemed. It was a bond with Israel based on love and loyalty between the Lord and His people. God warned His nation that they were to have "no other gods" before Him (Exodus 20:3). He wouldn't put up with being irreverently double-crossed and rebelliously two-timed. That is why Israel's eventual idolatry was a defiant affront to the Lord's righteous Name, a Name that alone was worthy to be praised and worshipped as the one true God.

The Lord, however, held up His side of the covenant He made with His people, even when aspects of the covenant were unconditional (not dependent upon Israel to sustain it). The nation would repeatedly break the holy commands of their benevolent God and consequently their covenant with Him as well. When they obeyed God's decrees they would be blessed; when they failed to, it resulted in a curse upon them. The prosperity and vitality of Israel as a covenant people hinged upon them being right with their God.

They were to function as a righteousness-emanating lighthouse to the pagan people's and nations' darkened understanding of God surrounding them. However, Israel, to their national and spiritual detriment (and to the detriment of their covenantal relationship with the Lord), were frequently caught with their spiritual guards down, a recurring problem that left them wide open to being influenced and even led by the pagan people. Consequently, we have account after account of God's people needing to be physically (and spiritually) rescued and revived. It became a pattern as well as the legacy of the ancient Hebrews (Israelites).

What about us? What legacy are we as individual believers and as the Church of Jesus Christ in this early stage of a new millennium leaving behind for those who will learn about us later? What will those believers who come after us say and think about the quality of our spirituality? Will they say we resembled more of the carnal culture we were saved to impact than the Person of Christ Himself? Will they dub us "neo-Israelites" who were unable to learn from their history as a people of God? Will they say that we obviously forgot who we belonged to?

Living for God while we're still in the world we've been called out of as His Church is a spiritual conundrum worth exploring. The familiar words of John 3:16 tell us that "God so loved the world that he gave his one and only Son." Jesus died for the people of the world (indeed to bring wholeness and order to all of creation). But where does that leave the Church *in* the world? A connecting theological principle between John 3:16 and 1 John 2:15–17 teaches us to walk the taut spiritual tightrope between loving people in the world and loving the values of the world that inhabit the people.

God commands us not to walk (or fall) on the side of life where we begin to find our meaning, identity, and fulfillment as His people wrapped up in an affectionate "love" for the attractive trinkets and bobbles the physical world has to offer (which operate in the fallen realm of our existence). As individual Christians and as the Church we can subtly adopt and even fall madly in love with the standards, ideologies, and philosophies of the world that are spiritually counterproductive and even lethal. Our history books (including the New Testament) clearly spell out how prone God's people have been throughout the Church age to getting spiritually waylaid and into trouble that way. Lusting for power, prestige, and possessions, for instance, got the better of the Roman Catholic Church in Martin Luther's day.

The kerosene of Luther's actions helped spark the fire of biblical accountability that became the schism in the Church known as the Protestant Reformation. Martin Luther came along at a time when the practices of the Catholic (Roman-based) Church had become thoroughly depraved. The German priest and theologian grew particularly hot and bothered over the Church's selling of *indulgences*. The attitude of the church's clergy, more or less, was that it didn't matter how you lived; as long as you put enough money in the church's coffers, you'd be forgiven.

Luther, with the look of one who had "the buck stops here" plastered all over his face, took a righteous stand and nailed his Ninety-Five Theses to the door of All Saints' Church at Wittenberg in 1517. Luther and a spate of other church leaders at the time were indignant at the corruption of the Catholic

Church. It wasn't their intention to reword the Scriptures but rather to call for their correct interpretation. They never sought in their protestations to bring about an entirely new branch of theology either (though that is what happened). Neither did they aim to spearhead a new strand of the Christian Church (though that came about as well). The predominant quest Martin Luther and the other reformers had was to bring the Church back to an obedience centred upon and adhered to the intended teaching and application of key Scriptures, especially those that pointed to *sola fida* (salvation through faith alone) (see Ephesians 2:8).

It was plain to see that on the cusp of the Reformation the Church was a revival needing to happen! Though the Roman Catholic Church ended up settling for their own reforms, the efforts of Luther and others sparked biblical teaching and preaching that is heard from pulpits all over the world today: the biblical truth that we are saved by the grace of God, through faith in Jesus Christ, and in that way become co-heirs with Him in the spiritual riches of the Kingdom of God. The only organized "Christian" Church in the time of the Reformation needed to remember that they belonged to God and the purpose for which they were called out and away from the sin-compromised values of the world that were contrary to those of the Kingdom of God.

The apostle Peter penned words in his first New Testament letter that were designed to make an enduring point of how distinctly blessed we are as a people of God. "Once you were not a people, but now you are the people of God; once you had not received mercy, but now you have received mercy" (1 Peter 2:10). Peter was steering his first century readers to live in the light of who they had become *in Christ* and to not only appreciate that truth but to appropriate it as well. Christians are to be a people who live so as to not take the longsuffering grace and mercy of God for granted. We all fail in our spiritual lives; God even expects it. However, we must never fall back on our sinful nature and use it like a "note of excuse," as it were, to explain to others why we've sinned against them.

We're all familiar with the convenient badge of false humility some Christians pull out and flash whenever they feel they're in need of putting their sin into spiritual context, the one that states, "Christians aren't perfect people, just people who are forgiven." The underlying truth in such a statement, however, is often misconstrued; because of that, it's also misapplied by a lot of Christians.

We have been "forgiven" in order to "keep in step" with the Holy Spirit's indwelling of us. The opposite of forgiveness isn't perfection; the opposite of forgiveness is guilt for sin. Therefore, if we have been forgiven by God, it must show not in perfection but in lives that are guilt-free because we choose to live righteously. When the world points out our (as well as the Church's) sin to us, perhaps we should rather adopt the comeback "Christians are people who can be guilty of sinning, just like anyone else."

If we're so advantaged (some would say blessed) by God as His people and Church (in the West), why is it that we continuously find ourselves hoping and praying for "revival" to hit our churches, cities and countries here in North America? Could it be that spiritual blessings (in the form of religious freedom, affluence, and the absence of persecution in the Church) don't necessarily equal or guarantee *spiritual maturity* in the lives of God's people?

David Kinnaman, president of the Barna Group, in the insightful, thought-provoking book *UnChristian,* estimates from one survey that approximately 3 percent of young people who profess Christ as their Saviour have a biblical worldview. Add to that the findings of the Barna research people, who say 80 percent of those reared in the Church will likely be disengaged by the time they are twenty-nine years old.[28]

These staggeringly discouraging statistics are nothing short of a spiritual heartache, but also a wake-up call. Could these findings be due in part to the fact that so many who claim to be disciples of Jesus have yet to engage the heart-burden of God for their lives, their families, and communities as they ought to have by now? If those who profess to belong to Christ can't even grasp how they should view their own spiritual lives, let alone how God views the world, how will they ever be able to know the difference between what a godly walk in life looks like and what a "worldly" one does? Christians belong to God in order to *redeem* their world, yet it seems harsh to think that perhaps many have allowed the world to redeem them back!

Where are the persistent and mature legs, arms, feet, and voice of Jesus in our churches going to come from, even twenty years from now? Where will the efforts for evangelism and a mobilizing passion to see the spiritually lost redeemed arise from if a generation of young people are now so uncommitted to biblical values and to the faith and ministry of the Church?

The truth is, sometimes the world redeems their own in its own way. And the way they go about it, even though it falls short of salvation, frankly often convicts me as a follower and disciple of Christ.

Ted Williams—not the late iconic Boston Red Sox baseball player but the one-time street panhandler—wasn't a household name. In fact, he was on the streets of Columbus, Ohio, holding up a weathered sign asking for work and money while sharing about his abuse of alcohol and drugs with all who would give him an ear.

Someone filmed Williams and put the footage on the instant-fame cyber engine YouTube. That was when a producer from a television show discovered that the intriguing homeless man was a former radio announcer who still had an astoundingly rich, deep voice. They took Williams to Hollywood for a voice-over tryout—and the rest, as they say, is "history."

I find Ted Williams' story incredibly fascinating. It's fascinating because we are not used to hearing of people going from "rags to riches" overnight. A freezing street person one week, an employed media darling the next! His story underscores what a life can look like after it has experienced redemption of sorts, how a life going one way can end up in another, much better, way.

We should be cut to the core of our hearts in praying for revivals to head us off at the pass as we see the Body of Christ going one way when it really should be going another. Any hope for revival will not come about by means of cheap-talk or flippant words that lack spiritual dent and grip. Rather, our desire for revival and renewal to take hold of our lives and churches requires not only the traction of *faith* but the identity of a *face*; that is, if we really want it, we've got to own it. The definition of revival, therefore, is really you and me, our collective need and burden for it.

2 Chronicles 7:14 teaches us that because we *belong* to God and because His *name* is on us, we must therefore also be in a right relationship with Him.

AS GOD'S PEOPLE, WE MUST BE IN A *RIGHT* RELATIONSHIP WITH HIM

If we were to look at all the names of God in the Bible and what they mean, we could comprise a rather lengthy list of adjectives: merciful, gracious, patient, full of loving-kindness, truthful, forgiving, just, faithful, almighty, and righteous. God, as our Heavenly Father, left us the best kind of inheritance that any loving father could leave his children: *His good Name.* How, then, could we not be right with a God whose name means so much to us in terms of the promises and assurances we have from His Word?

It still blows my mind that God allows you and me to take on His good and holy Name, and yet it's our relationship with Him that makes this possible. The Church represents God to a world that has lost the sacredness of His Name and what it means to be in communion with its Creator. To be a follower of Christ is to be a "Christian," and in order to be a Christian, one must be rightly related *to*

Christ! We can't claim the one thing (being a Christian) without actually having the other (a saving relationship with Jesus).

The Greek word Χριστιανός (*christianos*), meaning "follower of Christ," comes from Χριστός (*christos*), meaning "anointed one," with an ending borrowed from Latin to denote "someone adhering to" or even "belonging to" as in "slave ownership."[29] If you are a Christian today, you are property as well as a bondservant of Jesus. As a child of God and follower of Christ, you really are our Heavenly Father's adopted "next of kin"! In other words, you're *related* to Him!

Like you, I too have seen just about every cheesy-looking "Christian" shirt that has some sort of biblical one-liner pertaining to our relationship with Jesus written on it: "He's Lord Of All, Or Not At All"; "Hang with Jesus: He hung out for you." I don't have anything against God's people wearing such outwardly religious messaging on shirts, though I seldom do. However, if we're going to don one of them, let's do Jesus proud by living out whatever "truth" we're carrying around and advertising like a human sandwich board for all to see (and perhaps mock).

So the next time you spot someone with a Christian "fish" symbol on the back of their vehicle whooshing in and out of lanes and speeding, I dare you to catch up to them and give them the finger (that is, point them back to the name they are bearing on the back of their bumper!). If we're going to let motorists know we're Christians (and thus related to Jesus), we'd better drive like our Lord would!

The lesson is as simple as it is serious. Wherever God lays His good Name, He lays His reputation too! The saying is true—we may be "the only Bible" someone around us may read and come to know God's Son by *before they die*. To those we know who lack even a basic knowledge of Scripture and of Jesus Christ as the Son of God, we may just be defining how they perceive God and what they think of Him. The central task of the Church is to remain a spiritually clear and biblically grounded life-preserving voice for Jesus Christ as it swims in the religiously pluralistic and deceptive ocean of our culture.

If we're missing this vital element of our faith, we may well be relegated to living life in the regrettable shadows of "what-could-have" and "what-should-have" been as Christians and as the Church. We've got one shot at being the people of God to this world; one shot at being channels and reflectors of His goodness, mercy and power, in bringing an eternal perspective and hope to the current global madness. The world's best-case scenario is for the people of God to be right *with* their God so that they might be blessed beyond their ability to conceive, for out of the righteousness of nations comes the overflow of divine favour. "Blessed is the nation whose God is the LORD" (Psalm 33:12).

Second Chronicles 7 finds King Solomon (after the temple has been built and dedicated) being addressed by the Lord as a response to his prayer on behalf of Israel. The message from Heaven is elementary: God would pour out His blessings from above on His people of Israel if they'd just seek to honour Him and live before Him in humble surrendered obedience.

The Lord explains to Israel's king that His displeasure with the nation would result in such things as "famines" and "plagues" being visited upon the land and the people. However, the consequences of Israel's disobedience could also be reversed. If the spiritual compass of God's people pointed back towards the Lord once again, they would experience not just a reversal of their fortunes but a revival in the very heart of the nation in return. This was a conditional promise in that it depended on Israel exhibiting *four* key things of a spiritual nature.

Let's look at what they are. *"If my people, who are called by my name, will humble themselves* [key element: an attitude of the heart] *and pray* [key element: an attitude of faith] *and seek my face* [key element: an attitude of perseverance] *and turn from their wicked ways* [key element: an attitude of obedience], *then will I hear from heaven and will forgive their sin and will heal their land."* If the people of the world were to be blessed through God's people (Genesis 12:1–3), then the people of God had to be in a position *to* be blessed! The Lord's counsel to King Solomon in 2 Chronicles 7 provided the spiritual template for that to happen. God concerns Himself with the state of our hearts, with the quality of our faith, with our willingness to persevere in His presence, and with our resolve to live in obedience.

It's the same spiritual template *we* stand to gain from today as followers of Jesus Christ, the same divine blueprint that builds godly lives so that we as Christians can be a blessing to all who come into contact with us. In order for revivals that usher in spiritual reformation and change to come about, God's people need to *cry out*, "Lord, we've failed You!" "Lord, we haven't been living the way You've called us to!" "Lord, please forgive us and restore our relationship with You; revive and renew the cause of our faith in this world."

We have so much iniquity littering the grounds of our spiritual lives (and churches), and yet we have much more grace from Heaven's storehouses to claim in exchange to clean up the messes we've made. The psalmist says that if we harbour sin in our hearts, God will not listen to our petitions (Psalm 66:18). But

2 Chronicles 7:14 says that if we go to Him with the right heart, He promises to bless that.

In his classic book *The Revival We Need,* Oswald J. Smith recounts a time when a young lawyer came to faith in Christ in the year 1821. God filled that lawyer with such fervent power of the Spirit that his ministry as a Presbyterian minister and evangelist became remarkably fruitful. Charles Grandison Finney along with a few others was convicted to pray extensively for the power of God to hit the eastern region of the future United States. In response to their prayers, a movement of God occurred that later became known as the Second Great Awakening of the early nineteenth century. On one occasion, the Holy Spirit was poured out so fiercely that even before Finney arrived at a particular place to preach, the people were already crying out for God to show "mercy" on them.[30]

Ultimately, then, our hope for revival and spiritual renewal will always rest on each one of us who professes Christ. It's not a question as to whether God wills to revive us continuously. Rather, it's a question embedded in the church's court of decision: *how badly do we want it?*

It starts with a godly discontent for the state of our spiritual lives and the Church; it results in the holy favour and power of God's Spirit filling us and empowering our lives and ministries to affect our world, one Christian and one church at a time! Certainly, God's chief purpose in the event of revival and in seasons of renewal is to make His people spiritually fit by the Holy Spirit's ministry of grace upon them.

I would like to think that when true revival strikes down on God's people, there will be outward manifestations of spiritual fruit: contrition for one's sin and a sorrow for the quality of one's spiritual life, reconciliation, an awakened grief and burden for lost souls, endurance to keep on going for God in the midst of personal struggles, and an emergence of divine strength and resolve to serve God more consistently. If that were to happen in the lives of Christians in *any* given church, I believe its community wouldn't be able to shade their eyes from the glow that would seep through every door and window where a believer lives.

Spiritually exiled Christians (throughout the Scriptures) are continuously invited home to the heart of God so that they may be revived and consequently thrive for Him! Second Chronicles 7:14 is just one place in which we can find such an invitation. Though we cannot force God's hand in such an event as revival, He still wills to answer prayers like that of the psalmist: "Will you not revive us again, that your people may rejoice in you?" (Psalm 85:6).

CHAPTER 8

BE AFRAID, BE *VERY* AFRAID; IT'S GOD WE'RE TALKING ABOUT!
A Revived Reverence for the Almightiness of God

My wife, Elaine, and I, out of curiosity once attended a taping of a nightly talk show in downtown Toronto. While we and many others were waiting to file into the studio to take our seats, cards were passed out asking everyone to let the television station know a little more about themselves. Once we were seated in the actual studio, a representative of the show proceeded to highlight a few of the cards that were filled out. The one that stood out to me the most was where one young man wrote that he was "fearless."

When asked what he meant, the young man reiterated that he pretty much feared *"nothing"*; even if he was to see a shark coming towards him in the water, he'd "swim right up to it and punch it in the face." Perhaps someone influential in his life should tell the young fellow that possessing a healthy fear of some things in life (especially a shark) is actually a *good thing!*

It reminded me of James "Buster" Douglas (who was deemed a can't miss underdog by "experts" in the sport of boxing). Shortly before his 1990 bout with the then undefeated and much feared heavyweight champion Mike Tyson, he was asked if he at all was afraid of stepping into the ring with his opponent. Douglas humbly but stoically responded, "I fear no man. I only fear God." Douglas ended up shocking the boxing world shortly thereafter by doing the inconceivable: *knocking Tyson out in the tenth round!*

Perhaps the New Orleans Saints of the National Football League could have used a little fear of the potential punitive consequences of carrying out a "bounty" system. Players on the team were given financial incentives to "take out" certain players on opposing teams, even if it meant that those same players could be injured in the process. It was a scandal that rocked the league and left the commissioner, Roger Goodell, no choice but to discipline the team in record-breaking fashion, which included the loss of draft picks and lengthy suspensions to personnel. I couldn't help but chuckle at a headline I read pertaining to "Bounty-gate": 'The Wrath of GOoDell hits his unholy Saints!"

Fear: it's good to have some rational aspects of it in life, and yet it's to our detriment to fear things we really ought *not* to.

We often underestimate just how relentless the devil can be in his pursuit of keeping God's people shrouded in a cloak of needless panic and fear. The sinister plan and plot of the evil one is to inflate the actual size of *rational* fears we possess. The devil aims to increase our preoccupation with suspicion and hysteria as far as they relate to *possibilities* in our lives that would bring trial and tribulation but as yet are not a *reality*. In short, Satan is like the phantom "boogey man" we're all familiar with from our childhood, who tries his best to convince us that he still resides behind the doors and under the beds.

In the Bible, the Greek word for fear, φόβος, phobos, is the root of where we get our English word for *phobia*. A phobia is a type of anxiety disorder usually defined as a persistent fear of some object or of a certain situation in which the one who suffers will go to great lengths trying to avoid.

However, there are some fears that we *should* have!

I should fear, for instance, jumping off a tall building without a safety harness (even with one!). I should fear putting my hand on a hot stove element. I should also fear what might happen to my marriage if I were to mistreat my wife or dishonour my wedding vows. Spiritually speaking, I should fear what could happen to me if I were to allow sin to mount up in my life.

There are natural human consequences built into rational fears. Yet the central spiritual principle (and command) of God's Word is that we are to "fear the Lord" above anything else.

Why should we fear the Lord? Does it mean that God is onerous and wrought with a short-fused vengeance? Should we be cowering and trembling under His rule? Not really. Though it's a *good* thing to fear God, a careful study of the term "the fear of the Lord" can be a helpful and liberating spiritual exercise.

We are to "fear" the Lord not because He will strike us down if we live like we're unafraid of Him and indifferent to His will, but because it is "the beginning of knowledge" (Proverbs 1:7). A respectful and loving reverence for God and His commands leads to a life of peace with Him and to the acquisition of His favour and blessings in our lives. "The eyes of the LORD are on those who fear him, on those whose hope is in his unfailing love...We wait in hope for the LORD; he is our help and our shield" (Psalm 33:18–20). By contrast, the Bible says that someone who rejects God and does not fear Him, continuing to do evil, is "a fool" (Psalm 14:1).

To "fear" God, then, as His people, is not some quacked descent into spiritual paranoia or extreme religious ideology. Rather, choosing to *fear* God is a thoroughly rational yet entirely spiritual decision of the heart each one of us must make. However one chooses when confronted with the decision (whether to truly fear God or not) will either reinforce one's *disobedience* to Him or redirect one's will Godward in living an obedient life by faith in Jesus Christ. As well, Christians will never experience the true joy of their salvation if they cherish and nurse their petty divisions and conflicts at the expense of a fearless view of their accountability before God.

Chances are, at one time or another we've all gotten caught up in the ever-churning gossip treadmill of church life. If there's one thing I know about that kind of deal, it's this: *murmuring and indulging in speculative and harmful rumour as a child of God is a colossal waste of spiritual strength that only leaves the spirit of a Christian distracted, wounded, and open to satanic attack!* Believers who internally yearn for a revived "fear of the Lord" in their lives know how much a righted self-view of who they are in light of their Holy Creator is needed. If there's a more vital spiritual variable that's paramount to growth, maturity and unity in the Body of Christ than our collective need as Christians to fear God, I haven't seen it!

In many areas within Scripture, God's people of Israel were specifically commanded to fear nothing else but their God. In Deuteronomy 10 we find one such example. The Israelites had not yet taken hold of the Promised Land of Canaan, something they'd eventually do under the leadership of Moses' successor Joshua. At this point in Deuteronomy, however, Moses, the much-maligned and yet highly decorated leader of the Israelites, stepped up to his makeshift pulpit and continued to exhort the people of God towards compliance with His commands. The overriding theme of the patriarch's message: the people of Israel were to "fear the Lord."

"And now, O Israel, what does the LORD your God ask of you but to fear the LORD your God, to walk in all his ways, to love him, to serve the LORD your God with all your heart and with all your soul, and to observe the LORD's commands and decrees that I am giving you today for your own good?" (Deuteronomy 10:12–13).

God doesn't merely *advise* His people to obey His commands; He *commands* us to obey them! We're informed throughout the Old Testament how "stubborn" and "stiff-necked" Israel was as a nation. They always schemed to stretch the boundaries of their covenant with the Lord as if it were elasticised. The only difference between the Israelites and the other scattered nations that inhabited parts of the land of Canaan is that Israel could honestly say they *knew* what God required of them, morally and spiritually.

The general rule of worship is that the character of *what* we are worshipping is reflected by the way we live. So if, for example, a teenager idolizes a certain celebrity, chances are that young person will arrange his or her life so as to resemble the personality and look of that celebrity. Since the earliest forms of ancient cultic worship, tribal nations and pagan people throughout the world have emulated the gods they worship with all their requirements and rituals.

Nothing has really changed in that way. Many tribal nations throughout the world today still practice certain "religious" routines and perform various sacrificial rites and rituals as part of their belief system and understanding of the deity they worship. How many of these peoples and nations, though, actually know and fear the One true "Almighty" God who stands outside of us as sovereign and as the ultimate judge of our lives? Although God has made not only His existence but His will for us as His creation known to us, you'd think by how we're living as a human race with such a total disregard for the "fear of the Lord" that we want (or know) nothing of it.

The tragedy of civil wars and the ensuing humanitarian crises that usually accompany them are engulfing various countries in regions throughout the globe today. Many of these wars reveal the darkest side of humanity. Recently an art exhibition entitled "Children Drawing Freedom" was displayed in an art gallery in Toronto. The artwork of young children in Syria captured the horrors of the violence-wracked country. The graphic pictures depict armies shooting civilians and blood-painted streets, as well as funerals being held for the dead. Some of the children who drew the pictures lost both their parents in the ongoing civil war.

New reports that reveal the increasing amounts of political and social instability spreading with prophetic speed throughout the Middle East often cause my thoughts to digress to how our world seemingly possesses precious little thought (and fear) of a future day of reckoning, a designated day when we'll all have to answer to God for how we've lived this life. Even more disturbing (yet also biblical) is the fact that global unrest is escalating at a time when the dawning of Jesus' return to this earth is closer at hand than ever before.

God is clear by what He means when He commands in Scripture that He be feared. The fear of the Lord is to "hate evil" (Proverbs 8:13). If one word comes closest to describing the spirit of our age in these last days and end-times, it is *evil*. The fear of the Lord is as hard to find in people today as a tooth in a snow bank. You hardly hear anyone outside of the faith anymore refer to God in such light, that He is to be feared.

One of the Hebrew words for the word *fear, yir ah,* can be interpreted to mean awesomeness or the majestic reverence one feels when in the presence of God. The Bible says that God is *holy*. We can see Him as coddling and teddy-bearish all we want, but we'd better see Him as holy too. Holiness is His crowning attribute, His preeminent character. The primary word for holiness in the Old Testament means "to cut" or "to separate" away from what is unclean. In applying this term to God, it means moral perfection; it means sinlessness, His righteous transcendence over all creation.

This is the central spiritual truth reflected in the precepts and standards of His self-revelation to us (Scripture); it's what sets God above and apart from us. Therefore, the Bible's message can never be tweaked to conform to public opinion polls or to the prevailing and yet ever-shifting consensus of worldly wisdom. Whatever God commands is righteous. Whenever He judges and whenever He delivers, both actions stem from His righteous character and sovereign purposes, and both operate in holiness.

I wonder how effectively we in the Church today are reflecting lives that show the world *how* and *why* to fear God. If believers are not consciously (daily) leading the way in living exemplary lives that clearly exhibit what fearing God looks like, how can we claim to have a righteous leg to stand on from which to encourage the *world* to fear Him?

In the book of Genesis we read of one who could, in fact, claim to have such a leg (not one, but two!). Enoch's days on earth ended quite unexpectedly. The Bible says God took His servant away and into Heaven, as we would say, "Just like that." Though we're not told why the Lord did it, we can make an educated guess. Enoch "walked with God," but not just that; we're told as well that his life "pleased" God (Genesis 5:24; Hebrews 11:5). Add that information to the fact that Enoch lived in a day when wickedness ruled the earth, and we have a bigger picture as to perhaps why God removed him from the earth. It's possible that God did so to reward Enoch for his righteous life. The brief account of Enoch's life strongly intimates that he was what we would call today a true "God-fearing" man and a person God could trust with His reputation.

For our own spiritual good and for the sake of our testimony, we as Christians have more than enough motivation to live righteously by showing a healthy spiritual respect for the Almighty nature and holy character of our Creator. If as God's people we are not living our lives in "fear of the Lord," we can't reasonably expect the unsaved to do so either.

When I was a child my mom used to tell me that eating the green cardboard-like little balls on my dinner plate (peas) was for my "own good." She'd tell me that eating the crust of my bread would make me "really smart" as well. To this day I'm not really a lover of peas; nor do I enjoy eating crusts. Who knows, though? I may be healthier today, *and wiser,* because I was forced to heed my mother's advice in eating my peas and the crusts of bread as a boy!

God parented Israel by giving the nation the best-possible spiritual pointer, in the form of the divine command that He be *feared.* It was also a command the Lord gave to His people for *their* "own good" (Deuteronomy 10:13). Israel was to fear the Lord for the good of their nation's welfare. Their prosperity and protection as a people being watched and plotted against by their many enemies hung in the balance. The blessings of God would be the natural result of their obedience, but trial, curses, and suffering would surely come upon them if Israel disobeyed the commands of the Lord.

Sometimes the Israelites would get it right as a nation, while at other times they faltered, even greatly, as a nation. Oftentimes a failure to uphold God's righteous commands by even one individual caused the *whole* nation to suffer.

When the Israelites took the city of Jericho, one man (Achan) from the tribe of Judah was overcome by his "sticky-fingers" and took some items that were devoted to the Lord. The whole nation of Israel would pay the price for Achan's sin (along with Achan himself, who was put to death). The consequential damage for Israel wouldn't be minor. The Israelites were subsequently hammered in battle and incurred the loss of a great number of its warrior-men in a fight against the men of Ai (see Joshua 7). To think of what could have been avoided in Israel had Achan for starters feared the Lord!

For some, the thought of living under a God whom they're supposed to *fear* can seem like the spiritual equivalent of driving down the road with a police car tailing them. They're tense as a stone behind the wheel, overly cautious to keep the speed limit in case they'll be pulled over for that, *or something else!*

However, our need to fear God, as His finite created beings, should be understood in a much more gracious light. God knows we are but "flesh" and prone (by virtue of our sinful nature) to wandering into hazardous and bumpy spiritual territories. He knows how easily we are taken away from Him by the potent wiles of His adversary (the devil). God sent His Son to suffer and die for us so that we might resist the kind of *fearless* life that willfully rebels against Him. Jesus came to free us from a life chained to Satan's deceptions that wills to drag us to an eternal separation from God upon our physical deaths. God, on the other hand, wants us to enjoy Him forever where He resides in Heaven. The God-fearing life, the life that does the will of God, is the life that lasts "forever" (1 John 2:17). It's for our own spiritual and *eternal* good, then, to fear the Lord and uphold His commands, something that shouldn't be a burden to those who love God, who empowers us to overcome! (1 John 5:2–3).

God has put His Word forward to be obeyed, not to be *debated,* as is so often the case, in revival-needy lives. There are great rewards for godly living and for spiritual steadfastness. God desired that Israel have the best of the best, yet the promise was conditional; it required that they feared Him. What's the promise of the very first psalm? "Blessed is the man who does not walk in the counsel of the wicked…Whatever he does prospers" (Psalm 1:1–3).

Though I am not a proponent of prosperity theology by any means, it's still encouraging to remember that our Heavenly Father honours and blesses the obedience of His children. As finite creatures we will always be subject to our Creator. We are totally at the mercy of our good God's benevolence towards us, a goodness that demands we, in turn, live our lives worshipping Him in the fear of the Lord, as a proper response to His Majestic Person!

We were made and are owned by a God who's sovereign over our lives, someone who weighs our "motives," who "works out everything" in our lives according to His purpose, and who "determines [our] steps" (Proverbs 16:2, 4, 9). This was Moses' point to Israel in the Deuteronomy 10 passage mentioned earlier in the chapter. "To the LORD your God belong the heavens, even the highest heavens, the earth and everything in it" (Deuteronomy 10:14). The writer of Psalm 50 was obviously mindful of that theological fact, as indicated by his inspired words that the Lord even owns "the cattle on a thousand hills" (Psalm 50:10).

God gave the Israelites some fascinating "sermonettes" pertaining to the subject of His sovereignty and how that played out in terms of their divine election; that is, though everything was made by the Lord, and thus His to own and sovereignly rule over, not every people or nation was originally chosen to be His covenant people. (Only one was, Israel!)

Just as God chose Israel, He also chose you and I to accomplish His purposes in the world today. Why did God convict our hearts and tap on our shoulders in choosing to have mercy on us? Who are we? The Lord does as He wills, and no amount of human interference can frustrate His ultimate plan for our individual lives or for the world. Jesus' going to the Cross is the best example of that truth.

The unbelieving Jews, and indeed Rome, figured they were removing an annoying gnat whose buzz was an inconvenient truth. But all that the crucifixion of the Author of life at the hands of Jesus' enemies amounted to was to play perfectly into the redemptive plan and purposes of God for humanity. Brilliant! The judgment of God upon the unbelieving world flows from the rejection of its only Saviour. The ugliness of Golgotha's scene that first Easter is a vivid reminder of God's sovereignty over the powers and kingdoms of the world and why fearing the Lord is a command to be obeyed.

So we are not to fret under the weight of scary current-day headlines that encroach so mercilessly in layers upon us. We are to fear not these realities but *only God,* who is in complete unbridled control over all things and who reigns supremely over all leaders and rulers in the world. The apostle Paul said, "For there is no authority except from God, and the authorities that exist are appointed by God" (Romans 13:1 NKJV).

A revived and spiritually renewed Church will feature Christians who humbly recognize that each leader among them has been put into service and been given a trust by God Himself. The best thing we can do for our spiritual leaders in the Church, as well as for the leaders of the world's nations, is pray for them, for one day they will have to account for their leadership before God.

Christians who fear God will be cautious in how they treat their assigned leaders, for the One who judges the leader and holds *their* ministry accountable is the same One who will hold *every* believer accountable at the judgment seat of Christ. An ounce of fear now will prevent a pound of red-faced shame when we go before God one day to answer Him. There at God's throne, the amount of fear we have for the Lord in *this* life will ultimately be revealed in the next, our lives judged for the things we did "while in the body" (2 Corinthians 5:10). God is fair in how He deals with our sin. We can rest assured, then, that He'll be fair with the totality of our lives when we go before Him in eternity.

Someone who lost his father asked if I thought his dad would make it to Heaven. I couldn't be absolutely certain myself that the man knew Christ, and the best way I could respond was by clinging to the fact that God is a fair judge. We have the hope in eternity that when God weighs our lives, because He is all-knowing He will take into consideration the many variables surrounding our lives that no one else is privy to. He will know, for instance, those who privately (even at the last minute of their lives) acted in faith by yearning for His Son, and those who did not. God takes every second of our lives into account; He will not fumble the souls of men.

In this life, full justice concerning any circumstance and any life will not be served in full. People have been executed for crimes over the years who were actually innocent of them, while people who've committed heinous crimes are walking free. There are people who are being plundered and pillaged in countries around the globe for no other reason than that the greedy know they can take advantage of the vulnerable. There will not be total justice in this world. That being said, there's a God in Heaven (who's to be feared) who hears the cries of the oppressed innocent and the laments of all those who live under the seemingly immovable and equally cumbersome realities of earthly injustice.

Chapters 40–43 in the book of Isaiah are often referred to as *messianic* in nature (pertaining to the coming Messiah). They're also known as the "Servant" passages that prophesy about God's ultimate Ruler, whom He would send to deliver His people and lead them into the eternal Kingdom the Servant would be given. We know that "Servant" as Jesus Christ. In Isaiah 42:1 we read, "Here is my servant, whom I uphold, my chosen one in whom I delight; I will put my Spirit on him and he will bring justice to the nations."

When Jesus came He showed us how to love those who appeared unlovable, people whom others discarded and even treated as subhuman: the poor, the demoniacs, the lepers, and the riffraff of Jesus' day. In His ministry Jesus pursued and granted justice and dignity for people who came across His path.

We need a revived outlook on our own priorities as believers who live in the increasingly "I've got my own problems" world of the twenty-first century. We need a renewed resolve to live up to the standard of righteousness and godliness God calls us to and *expects* of His people. Christians should be the first to act justly towards one another, as well as the first to cry out for justice to be done in our world; after all, we are a people who've been shown much mercy!

Jesus is gracious, and so should His disciples be. During His ministry, the Lord looked after the cause of the fatherless and the widow; He loved the "aliens" around Him. So too, then, should those who bear and serve in His Name (the Church)! The reality of bottomless needs surrounding us calls for the people of God to act, for no other reason than because we fear the Lord, instead of responding by turning a blind eye or by turning our backs.

The Christian life may be about many things, but at its spiritual bull's eye it's absolutely about remaining faithful to Jesus Christ as well as the *cause of Christ*.

Much like the Church today, the earliest believers of the first century were situated amongst a wide swath of societal philosophies and religious beliefs that communicated spiritual values and ideas opposite to theirs. The Romans were very suspicious about their spiritual life; they internally skulked under the pagan gods they believed to be serving. You could say that the Romans and indeed many other pagan peoples worshipped under a lead-weighted cloak of paranoia. They were walking on "eggshells" at times so as to not upset any of the voracious too-many-to-count gods they served, for fear of retribution at the hands of one of them.

Thankfully, we don't have to fear God in that way. Our God is a personal deity; a knowable One who doesn't make His creation guess about Him. He's revealed His holy character and has made His divine intentions and purposes known to us through His Word and through the incarnation of His Son Jesus into our world. God won't suddenly become someone we can't recognize from Scripture. He is who He says He is!

Proper theology tells us that even when we are unfaithful in terms of our relationship with God, He will always remain faithful to us. We wouldn't want anything less from God, would we? The Bible says, "If we are faithless, He [God] will remain faithful; He cannot deny Himself" (2 Timothy 2:13 NKJV). Isn't that wonderful?! It is a faithfulness that's unparalleled and unseen in our world today.

The man who penned the Christmas carol *I Heard the Bells on Christmas Day*, Henry Longfellow, wrote the words as a hymn during a time of intense fighting in the now United States of America. In 1863, the fledgling country was bogged down in a bitter civil war that pitted the north against the south. A distraught Longfellow surveyed the situation and feared that evil and strife would rip apart many more lives.

But then he heard church bells ring at midnight one Christmas, and he remembered the gospel message proclaiming peace on earth and goodwill extended to men. Surrounded by death and hatred on all sides, the bells, to him, rang like they never did before! The sound strangely reminded him that God's work in the world wasn't finished and that He would not forsake His people. The bells of God's faithfulness, as it were, refreshed Henry Longfellow and struck in him a chord of the awesome *fear of the Lord*.

Buckskin Brady was a cowboy turned evangelist at the beginning of the twentieth century. He left home to find work at the tender age of eight after his father died. The only work he could find was at a ranch where horses needed to be rounded up. Just before he rode off on a pony his mother offered him a few things: a prayer to send him on his way, a math book, and last but not least, a Bible. In his account of his life Buckskin Brady said, "Every day I studied my math book to keep me square with my employer, and every day I studied my Bible to keep me square with God and the world."[31]

As the nation of Israel was commanded to long ago, may we today as Christ's Church heed the same command and remember the spiritual implications of what it means to truly possess the "fear of the Lord" in our lives and ministries.

May it be our prolonged burden to acquire a spiritual transformation that squares us not only with God but with our fellow Christians as well. In this way we will stand a better chance of staying square with those *outside* the faith who may be studying our "God-fearing" lives to see if they line up with our beliefs. The best way we can begin to see this reality come to fruition in our Christian lives is to fall on our knees. We need to get into that place where hearts are changed and burdens lifted up and taken away by the reviving and renewing power of God in the *presence* of God.

CHAPTER 9

Moving Mountains and Erecting Monuments in Their Secret Place

A Revived Passion for Closet Prayer

Each year the world remembers the anniversary and events of the horrendously sad and heartbreaking day of September 11, 2001. It's hard not to think of all the calamity, heartache, and loss of life that filled that fateful day whenever the anniversary rolls around. A silver lining from that day, however, will remain visually captured across the screens of our memories forever. I'm referring to the many heroic and sacrificial people, such as police officers, firefighters, and other volunteers, who selflessly and valiantly raced against time to save lives trapped in the two collapsing and fiery twin towers of Manhattan.

However, what boiled to the top of most hearts in the days and weeks following the terrorist attack on the United States was the dross of a dense anger. There was incredible dread and trembling filling people around the world as well. But what was most telling, perhaps, was the hunger many people possessed for divine answers.

As a result of that ultra-yearning, a phenomenal unprecedented event took place at the old Yankee Stadium in the Bronx, New York. There, just days after 9/11, about 40,000 people from all walks of life and of different colour and faith backgrounds linked arms in prayer for their nation. In fact, prayer vigils were held all over North America and the world as people united in grief sought God in prayer.

At that moment, as has been the case at other times throughout history, people believed that prayer was for real, appearing to instinctively grasp that petitioning God was the foremost need in their lives. There are just times when the world gets that prayer has something to do with addressing the human problem and with combating injustice on the earth.

A mainstream news publication credited the united prayers of both Christian and Muslim women with the sentencing of the Liberian dictator Charles Taylor. One Liberian woman believes God spoke to her to "gather" women together to "pray for peace." In 2002 a group of women indeed began to meet for prayer in a Monrovian fish market. Columnist Lorna Dueck wrote,

> Sometimes there is an opportunity to document that the power of God is real…As women of different faiths prayed, they bolstered each other in courage and strategy. Some lobbied their imams to pressure the warlords, while others lobbied the government. By April of 2003, the women had obtained an audience with Mr. Taylor to demand that he begin peace talks. The rest is history…They went on to drive the election of Africa's first female head of state…who after a period of transitional government succeeded Mr. Taylor as president of Liberia…Their [the praying women's] Liberian story is proof…that what happens in prayer can be enough to equip us to heal our world."[32]

Such events point to the truth that God cares about our lives and He is moved by our sincere prayers and by our trust in Him. Though our greatest need as a human race is to be in communion with the Heavenly Father, sometimes it feels like our world takes the idea of petitioning God in prayer about as seriously as it finds it easy to mock: a la the popular impersonation of prayer that has become known as "Tebowing" (acting as if one's praying on bended knee) as envisaged by the iconic statue "The Thinker." What is referred to as "Tebowing" is of course the mimicking of the American football player Tim Tebow, who's been known to drop down on one knee during games to pray on the sidelines of the field.

Despite how frivolously our culture at times tends to treat the sacred and solemn nature of prayer, it doesn't change the mammoth need we all possess as finite creatures living in treacherous times to bring our cares before a loving and merciful God.

As I discussed at the beginning of the book, we are confronted on a daily basis with the reality that our world has become increasingly chaotic and unstable. If the present realities of our time aren't enough to turn us into people who earnestly seek out God in prayer, I don't know what will.

It's been said by some that in the age of advanced science and technology the need for "prayer" has become obsolete; humanity has taken us, they say, where faith cannot. Such a view, however, fails to take into consideration a couple of vital spiritual realities: the sinful nature of human beings and the sovereignty of Almighty God. We live in a day that is moving ever-closer to the point in the history of the world where it will witness the return of Jesus Christ.

In light of that certain event, God's people need to be ready for the spiritual bracing they'll need as the amount and the intensity of satanic offenses against the Church rises. In those final days (and they are fast approaching), Christians will have to take a more visible stand if they're to remain steadfast in their faith.

The founding fathers of the early Christian Church, along with many personalities within the monastic communities, consisted of men of God who saw intently into the spiritual battle all believers face. They consequently made prayer and meditation the utmost of priorities in their faith experience. Perhaps not until the later 1700s did the importance of prayer explode in the Church once again, leading to many of the revivals in the North Eastern United States.

Is there a more talked about and yet less-activated aspect of the Christian life than *prayer?* Most if not all believers you discuss the subject of prayer with would readily admit that they don't spend nearly enough time in God's presence. Truthfully, no matter how long we've been Christians, prayer *can* seem to be a perfunctory exercise at times; something we keep putting off until everything else we need to do is done. Perhaps this is why some of us believers experience heart-probing feelings of self-examination and self-indictment coming over us whenever we hear a sermon on prayer, read a book on the topic, or hear another believer talk about how important their "prayer life" is.

Christians, above all people, should realize just how imperative and medicinal prayer is for their souls. Clearly, we can never get away from the Bible's ever-imploring of us to get into prayer formation in order to cultivate the relationship we have with God and to be changed by His transforming power.

The Bible teaches us that God has made us for Himself. He created us to be able to respond to Him. He made us response–*able,* just as much as He has made us respons-*ible* to Him. Prayer is not merely to be "a part" of our lives as followers of Christ but to characterize how we *live* our lives. When we strip away all the spiritual and theological implications of what it means *to* pray, prayer is essentially *talking* with the God of the universe, the One who spoke all things into being! Prayer, for that reason, should be a perpetual practice in reverential awe. We are never to grow too comfortable with being in the presence of Almighty God.

As is the case with any conversation, we can speak to God, but we must also keep a thirsty ear in order to listen to and hear Him as well.

It still marvels me that our Heavenly Father can hear me and you just as if we were the only ones speaking to Him. And just like God can hear Frank across the world in Italy (in his language), as if he were the only one in the world speaking to Him, God can hear His child Minga over in China (in her language) just as if she were the only one in all the world talking to Him.

If millions of people were speaking at us all at once we would only hear an overwhelming verbal drone, a sound so loud and piercing that it would surely split our heads apart, never mind bust our eardrums! Thankfully, God can handle lending His ear to zillions of petitions voiced at once and hear them as if they're individually spoken! That's why He's God! Pray all day, and God will not miss a single syllable we utter!

The Church, in these last days, desperately needs a revived burden for the necessity of a sustained and prioritized private prayer life to a God who tirelessly listens to the cares and concerns of His people. Prayer sets the spiritual table for lives to be changed; it always has and always will! We need a renewed perspective of how God views the prayers of His people, even more, a rediscovery through prayer of the kinds of grace, power and wisdom that are ours for the having to stabilize as well as mobilize our spiritual lives.

If we as God's people could abandon the tyranny of our overly demanding environments long enough to get into that secret place of prayer, imagine how powerful a force we could be as an army of God in this world!

When we gaze into the fascinating and quintessential teachings of Jesus in the Sermon on the Mount, it shouldn't surprise us to find the Saviour teaching the world's best seminar on the subject of prayer.

Though our Lord didn't wear a T shirt reading *"Prayer Is For Real,"* He not only talked about it in that light, He prayed like it! Jesus could speak with great authority when it came to the discipline of prayer. Whose prayer life was more engaging, important to observe, not to mention more fruitful than that of the Saviour's? Jesus was and is the all-time grand-master prayer-warrior. It's not surprising then why the Gospel writers recorded some wonderful examples of what the prayer life of Jesus Christ looked like. Like no other person before Him on the face of the earth, Jesus demonstrated what a life fully devoted to prayer was capable of.

Aside from the fact that He walked the earth as Almighty God (in every sense of the term), He also possessed an authentically human body in every sense of the word. Though He possessed every attribute of the Divine, in His humanness He possessed every ounce of our intricate weaknesses (except for a sin nature). All this to say that Jesus knew how much He needed to pray to His Father in Heaven!

There was just something about the prayers of Jesus that made His followers (who were a spiritual work in progress) drop what they were doing *or thinking* and take notice. Luke tells us in his Gospel that the disciples, though they were Jewish men who would have been taught something about prayer as young boys, after hearing Jesus pray one day asked their Master, "Lord, teach us to pray" (Luke 11:1).

Jesus' disciples wanted to know what the missing ingredients were in their own efforts in prayer compared to how He prayed. They were obviously taken by Jesus' close relationship with His Heavenly Father. This was evident not only in how the Lord *prayed* but by the *time* He devoted to prayer. The Lord went to great extents in order to clear away the clusters of need that were constantly circling like a ring of humanity around Him. He did it in order to spend meaningful prolonged periods of time in prayerful solitude.

In Matthew 6, with His disciples huddled around Him, Jesus converted a hillside into a makeshift jam-packed class on Christian ethics and practice. The Lord went into full rabbi-mode and shared with the people the values of His Kingdom, with one of the topics of the day being *prayer.*

Jesus seemed to be just as concerned about the motive and content of prayer as He was about the physical place in which one prayed. The Lord pointed out some key attitudes that His disciples would need to bear in mind and adopt towards prayer that were tantamount if their petitions were to please the Father and bear spiritual fruit.

What's notable from the Matthew 6 passage is that three times Jesus used the common phrase "when you pray." Each time He used the phrase He taught us something about the role and place of prayer in our lives. "And when you pray, do not be like the hypocrites, for they love to pray standing in the synagogues and on the street corners to be seen by men. I tell you the truth, they have received their reward in full" (Matthew 6:5).

It was Jesus' intention to communicate that one could possibly end up putting themselves in a hypocritical position when they prayed. As someone who has been walking with the Lord for some years now, I fancy that we do this far more often than we may actually realize. We can carry short memories of our own iniquity to prayer while possessing a long finger that we sometimes use to point at others who have sinned when talking to God.

Jesus called us to be mindful of our motives in prayer so that we are not practising personal piety (which is spiritually overrated and unattractive, anyway) whenever we pray in a public setting. There obviously were people all around the Lord who were fostering prideful hearts as they were praying; their choice words as they petitioned God no doubt giving them away! To Jesus, self-righteous prayers were *no* prayers at all; on account of that, He sought to make an example of such persons.

Who were the people praying in such a self-elevating manner? We can surmise from whom Jesus referred to as "hypocrites" on more than a few occasions in the Gospels that He was largely calling out the usual suspects known as the *Pharisees*. They were an elite conservative political party and religious school of thought carved within Judaism. The thing about this group that rubbed Jesus like a prickly garment on His divine skin was the fact that they enjoyed their notoriety and respected profile in the nation *way too much!* There's no easy way to put a godly shade of makeup on the face of legalism! The public gatherings of the Pharisees and other religious leaders resembled more self-preserving power-*paloozas* than conclaves of religious men saddled with the responsibility to seek the heart of God and His true will for His people.

The charade of this upper religious echelon within Israel came across to Jesus as a walking, talking poke in the eye to the face of proper righteousness. However, the Lord issued a long-overdue spiritual "memo" to the Pharisees and others like them (the elders and chief priests) that they were not above His rebuke, for He knew that when they prayed they actually showed their true spiritual colours. For Jesus, such prayers (no matter who mouthed them) were incurably arrogant and irreverent to the Father He knew in Heaven.

The front-end of Jesus' remarks when He referred to such hypocritical people actually made them sound quite spiritual and exemplary: *"they love to pray."* Who wouldn't want to hear that being said about them from the Saviour of all people?

In the local synagogue one person was usually invited to come to the front to offer up prayers on behalf of those in the assembly. To be asked to do so was considered a high honour. This particular person would have the aura of being distinguished. There was nothing wrong with that, per se, yet Jesus knew that what the "hypocrites" loved more than anything else was being thrust into the top-billing of religious notoriety. They obviously appeared to our Lord as relishing the "camera-eye" and the opportunity afforded to them to parade their self-righteousness before the worshippers.

The Pharisees and others may have thought they could fool most of the people most of the time, but Jesus would have them know that they could never fool God *anytime!* Most devout Jews prayed at least three times a day, and oftentimes while they prayed they stood, which was the standard posture for prayer in the synagogue. It's probable that the hypocritical bunch either purposely waited until when the temple courts were filled to high capacity to start praying or moved out closer to the street at a point during the afternoon time of prayer when there would be a high volume of people present and begin to pray in that setting.

All of the religiously stinky carryings-on must have sickened Jesus' heart, for He knew the underlying motives of all people. The Lord knew those who prayed in such ways did so not to please the heart of God but to "be seen by men" and to score the adulation of mere human beings. If that was their sole *aim* (the applause of people) when praying openly, Jesus made sure they knew that that would be their sole *gain!* He then sealed His spiritual point to the disciples (and us for that matter) by insisting, in effect, "Don't be like them!"

All that their efforts before the masses to appear pious and spiritually polished brought the Pharisees was Jesus' charge of *hypocrisy*. They were those who would "honor" God with their "lips," as Jesus would say, but whose "hearts" were actually miles and miles away in spiritual-distance from resonating with His. The Pharisees may have been "big kahunas" in the eyes of many, yet their self-infected prayers dwarfed them in the eyes of God.

It's not that public prayer was forbidden in Israel or that praying out on a street corner (although it wasn't highly practiced) was not honouring to God either. The spiritual take-home lesson here is that it is in the public or corporate forums of our lives, Jesus says, that we, like the Pharisees, may be all too prone to forgetting what the true essence of prayer is: *a child of God in communication (or in communion) with their Heavenly Father.* God should be the only audience one focuses on when they pray, especially in public.

Billy Graham stated over the years that because of the trust given to him by many sitting presidents in the United States and leaders around the world, he was often tempted to use his influence as power whenever he prayed in public settings. Graham realized that we can get spiritually ambitious and take our eyes off the purposes of God when we are popular and much sought after figures in the public domain.

Jesus knows the heart-intent of all people when they pray and is perfectly aware of the hidden motives of those who pray in a hypocritical fashion. If we are not careful with our intentions in prayer, *we* could easily become one of those people. Our sinful nature makes us susceptible to lapsing into hypocrisy daily, and our prayers, whether private or public, can reflect it.

If it is the accolades of those around us and their "pats on the back" we seek through our public prayers (and that desire can subtly creep up on us), we shouldn't expect God to be so moved as to reward us in some way. The only "reward" we'll receive is simply the cheers of people, the very shallow recognition we craved, with nothing left owing from God. Jesus, as well, knew how spiritually leaky the praises of people could be; they were of the what-have-you-done-for-me-lately commodity (here today, but probably gone tomorrow). The bottom line here: it's always better for us to impress God when we're praying in public than to use our prayer language to turn the heads and ears of people and secure their admiration!

The fact is, Christians pray best when they pray with God's burdens in mind. We're all tempted to sound "deep and spiritual" in public prayer, yet what our Heavenly Father desires from us is much more underwhelming to our intellect. He's simply concerned with how we're relating to *Him* and responding to *His* priorities *as* we're praying. That must be our heart's (and our words') target, whenever and wherever we pray.

In this age of uncertainty and anxiety where growing opposition to the gospel in our world kisses the ever-developing opportunities for Christian witness and ministry, God's people must meet that challenge by a renewed spiritual resolve to pray. In these last days the people of God need to regain a biblical understanding of their place before God and be convinced of the important role that their prayers play (as measly as they can seem) in His redemptive plans for the world.

I believe that Christians pray with more transparency and zealously intercede on deeper levels when they pray believing that their prayers inherently possess the very power of God. Perhaps some of us need revival and renewal in this area of our lives because we've stopped believing (or at least praying like) our prayers move the hand that moves the universe!

Though it is God who makes our petitions to Him filled with the potential for world change and not the physical mode or place in which we pray to Him, Jesus nonetheless encouraged people to make *private* prayer their priority.

There's something to be said about being alone with our Saviour where His presence enfolds into us and we into Him, like how our hand fits into a nicely fitting glove. "But when you pray, go into your room…Then your Father, who sees what is done in secret, will reward you" (Matthew 6:6). As Christians we've come to call these "quiet times." They're moments when we come away to be alone with God in prayer. Most of us see them as essential for our spiritual lives to be strengthened and refocused. Nothing brings us back to square-one spiritually, nothing empowers us to live as Jesus would have us, more than being in His peaceful but powerful presence.

Unfortunately, it seems rather normal today to hear Christians increasingly admit to struggling to maintain consistent quiet times of prayer. God's people very often fail to get into that secret place with Him. God is waiting, but we aren't showing up. As people we are used to making time for things that are close to our hearts. For instance, we may have a favourite restaurant we always go to with a friend. Or perhaps there's a weekly function we attend that we hate to miss. However, when it comes to prayer, do we have a reserved non-negotiable time-period and sacred space where no one can gain access to us but God? Is this kind of thing even a priority for us?

Elaine and I know of a woman (the wife of a pastor) who would go into the washroom once a day to pray. It was her way of escaping the chaos of her life as a mother with young children. "The water-closet became my prayer closet," she would say. We may not choose a washroom, but we all need that "secret place," a room or area where we can totally be ourselves and where no one else is listening to us but our Heavenly Father.

Jesus may have been alluding to the storeroom of one's home when He advised His disciples to go into one's "room" to pray. In the Lord's time most homes had a so-called "inner room" that was secluded and had no window. In Luke 12, Jesus mentioned these rooms when He taught His followers not to worry about what they had to eat or wear, because God fed even the "ravens," who did "not sow or reap" and who did not have any "storeroom" (Luke 12:24). Jesus is calling us, as His people, away to the storerooms and inner rooms (He'll even settle for the bathrooms) of our lives.

He compels us to make it a habit of praying there, because He will reward His people for what is done "in secret," whether it be giving, serving, or praying. It's in these secret storerooms of our lives that we are changed and shaped by the inward working and power of the Holy Spirit, where we're guided and given knowledge and wisdom for daily living.

Sometimes we need to use fewer words in prayer in order to allow enough room for silence, even pausing for periods of time in order to ask God, "Are You speaking to me today?" God mainly speaks to us by His Word, and yet He can speak to us in prayer as well. Jesus in John 16:13 said that when the Holy Spirit came, He would act as our Counselor and "will speak only what he hears, and he will tell you what is yet to come."

God's Spirit speaks the deep things of God into our lives that come straight from the heart of the eternal throne of grace itself, where Jesus intercedes for us at the right hand of the Father. Throughout Scripture God invites us to inquire of His goodness and wisdom in prayer. "Call to me," says the Lord, "and I will answer you and tell you great and unsearchable things you do not know" (Jeremiah 33:3). We can be certain that our human finite prayers spoken in the quiet unseen moments of our days incredibly become insurable and transferable addresses to Heaven that assure us of God's response.

The late former boxing champion Joe Frazier (who had those classic bouts with Mohammed Ali) shared his secret for how he prepared for his fights. Said Frazier, "The work you do, or don't do, in the early dark of the mornings, will show up under the lights of the ring." This simple and yet profound principle from the sport of boxing analogously correlates to the kind of efforts we make in the secret place of prayer; that is, a lack of it will show up in the light of our everyday lives! Sweating it out in prayer in the darkrooms of God's spiritually developing and conditioning presence makes us fit for the battle that is the Christian life.

Another powerful lesson on prayer Jesus sought to teach people was to be *specific* in our petitions when we pray. "And when you pray, do not keep on babbling like pagans, for they think they will be heard because of their many words…your Father knows what you need before you ask him" (Matthew 6:7–8).

John Stott in his commentary on the Sermon on the Mount stated that various papyrus findings from the first century show that the prayers of the "pagans" Jesus talked about here were more of the magical "incantation" sort. They would sound like meaningless repetitive vowel sounds. It was thought that such incantations could wear down the gods and plague them into giving what the petitioner wanted.[33]

But Jesus took exception to that approach to prayer because the pagans prayed from a stance in which they implored gods whom they thought were impersonal (and whom Jesus knew were non-existent anyway).

His disciples, on the other hand, were not to think of God in the same terms the pagans thought of the false gods. Jesus taught that the Father was neither ignorant or impassive and did not need to be instructed or persuaded by endless nagging chants in prayer. The Lord assured them that God "knows what you need before you ask him" (Matthew 6:8).

The point Jesus makes here is this: keep it plain and simple with God in prayer, because He can already read our minds! In fact, the Greek word for "babbling" that Jesus used in Matthew 6:7, *battalogeo* (which even sounds strange), actually means something close to "much words or speech."

It's not that the Lord was prohibiting any and all use of repeated phrases when one prayed to the Father but that using mindless and mechanical terms when we're praying is terribly unnecessary.

When I was in Bible college sometimes the professors would ask a certain student to pray before the class commenced. I can still remember one fellow who used to be quite pedantic in the way he prayed. He would say something to the effect of "God, we praise Your Name. God, we ask that You would direct us today. God, that You would open our ears and hearts to Your Word. God, that You would…God this, God that…" By the time he was finished all you could remember from the prayer was how many times he uttered God's Name! To my ears, it was a bit distracting to say the least, but I do think the Lord got the drift that He was being petitioned!

It doesn't really matter to God how many words we utter or even how flowery or eloquent we are when we pray. What matters to Him is that we remain mindful of Who we are speaking to and that perhaps we say more in prayer by actually saying less. This means that our prayers for revival don't necessarily have to be long and drawn out either. We can get to the point with God! Even the apostle Paul, the great prayer-warrior that he was, stated that he would "rather speak five intelligible words to instruct others than ten thousand words in a tongue" (1 Corinthians 14:19).

God is not stirred by well-flowing and deep theologically crafted petitions; He's moved by the *heart* of our prayers. Some of the religious leaders of Jesus' day may very well have been men of powerful sounding prayer whose spellbinding words held all listeners captive. That reality aside, Jesus still pressed for *authenticity* in prayer and for genuine introspection and humility to underline our motives when praying to God. It's always the sincerity of our inward life that gives our outward words and service credibility in the eyes of God.

The Lord wants us to remember that God looks for spiritual substance when we talk to Him, not style. After Jesus arose from prayer when He was in the Garden of Gethsemane and soaked in His own sweat, He came to His disciples and found them asleep with their mouths catching flies. It was the moment of all moments when they should have been praying to not be overcome by the temptation to desert Jesus. The Saviour was not impressed. These were the same men, remember, who only a few hours earlier were willing to die for Jesus. However, in that all-important hour of need, Jesus' disciples couldn't even bring themselves to deny one of their physical needs and pray with Him. Our Lord wasn't asking them to begin a lengthy fast; He wasn't asking them to sing a hymn or for an impromptu homily. He was simply asking them to pray for their own good!

It's ironic that in some ways it may be easier to die for Christ than to live as He has called us to live for Him! This includes being the people of prayer our Saviour taught us to be. We want our spirituality compartmentalized for easy use. We want it convenient for quick consumption. We want results in prayer, but we're hoping that'll happen in spite of our poor efforts *to* pray.

There are too many times when we as believers don't want to go into the secret place to spend time with God. We'd much rather have our swiftly uttered token-prayers taken for what they are. We convince ourselves that it's God who needs to adjust to *our* priorities, not the other way around; after all, we're busy people. God should understand!

However, there's an old saying that goes, "When people work, they work; when people pray, God goes to work." God made things operate in such a way that His people must pray, and endure in prayer, for certain things to happen.

John Devries, the founder of Mission India, powerfully extrapolates on the necessity of the Church to pray, in terms of their partnering role with God in bringing salvation to the peoples of the world.

> God intended for prayer to be the means by which we join with Him in His work of redeeming the world. When He invited us to "ask and receive," He was not implying that He would "do it anyway"... He chooses to work through us. And there is a whole world out there in which we can say with confidence that God will not act unless we pray! Why else would God say to the Son, "Ask of me, and I will make the nations your inheritance" (Ps. 2:8)? Is God lying when He tells us that the primary method of delivering the nations to the Son is through prayer?[34]

One of the most underestimated challenges in the Christian life is that of spiritual warfare. Even our societies' obsession with dark themes and cultish practices speak of an ever-heightening consciousness and acceptance towards the existence of the spiritual realm.

The editor of *Leadership Journal*, Marshall Shelley, writes,

While many in the modern world deny the existence or relevance of evil spirits, the battle with these adversaries has been part of the Christian life…In contemporary American culture, there's a growing interest in the paranormal, from Harry Potter to Twilight, from fascination with angels to fascination with vampires…the spirit world is no longer denied… believe it or not, spiritual warfare is a part of our world, part of our ministry, part of the cost of our daily discipleship.[35]

Prayer works as well to thwart and even defeat the plans of our enemy. Therefore we must see ourselves as rulers with immense spiritual power at our disposal over evil through prayer in the Name of Jesus.

One of my favourite stories stemming from the days of the early Church was penned by Athanasius. The third century theologian in his work *The Life of St. Antony* portrays a man named Antony (an Egyptian by birth who grew up in a Christian home) as leading an extraordinary life that was both fruitful and glorifying to God. Antony was convinced that God was calling him to sell his possessions and to enter into an ascetic lifestyle. This he did while remaining devoted to such spiritual disciplines as prayer in seclusion, fasting, and the giving of alms.

Alluding to how Antony overcame the onslaught of satanic attacks he experienced while in isolation, Athanasius noted how the devil solicited Antony by bringing to his mind all the "amenities of life" in an attempt to try to get Antony to "abandon his set purpose." The result of this encounter was described by Athanasius as a sweeping victory for Antony over the enemy of his soul. "The Enemy saw, however, that he was powerless in the face of Antony's determination…being bested because of the man's steadfastness and vanquished by his solid faith…constant prayer."[36]

Christians have a great need to be wide-awake spiritually today, to be diligent in prayer and in the binding of the ultimate spiritual provocateur (the devil). God's people will need to be prayerfully armed if they're to successfully jump the shark that is Satan's counterfeit work closing in and around them in these last days.

When Jesus' taught His disciples "how" they should pray, He instructed them to ask God to "deliver" them "from the evil one" (Matthew 6:13). Satan will be pulling out all the stops as a barrier to the work of the Church leading up to the second advent of Christ.

Wesley Duewel, a former missionary to India, once shared about his mission struggling for twenty-five years to plant a new church every year. The mission workers came to the conclusion that something of a grand spiritual nature was very wrong. To combat this, they enlisted 1,000 of their supporters to pray daily for their ministry in India. The prayers of God's people resulted in the planting of 550 new churches and a conversion count that rose from 2,000 people to roughly 75,000.[37]

It is we, the Church of Jesus Christ, who have the tremendous privilege of comforting and compelling our culture by means of the spiritual language of the ages: *prayer*. We should seek revivals in our churches and spiritual lives if for no other reason than for us as a people of God to get into our secret places of prayer more often.

Though the section we call "The Lord's Prayer" in the Sermon on the Mount doesn't list any examples of *answered* prayer, the fact remains that the righteous petitions of God's people can move the burdensome mountains of trials in their lives and erect monuments of answered prayer (as well as strengthened faith) in their place (see James 5:16).

While not calling us to neglect corporate (or public) prayer as worshippers, Jesus *is* calling each of us to go into the "secret" rooms and places of our lives and to a deeper, reflective prayer life. It's all a matter of priority, is it not? But let us encounter more of God in prayer, for not only does the empowerment of our spiritual lives and the mobilization of our ministries depend on it, but our broken lives require it as well.

CHAPTER 10

BROKENNESS LOOKED IN THE MIRROR AND SAW AUTHENTICITY

A Revived Desire to Exhibit Spiritual Genuineness

Biblical wisdom points us to the reality that in order for true revival and spiritual renewal to take place in the Church, the need for it must first be realized; secondly, the need must also become a full-blown desire. Before the spiritually medicinal work of the Holy Spirit can infiltrate the lives of God's broken people and affect a therapeutic wholeness in areas that lack it, there must be a desperate cry for such an occurrence within the core of one's heart.

It's only in accepting that our lives are capsules containing pressure-points of brokenness that we can realize the prayerful need we possess of the Spirit's inward reviving and renewing to strengthen our spiritual resolve on an ongoing basis. There's hope and the potential for joy and fulfillment in our varying states and levels of brokenness, for God wills to hold our lives and to put pieces of it back together.

We seldom see how the words *broken* and *blessed* could possibly be pressed together in the same spiritual sandwich. Nothing in our lives appears blessed when we're conscious of our spiritual brokenness and trudging through a tunnel of personal darkness. As God's people, none of us are spiritually bulletproof. When the problems of life and when angry spiritual-torpedoes come shooting at us, we can take quite a hit;, even with our "Ephesian 6" under-armour in place!

I know of a good number of godly Christians who suffer from acute depression during certain times of the month *and year,* as well as those who continuously battle with self-esteem issues. Chinks in our spiritual armour (as a result of our fallen nature) will always leave us open to sin, spiritual setbacks, and all-out attacks.

The Bible says there's "a time for everything, and a season for every activity under heaven" (Ecclesiastes 3:1). There are periodic times in our Christian lives when we feel the muscle of our faith has turned to flab and when our heart is so heavy it sinks like a stone to the bottom of our chests. There are times when our struggle spiritually is so intense that our days just seem too long for us. There are nights when sleep comes slowly, if at all, and when our heads seem to be crazy-glued to our pillows the following morning, times when tears quietly but frequently blur our eyes.

There are durations in our Christian experience when we deeply sense that we're broken up inside, when we possess an emptiness and sorrow that knows no comfort, a wound for which there is no apparent healing balm.

The reality of spiritual brokenness, in the lives of Christians, however, runs deeper and extends beyond the intermittent seasons when we *feel* we're broken. Our brokenness, rather, is innately wholesale in our being; it's an unwanted and constant lifelong spiritual condition every human being carries with them to the grave. Accepting this can lead to a more freeing and spiritually shape-able life as a Christ follower; it can also assist us in cultivating a life of *authenticity*.

Who was more authentic and spiritually genuine than Jesus Christ? Has anyone displayed more brokenness in their humanity than our Lord did in the Garden of Gethsemane or at Calvary's Cross? Knowing the limitations of His humanity (albeit not saddled by a sin nature) and intimately knowing the love of His Heavenly Father allowed Jesus to exhibit an appropriate vulnerability and brokenness of person. In order for us to put our humanness in a spiritually correct context and develop a healthy spiritual self-awareness, we need first to accept who we are (finite and sinful) in light of the attributes of our Creator (infinite and holy). A healthy knowledge of who our God is aids us in our brokenness.

We feel the reality of our own brokenness because we sense how unholy *we are* in comparison to our perfect Creator; a holy God can only command His people to be likewise! However, there are pockets of time throughout our pilgrimage of faith when we can feel like the only thing "holy" about us are the copious amounts of sinful holes that can appear to characterize the spiritual surface of our lives. The hardest thing to do as a child of God is to ask the Holy Spirit to reveal all the coarse and cold religiosity and hypocrisy submerged within us; it's as much an exercise in prayer as it is in cringing! Honesty is not only the best "policy" in life; it's integral in terms of the admission price every Christian needs to pay if they're going to get beyond the penitential door leading to the place of revival and spiritual renewal in the Body of Christ.

John Wesley, the great frontier revivalist preacher of the eighteenth century, was often "shown" the door after he had preached at certain churches. It was difficult for some of God's people to absorb the convicting tone of his messages. Wesley would reiterate in his sermons how Christians often failed to allow God to break harmful growth-strangling strongholds in their lives that stemmed from their spiritual poverty and human brokenness.

As was the case in John Wesley's day, teaching on spiritual brokenness today can be extremely unpopular as well. However, Jesus was as clear as a freshly Windexed-window that those who were "poor in spirit" were actually in a position to be "blessed" eternally! (see Matthew 5:3). For the Lord, then, brokenness and blessing are actually related to one another; they're connecting spiritual blocks that work together to build a life that God can work in and glorify Himself through.

Each Christ follower must be willing to "man up" about the state of his or her spiritual life; its quality, vitality, and usability for God's purposes must all be laid on His examination table. That being said, exhibiting some "gut-honesty" before the throne of Heaven is something that's easier to *think* about doing than *actually* following through with. But if it only takes "one spark" to make a "fire," then it can be argued that it only takes each individual Christ follower pursuing the cleansing inferno of revival and spiritual renewal in their own personal life for the rest of the Body of Christ to be engulfed by the same flames!

Oh how we need more "real" people in the Church today! The Church is starving for believers who can readily admit their shortcomings and who have no problem with being spiritually transparent as a part of building an authentic spiritual community.

One of the many things I appreciate about the Bible is how real the people in it are. How could we not relate to a person like Moses? We can see ourselves in him a lot: the self-doubt, the questions he had for God, his missteps and frustrations. All his personality warts are owned by *us!* We can hook with the blips and glitches on the radar of Moses' character, even if they were experienced by a great patriarch of the faith!

Why does it often appear in the Church as if we all have holy crushes on such biblical titans as a Joshua, David, Daniel, and Paul, wishing that our lives resembled the depth and breadth of their faith and glowing servant's track record? I find that as I interact with God's people in various Christian circles, a good number of them appear noticeably uncomfortable in their own spiritual skins.

Whether it's a marked low self-worth in the lives of Christians as to their perceived value and pecking order within the Body of Christ or just the amount of jealousy that's exhibited of other so-called "successful" believers, it seems to me that our brothers and sisters in Christ (like any other person outside the faith) battle intensely with identity and self-acceptance issues.

This reality can give way to an awkwardness within the Christian (church) culture. Many believers feel such personal struggles have no place in the life of the child of God. Unfortunately, there are some Christians (though well-intentioned) who hastily brand every difficult situation in life as being a satanic overture and end up low-blowing their sister or brother in the Lord by diagnosing their insecurities as being unequivocally *demonic*. Such insensitively over-done "spiritual" sentiments can make the more immature and under-grown Christian feel like they've somehow been possessed by the devil; they also fail to take into account the normalcy of such human feelings and the possibility of them being a by-product of a common human brokenness.

Why can't we feel more free in admitting to how we are feeling without fear of having another believer jump on our vulnerability as if it's somehow taboo? Why can't we, for instance, be our remorseful selves and champion the things we wish we had done or said better and find a genuine rooted contentedness in that? Not that we should continue to punish ourselves and stay in a kind of spiritual "rut" mode forever, for that is not God's will for His redeemed people; neither would such an attitude in the life of a Christian bring Him glory.

However, why can't we wear our life-sized goofs and gaffes as if they were badges of authenticity God can use to make us a more relational person to the average Joe or Jane (in and outside the church)? Where has all the authenticity in the Church gone? If the pew is meant to be filled with sinners, and if all worshippers are broken vessels to begin with, why are so many of our churches and so many Christians trying so hard to look so well put-together?

I find it extremely difficult to avoid periodic memories of my mistakes and failures as a Christian; they inconveniently find accommodation in my mind from time to time. Oftentimes I grieve at how much I fall short of the potential and capacity I have to be the person I was redeemed to be. At moments like that I find myself clinging with ease to Paul's refrain: "Not that I have already obtained all this *[made into the likeness of Christ, in its fulfillment]*, or have already been made perfect, but I press on to take hold of that for which Christ Jesus took hold of me" (Philippians 3:12).

Though we have spiritual wholeness and completion awaiting us in Heaven, we yet have a brokenness of person to still deal with on this side of eternity. In Heaven we'll be untouchable in terms of pain and heartache (for they won't exist); on earth, however, we can't help but bump into tribulation. We're all in the same dirty playpen, so let's be brutally real about it without slinging mud! Though it may be difficult for some of us Christians to be vulnerable before people, we must absolutely be at our most vulnerable before the throne of God. It is there, after all, where God purposes to make us more spiritually authentic, for authenticity is the greatest advertisement any Christian or any church can possess to lead people to the Saviour.

We're all delicately emotional and highly breakable spiritually. The next time you brush against a person on the street, on a subway, in a store, not to mention *in church,* be careful—they just might fall apart! We're so inwardly fragile as people that it doesn't take much for us to crack from the relentless stresses of life or to cave in under the weight of hurtful and critical words dropped on us. This is as true for Christians as it is for the non-believing person. Every human being has an invisible irremovable sticker slapped somewhere on their person that reads: *"Handle with care."* Like with fine china, we need to exercise the utmost caution whenever we're handling each other's lives.

When we as believers entrust ourselves to people who end up carelessly handling us, causing relational fractures to incur, no amount of conciliatory glue will hide the repair job that will be needed. When we've been hurt by other people there will always be memories of it to be overcome and degrees of trust to be re-earned.

Have you ever noticed how effectively music locates our emotional "centres" in that the most common and popular image we see in lyrics of songs is that of the broken heart or broken life? The reality that all of humanity is naturally (and inherently) in need of spiritual wholeness, rebirth and renewal is captured in the words of Steven Curtis Chapman's song "Broken." On the surface of his life, Chapman admits in a lyric from the song, "I'm just a well dressed wreck, I'm just a made up mess."[38]

I feel like a great number of us as Christians make a habit of flipping down our protective spiritually cosmetic "Sunday" disguises whenever we enter a church. It's like we're goalies making sure our hockey masks are in place before "the puck drops." We can feel like we're in the minority in the Church because we have big, ugly, monster-like problems, despite the fact that a lot of people (even Christians) secretly masquerade as the more-acceptable "Dr. Jekyll" in order to avoid their believers' version of "Mr. Hyde" from being noticed by others.

There's that part within every one of us (whether we are Christians or not) that is so wrought with a twisted and tangled spiritual darkness that we cannot know how bad off we are, let alone admit to it. What we fear the most sometimes is having that "other side" of us (that's sin-affected and God-disoriented) break out and attack others. Though we're not as outwardly "bad" as we could be and seldom show the maximum extent of our depraved nature (and brokenness), nonetheless we are utterly marred beyond our comprehension. "The heart is deceitful above all things and beyond cure. Who can understand it?" (Jeremiah 17:9).

In many ways we will remain a spiritual mystery to ourselves for as long as we live. The truth is, we're so broken as a human race that we couldn't even begin to know how it could be remedied. If it weren't for our Redeemer who came to show us the scope of our fallenness, we wouldn't know the potential our lives have, either, to be spiritually recovered, a process that will reach its fulfillment when we see Jesus. We must never forget that every Sunday when we take our place in the pews, we are sitting next to some "crackpot" whom God is shaping into another vessel for His glory (see Jeremiah 18:4), just as they are sitting next to someone like that: *you and me!*

Show me a Christian who seems to exude a life that's encamped on pretty solid spiritual ground, and I'll show you an authentic believer who still has scandalous issues harassing their redeemed life. As a Heaven-bound people of faith, though we are regarded as "saints," we are also a people whose unseen "halo" of an inward regeneration goes only so far. No matter how far we've grown in the spiritual life, we are in no way even close to being free of our sinner-ship, for we remain thoroughly broken and undeniably riddled with the destructive aspects of our sinful nature.

It's a grand satanic lie of Freudian and Marxist proportions that environmental stimuli is to be blamed for our human (spiritual) problem. It doesn't make our struggle with sin any easier knowing that even the planet we inherited at the moment of our birth is also broken (see Romans 8:19–22). It's a consequence of being born into a fallen world. Our very first breath as newborns inhaled the air of a realm in which its evil prince (the devil) eventually tempted us to realize the capacity we have to deny our Creator.

Like you, I too have met, and still meet, suffering Christians who inwardly "groan" to be free of pain and with their Saviour one day; nonetheless, they show a genuinely happy countenance, without a spray of pretentiousness about them. There are some believers who just possess an authentic "joy of the Lord." Joy is a wonderful Spirit-produced fruit and element of the Christian life; it also makes for a bad acting-job whenever we try to manufacture it in our own strength. People appreciate our honesty as much as they do our attempts to "suck it up" at times when life isn't going how we want it to. Paul's exhortation to us to be "joyful always" (1 Thessalonians 5:16) is compatible with the surface realities (circumstances) of our lives.

We can be joyful in the Lord yet not have that *joy* come off as disingenuous; that is, though the top of the waters of our lives can be tossed about as a result of trials and tribulations resting on them, we can yet have a calm, quiet, joy, and spiritual stillness in the depths of our lives, below the surface, as a result of our faith in Christ. If we can truly feel *and look* that way (spiritually joyous) and not just outwardly *appear* that way despite the presence of challenging circumstances in our lives, that is wonderful! What a great testimony!

However, my point is, let's not exhibit a false happiness or joy if it isn't really there! We're spiritual masterpieces in the making and yet walking heavenly construction sites, all rolled up in one. We never know who we'll be able to commiserate with and minister to, who just might need to see and hear a little honesty and authenticity from us before they'll trust us enough to share *with* us. Personally, I tend to be more transparent with people whom I sense lack an "air" about them and are devoid of spiritual superficiality. I find it almost impossible to relate with the person (especially the believer) who claims they are "excellent" every time I inquire of them. I find it difficult to accept as well when some Christians claim they're "great" or state the annoyingly overused "It's all good" when referring to how they're doing when I have more than a hunch that they're not really doing well at all.

Authentic fellowship always begins where *acting* in the Body of Christ stops. It's unfortunate when our brothers and sisters in Christ feel they have to feed us a "line" in order to come across as "godly" or as *spiritually correct* instead of just being honest with us. God gave us emotions and wants us to express them in a spiritually authentic manner. Though the promises and power of His Word ultimately realign our sin-infected emotions and cushion our trials by putting them both in their proper spiritual perspectives, we can still be real about the wear and tear our troubles are exacting on us *humanly.*

The presence of faith while we're stewing in our trials (the Christian hope), should never at the same time deny what we're feeling (the reality of pain). If we want non-believers to get real about their sin, let us first as God's people get even more-real about not coming across as religiously rehearsed. We need to relate to the lost world about as much as we need to provide an attractive spiritual alternative for them. It would help if we could see just how much our brokenness can reflect an authenticity that speaks spiritual volumes to people (even the unsaved).

We need to balance human reality with biblical possibilities and encouragements when engaging both the believer and nonbeliever. I think the last place a nonbeliever wants to be when their lives are less than okay is in a church. Should there be any wonder as to why? Could it be that they perceive or even worse get the impression from us that only those who have it "together" go to church? It's been my experience that that is largely how those outside circles of faith (the world) view and peg religious people (especially evangelicals). If they only knew how broken we are!

Many outside the Church find it too daunting a challenge to try to penetrate the impenetrable walls of faith culture many believers erect and cultivate in God's house. Have we somehow given an iron-clad message to the world that we're all "okay" in the Church? I think they know better, and so we in the Church must do better in terms of relating to the watching (and equally broken) world.

If our lives as Christians always seem to reflect a resounding story of success where all our trials get wrapped up with a pretty bow, topped off with a tag that says "Here's how I did it," then people will probably not want to be around us very much. I'm all for celebrating our spiritual victories in Jesus' Name. We should never rob God of His due praise! However, I wonder if there are times when in our attempts to bring glory to God that we actually end up making others feel worse in the process, leaving people wishing that they too could scale the same lofty spiritual heights we've climbed after our trial!

There are some people (a lot of them in the Church) who seem to be unable to come through their trials and tribulations very well *or at all.* There are seasons of extreme brokenness that appear to be so spiritually hopeless it gives the child of God every indication that there is no getting out of it.

This is often referred to as "the dark night of the soul," a term given to us by *St. John of the Cross,* who described his period of brokenness by such desperate terms. The Spanish Catholic priest and poet of the Carmelite Order in the 1500s endured a time in which God seemed profoundly distant to him. The seemingly steel-like ceiling his petitions hit on their way back down to him made Heaven appear as if it were locked and barred-off forever. It left St. John of the Cross feeling utterly imprisoned in his painful trial. As a result of some reforms he sought to bring to the prevalent laxity of his order, the Discalced Carmelites, he was taken captive by the Calced Carmelites and held prisoner at their monastery in Toledo, Italy.[39] St. John, for months following, was subjected to imprisonment, solitary confinement, and public beatings by God's own people.

Israel's King David suffered in ways similar to that of St. John of the Cross. Hordes of the king's own people sided with his son Absalom and were pursuant to take down David and end his life. David in Psalm 6, while on the run and enduring an intense period of brokenness in his life, described his plight by using such excruciatingly painful words as *agony, anguish, groaning, weeping*.

They're heartbreaking words, are they not? The beginning of Psalm 6 is uncomfortable to absorb for its blunt desperation; reading it is like receiving a letter from a hurting friend and experiencing them emotionally vomit all over the pages. David was a king who was crushed, in body and soul, under God's rebuke. Although he was a successful military strategist and leader, such qualities couldn't secure or guarantee spiritual strength and health. David was like everyone else: a broken human being who was prone to failure and constantly needy spiritually.

Further to the kind of brokenness experienced by the likes of David and St. John of the Cross, there have been others in and around the Church who lived their lives and who even went to the grave wondering about and questioning the faith.

The late Charles Templeton at one point was an evangelist and a close personal friend of Billy Graham's. For some years, though, Templeton struggled with doubt surrounding his faith and even wound up publishing a book entitled *Farewell to God: My Reasons for Rejecting the Christian Faith*. Brokenness comes in all shapes, sizes, and colours. If even those who once espoused the Scriptures with such passion and urgency can end up doubting the truth of those very same Scriptures (even outright rejecting the Word of God), then we can know with terrible certainty just how folly-prone and broken we are.

Try to recall at least one or two testimonies that you've heard from any Christian who put a great emphasis on their brokenness, even personal failure, and who left the microphone closer to that tone rather than ending on a predictable note of spiritual triumph. Author Phillip Yancey writes, "Modern churches tend to feature testimonies of spiritual successes, never failures, which only makes the struggles in the pew feel worse…Yet delve a bit deeper into church history and you will find a different story, of those who strain to swim upstream like spawning salmon."[40]

In my first book, *My Fanatical, Regrettable Tour of Ministry*, I sought to remove any semblance of a protective face-mask on my part as I reflected on some of my more trying experiences and ministry meltdowns as a church leader and pastor. So many Christians (many of them leaders on the frontlines) are just getting by day-to-day spiritually. In their moments of unbridled transparency some of them would perhaps freely admit that they constantly knead their theology and desperately struggle to remain close to their Saviour; they may even reveal that they harbour continuous questions about how their faith lines up with the unsolved mysteries of life and with the challenges of ministry.

If we have any hope of experiencing a deep spiritually invasive revival and renewal in our Christian lives and in the Body of Christ, we need to put aside our infatuation with being such great *pretenders* and get on with the much more spiritually worthwhile pursuit of becoming *contenders* for the visitation of God's power from on high. We're all familiar with the saying "If it ain't broken, don't fix it." Yet in pure spiritual terms, what *needs* fixing in our lives *has* to be broken in order for it *to* be fixed.

Thankfully, as God's people, we have a verse such as the one in Lamentations 3 to buffet us and to cling to as hope whenever onslaughts of our brokenness seem to slam into us and peek at certain times in our lives. Tucked into the spiritual gut of a very graphic and despair-filled biblical book depicting the devastating consequences Judah suffered for their disobedience towards God, we read of the hope His broken people had of gaining His mercy and that on a daily basis. "Because of the LORD's great love we are not consumed, for his compassions never fail. They are new every morning; great is your faithfulness" (Lamentations 3:22–23).

The spiritual sunrise that's slowly but surely peeking at the end of the dark regions of our current brokenness, spreading its light of hope over our lives, is the eternal reality that God's people will one day be made whole. God wants to bring each of us to the fulfillment of our future, a plan and a promise that takes even our present brokenness into consideration.

CHAPTER 11

I Believe in the Merits of Dead-Again Christianity
Reviving a Discipline for Self-Denial

The 2010 Vancouver Winter Olympics will go down in history as being dubbed a Canadian "love-in." The international sporting event was a spectacle in Canuck smash-mouth confidence and pride as well as a showcase of unapologetic and record-breaking partying! It was two weeks filled with many memorable moments that challenged even the most hardened of the unpatriotic in Canada to a duel. All this to say that most Canadians (of which I am one) were caught up in uncharacteristic revelry over our country's cleaning up in the area of medal-bagging. We not only wanted to experience a "gold" rush in terms of performing well in the games; we wanted to feel good about ourselves as well.

To sum it up in a word, for a few short weeks *(that even seemed too short)* Canadians just flat out "believed" in themselves.

The spirit of Canadian pride during the 2010 Winter Olympics was captured for national consumption in the games' theme song and anthem: "I Believe." The tune hit no. 1 on pop charts in Canada and was sung by Canadian jazz singer Nikki Yanofsky. With all due respect, hearing the song once, maybe even two times, would have been tolerable to my constitution; to hear it several times daily, however, was more than over the top. It got to the point where I personally was happy to see the Vancouver Games end just so that the song would peter out on radio airwaves!

The Vancouver Olympics reaffirmed to me something of a poignant spiritual truth: people's lives are enriched when they choose to *believe* in something greater than themselves. I was moved by my country's renewed spirit of belief in its ability to express our unique heritage and national strength on the world's stage.

Belief is a strong agent for cultural cause and social change in our world. It was almost as if Canada was revived in some way out of the doldrums of a passé presence and identity on a global scale. In hindsight, however, though the soap-boxy campaign in national pride and achievement that was the Vancouver Games built up the muscle mass of our collective patriotism and got us through the annual "February blahs," I couldn't help but feel a bit hollow once the event was over.

This perhaps speaks of the yearning each one of us has to possess something in our lives that grounds our desires and brings us a deeper immovable and inward satisfaction.

The pleasant distraction of the Vancouver Olympic Games played out a lot like the frivolous activities and distractions that Solomon sought to enjoy and fulfill his life by. The king, however, found out how quickly the appeal of his regal ventures could wear off and how they failed to replace the true need in his life: *the fact that life is meant to be enjoyed with God at the centre of it.* Without Him giving us an eternal perspective from which to view our lives now, all the things we come to do and believe in this world are ultimately "meaningless."

On the greater spiritual plain of life, it's not believing in some*thing* (for example, our cultural capabilities or individual abilities) that injects in us a sense of what the purpose and meaning of life is all about; rather, it's our belief in *someone!*

That is what faith in Jesus Christ does for the Christian "believer." Our belief in the Saviour gets us through the rough-and-tumble offerings and spiritual inclines of this world, all the way to the banks of Heaven's safe and happy shore. As the Church, we believe this without blinking. As Christians we have no trouble believing in Christ as the Son of God as the One who died for our sins, who rose again, and who will come back again.

But ask a Christian to believe in the merits of dead-again Christianity, and you may just come across as sounding heretical to them; perhaps like you're preaching "another gospel" other than the one they've already received, as Paul wrote in his letter to the Galatian church.

However, what I am referring to by the term *dead-again Christianity* is that aspect of Jesus' teaching and discipleship that challenges those who would follow Him to embrace a life of self-denial (the taking up of their "cross"). As a peacocking self-assured Pharisee, the apostle Paul must have swallowed hard at the prospect of living a life of self-denial, every Christian's "Damascan Road" reality! The Pharisee turned newborn Christian undoubtedly struggled with the thought of living lowly and humbly as a spiritually integral element of entering into discipleship with the Lord.

However, after Paul's conversion to Christianity found the apostle spiritually taken over by a zealous belief in and commitment to Christ, he couldn't help but communicate to the early Church his own radical spiritual recipe for godly living: the need for him to "die daily" to himself (1 Corinthians 15:31 NKJV). In fact, Paul saw his life as possessing inherent value *through Christ* alone and nothing more. "I consider my life worth nothing to me, if only I may finish the race and complete the task the Lord Jesus has given me—the task of testifying to the gospel of God's grace" (Acts 20:24).

We all know that merely verbalizing a belief in Jesus as our Lord and Saviour is the easy part in identifying ourselves as "Christians"; it's what that belief *entails* for our lives that challenges the rubber of our faith when it meets the spiritual road!

As counterintuitive as it sounds on a theological level to the resurrection-bound believer, "I believe in dead-again Christianity" is actually our everyday spiritual battle cry. If we were to sum up the Lord's response to those of His day who entertained thoughts of following Him, it would be: "Are you willing to die to yourself first?" Jesus let it be known to all potential disciples, "Whoever loses his life for my sake will find it" (Matthew 10:39). God will not use us and fill us as much as He could if we are still full of ourselves. For over two thousand years, aspiring disciples have been challenged to live by Jesus' directive to deny themselves as an act of submission to God in following the Saviour.

The events of a personal revival and spiritual renewal assist us in how we ought to view the *spiritual* life as being one of self-denial. The prophet Elijah, while engaged in a "my God is better than yours" showdown with the worshippers of Baal, called on the Lord to set fire to his water-saturated sacrifice of wood, stone, and soil in order to prove that Israel's God was the one and only God in existence. After fire indeed fell from Heaven and burned up Elijah's sacrifice, it was then that the people present dropped to a prostrated posture of reverence and submission before the Lord.

It was a scene of emulsifying revival and renewal within Israel. Elijah, just prior to his prayer for the Lord to set his sacrifice aflame with conviction, cried out, "O LORD, answer me, so these people will know that you, O LORD, are God, and that you are turning their hearts back again" (see 1 Kings 18:37–39).

Israel was a privileged nation, spoiled by God's loving presence and sovereign provisions; nonetheless, they would get to the sorry point where they needed to be revived and renewed in their obedience to the Lord again and again.

Likewise, the fattened blessing-bloated spiritual life of any Christian can end up turning away from the disciplines of discipleship and find itself in need of the heart-stoking fires of personal revival and renewal. We can be born-again and yet lack much in terms of being willing to die to ourselves on a daily basis.

Instead of seeing ourselves merely as people who are spiritually "alive" and therefore meant to be gorging absorbers of an abundant life, we need to be ever mindful of the spiritual poverty we *still* possess as well. Though we have been redeemed and cleansed by Jesus' blood, we nonetheless have endless amounts of recycling spiritual junk in our lives.

Oftentimes we overlook the need we have for the convicting fire of God's reviving and renewing Spirit to turn up the purifying heat on our Christian lives as if they were an offering laid upon the altar of His Lordship. Only the refining fire of the Word of God in unison with the Spirit of God can cause a greater obedience to take place within us in turning us back from the spiritual wastelands we amble into.

To be spiritually redeemed and therefore made alive in Christ doesn't in any way negate Scripture's call for us to empty ourselves of the items that take the place of our heart's allegiance to Jesus. Though the event of our spiritual rebirth (salvation) is a one time, one moment event, our process of sanctification (becoming more like Christ) is a day-by-day lifelong transaction. This is accomplished as a Christian embraces a lifestyle of self-denial (dying daily to self).

It's in light of God's "mercy" on us through His Son's life that was given for ours that we Christians are to then "offer" our lives, our "bodies as living sacrifices" and to "be transformed by the renewing" of our "mind[s]" (Romans 12:1–2). Although Paul's words to the Christians in Rome don't state it in so many terms, the apostle was clear that a spiritually alive church is also a body of people who become dead to themselves again and again.

From your own experiences in the Church, some of you (particularly those in active ministries) who are reading this may be thinking, "I know exactly what he means by *dead-again* Christianity; I see dead-again people in board and committee meetings all the time!" Perhaps there is a certain connection to death and God's people that we often *don't* overlook!

In all seriousness, however, Christians are complex mixtures of people who bear both salvation and a residing sinful nature all rolled up into one. No wonder so many of us in the Church feel as if we're a tad schizophrenic in our spiritual understanding of our own lives!

In that way we have a lot in common with those who were amongst the first to witness Jesus Christ in the flesh.

The Church observes and celebrates the truth of Easter quite well, and so it should; after all without the Resurrection we might as well put away our Bibles, close up the hymnals, shut down the PowerPoint, and go home. Yet there's a vital truth in our preparations for Resurrection Sunday that we often overshoot far too quickly for its spiritual efficacy.

Palm Sunday is the day we remember Jesus as He rode into Jerusalem sitting atop a young colt, as many fair-weather worshippers gave the Lord His "props," as they say. Titanic waves of praises appropriately met His worthiness.

However, it was a different kind of coronation, one that even the "rocks" themselves could witness as being a just and divinely regal affair. What the people were shouting "Hosanna" (meaning "Save us") that day is almost as key to understanding the person and mission of Jesus as the choice horse He was riding on; both are spiritual triggers for the Christian to remember in their prayers for revival and renewal in the Church (we need both a humility of person and a faith in an all-powerful God when we're on our knees).

It seemed like a great occasion with excitement levels off the charts. The hype surrounding the Lord's emergence moved from lawn-mover decibels to standing beside a jet engine. Many a Jew who had finally brought themselves to believe in this miracle-working prophet and teacher (Jesus of Nazareth) could almost taste the reality of their freedom from the clutches of the Roman Empire with every stride the colt made towards the Holy city.

Yet not all was as it seemed. The reality of the event we recall as Palm Sunday had a much darker and more spiritually ominous outlook hovering over it. *Jesus wasn't coming to the city to announce to Pilate that a new "sheriff" was in town but came to be crucified;* a prospect utterly unthinkable to all the messiah-huggers that fateful day. Though people had praises on their lips, Jesus had one thing on His mind: dying for the sin of the world.

By Jesus dying for the sin of all humanity, God would hold the world eternally accountable for how they'd respond to His Son. Likewise, Christ Himself, by virtue of His vicarious sacrifice would hold all His would-be disciples accountable for how they lived *their* spiritual lives.

Paul, in his life and ministry, was certainly one who got *both* drifts coming from the Cross of Jesus. The apostle, by evidence of the content of his New Testament letters to the first century churches, firmly grasped what the third Person of the Trinity's death would mean for those who would profess faith in God's Son. The thought of having to face his own martyrdom must have been foremost in his heart and mind when he put pen to paper in writing certain verses we find in the book of Galatians especially.

Have you ever wondered what Paul was really getting at with his readers when he stated words of ultra-devotion such as "I have been crucified with Christ" (Galatians 2:20)? The apostle wrote those words as a part of a rebuke to Peter for being spiritually two-faced in his dealings with the Gentile believers over the issue of table fellowship. However, in the course of his address to his fellow apostle Paul managed to leave the Church a timeless spiritual lesson in self-denial. Just what *did* Paul mean when after stating that he'd been "crucified with Christ" he said that *he* therefore "no longer live[d]"?

As a Christian and as a pastor, such a truth isn't the first spiritual inclination I have upon waking each day. In fact, I almost want to avoid this verse in Galatians for the sheer reason that the apostle's words seem to catch me like a spiritual paper-cut every time, because I naturally interpret my salvation as resulting from *Jesus* solely being on Calvary's Cross and not me along with Him. Sometimes I have difficulty handling this general truth about my life as a disciple of Jesus.

However, Paul got it right, didn't he? If Jesus was lovingly thinking of us when He was on the Cross, wouldn't that mean that we were co-joined there with the Lord in a spiritual sense? Though only He (Jesus), as the perfect sacrificial Lamb of God, could indeed die for us (who took the "punishment" for our sin, as Isaiah said), it was *our* iniquities in the first place that put Jesus in the position of being crucified.

The only reason there's a place for each of us today at the *foot* of Jesus' Cross is directly due to the fact that there was first enough room for each of us *on* the Cross with Him at Calvary. Paul owned such a spiritual view of his life. Therefore, Christians in all reality, though they are eternally alive should also be identified as a group of "dead people."

In the Galatians' passage Paul was simply saying that having faith in Jesus Christ involves a *death* as well as a *new life*. Could it be, then, that if our bodily resurrection can only follow our physical death, perhaps revival and spiritual renewal can only follow a new appreciation of our dead-again (dying daily to self) status?

If we know, in fact, that we are nothing without God, then there should be ample enough space within us for Him to fill us with His Spirit and empower us again and again.

A quick breakdown of Paul's words in Galatians 2:20 and following point to the reality that a genuine Christian is one who not only *believes* that they must be dead to self but who *behaves* that way. It's all about "attitude" in life they say, a piece of advice that could also be applied to the spiritual life. The believer in Christ must live as if they are literally dead to self, not only if they're to be continuously spiritually revived and renewed but because they are actually now *alive in Christ!*

We better believe that in coming to faith in Christ we have voluntarily buried our old selves (with its one-way ticket to eternal death attached) and that a new Christ-induced birth (with its one-way ticket to Heaven) has occurred in its place. In 2 Corinthians 4:10, Paul worded this spiritual reality of the inward Christian like this: "Through suffering, these bodies of ours constantly share in the death of Jesus so that the life of Jesus may also be seen in our bodies" (NLT). Because each day brings with it fresh challenges to our faith, we must remind ourselves on a daily basis that we have another life to live now, one that is not of our own making or of our own maintaining.

Any individual Christian or churches as a whole who seeks revival and renewal in their lives and ministries must first recall to mind that they have in fact already *relinquished* their lives to Jesus.

THE RELINQUISHED LIFE

Paul's way of acknowledging that central spiritual truth in his life was by issuing the theologically thundering and equally shocking statement "I have been crucified with Christ."

The apostle was saying, "I'm all in!" There were no "half-sies" with Paul. If Jesus was to be Lord of Paul's life, then the Lord had to be the sum of all its parts. Just as Jesus gave up His life to cover and pardon our sin, so we must relinquish our right to live our lives the way we used to prior to our coming to the Saviour.

However, the rather sad reality in the Church today is that many of God's people are said to be indistinguishable in their lifestyles from those who claim to hold no faith in Christ.

> Scandalous behaviour is rapidly destroying American Christianity. By their daily activity, most Christians regularly commit treason. With their mouths they claim that Jesus is Lord, but with their actions they

demonstrate allegiance to money, sex, and self-fulfillment. The findings in numerous national polls conducted by highly respected pollsters like The Gallup Organization and The Barna Group are simply shocking. "Gallup and Barna," laments evangelical theologian Michael Horton, "hand us survey after survey demonstrating that evangelical Christians are as likely to embrace lifestyles every bit as hedonistic, materialistic, self-centred, and sexually immoral as the world in general."[41]

Again using Paul's teaching as our spiritual blackboard, for one to decide to go along with Christ (that is, become a Christian and enter into discipleship with Him) must equal a life that's wholly transformed inwardly and outwardly *by* that decision. There can be no turning back to the life we once knew that was spiritually hollow and lacking God's inward redeeming presence, for we have already responded to Scripture's invitation to "Taste and see that the LORD is good" (Psalm 34:8). The author of Hebrews took this point a little further when he wrote, "If we deliberately keep on sinning after we have received the knowledge of the truth, no sacrifice for sins is left, but only a fearful expectation of judgment and of raging fire" (Hebrews 10:26–27).

For the apostle Paul, when people turn aside from lives of sin that resulted in Jesus going to the Cross, they must then realize that they have taken their place *with* Christ *on* that same Cross. Their lives that were once solely oriented towards sin's reign in them died along with Him there.

A renewed grasp of our spiritual depravity should always lead to our attaining a greater value of our spiritual rebirth; one cannot be divorced from the other.

In this way, revival and spiritual renewal in the Church should reignite that element of Jesus' message that implores those who would come after Him to count the cost. It's okay to be high on grace when we share our faith and when we expound from the Bible (for God *is* gracious), but God's grace must be communicated within the context of His holy character as well. We never do any potential believer (or Christian for that matter) any tick of spiritual good if we raise the bar of God's grace so high in our dealings with people that we create a spiritual imbalance where the scales of conviction and scriptural accountability are weighed down as a result. Following Jesus in a committed relationship is a spiritually challenging, faith-stretching lifelong endeavour, not some arm-in-arm stroll down spiritual "easy street," like a fan hobnobbing with some religious celebrity.

Jesus, using cultural motifs from His day, addressed the temptation some of those who were following Him might have had to turn back. "Anyone who puts a hand to the plow and then looks back is not fit for the Kingdom of God" (Luke 9:62 NLT). The convicting work of the Holy Spirit in our lives as Christians clears the cobwebs that impair our spiritual memory and reminds us that we have relinquished our life to Christ. Therefore, the reins to commandeer our lives must also be given up as well. God's power doesn't fully kick in if the Lordship of Christ in our lives hasn't first.

To embrace the Cross of Christ is to open our hearts to Jesus' Kingdom values with an *invitation* to live as sacrificially as He did. Doing so makes one spiritually fit for not only being able to enter into Jesus' Kingdom (Heaven) but for serving in it in the here and now. Jesus will never be the horse who follows *our* carrot of self-will. Rather, *He* is the One who must grab the reins of our lives and dangle His will out in front of us, steering us in its direction.

Jesus knew that when He was in the world (as the incarnate Son) submitting to His Father's will was the hallmark of His life. Our Lord didn't chase after self-preserving ideals and independent avenues; He denied Himself, even unto death. How eternally comforting a thought it should be for every believer that our perfect Saviour chose (in obedience to His Father's will) to sacrifice His very divine life for our sins!

Even though Jesus had battalions upon battalions of able war-waging angels at His sovereign command to slew His enemies, *He chose the nails* over self-will and remained glued, as it were, to the Cross, enduring its irreverent shame and unimaginable suffering. He may have done so "for the joy set before him" but also because He was selfless in making Himself "nothing" (Hebrews 12:2; Philippians 2:7).

Let's never forget how gruesome the execution scene at the Cross of Christ really was. The bones, tendons, and muscles of Jesus' wrists and feet were pierced-through by large merciless spikes and nailed into wood. Anatomically, and barring any supernatural stunts, there would be no getting off the Cross for Jesus. The Lord's divine blood flowed like a river in streaks down His body until the lines joined together to become a sea of red all over Him.

While His Son's life was slowly draining out of His body, the Father was beckoning the world not to let what Jesus went through be wasted, for God bids that none should perish eternally but that "everyone" would "come to repentance" by coming to Christ in faith (2 Peter 3:9).

The Cross of Christ, then, compels us not to turn back from our Saviour but to actually turn aside from our former life, a life characterized by its lack of God's forgiveness and its lack of peace with Him. That's why times of revival and renewal within the Church are needed for God's people to become resurgent in their ministry of evangelism. When we remember the depth and breadth of our sin's offense in the eyes of God, we'll gain a fresh appreciation for the massive coverage of His grace over our lives. We should want to communicate that kind of unseen grace and mercy to people who have not experienced it.

Though our faith in the Saviour of the world brings us a new forgiven and even abundant eternal life, it is still a life that calls us to acknowledge the relinquishing of our own.

For the apostle Paul, there was no letting his old self who died with Christ out of the spiritual cemetery, as it were. The truth and reality behind our relinquished life is that sin's power *over* us and its residence *within* in us can be overcome and overruled; that is, we are now born-again and free (empowered) to do what is right and pleasing to God. We are no longer helplessly enslaved to our sinful nature. The fact that this deems us a "new creation" in Christ means we've lost absolutely zilch in terms of the spiritually lost life we've relinquished (and which Jesus took to the Cross with Him). Our best life, our Heaven-realized life, is yet to come.

When James Calvert was sent to be a missionary to the Fiji islands, the people who were targeted with the gospel were known as common cannibals and savages. The captain of the ship who dropped him on the island sought to turn him back. "You will surely lose your life and the lives of those with you, if you go amongst these people." "We died before we came here," replied the stoic-faced Calvert. The missionary resolved that he had already exchanged his own life for Christ's. Even if his own physical life would be snuffed out as he evangelized in jungles riddled with spiritual darkness and danger, he couldn't possibly lose anything of *eternal* worth.

THE EXCHANGED LIFE
Believing in the merits of dead-again Christianity always leads us to remember that we have indeed exchanged our earthly dying and finite lives for the glorious and eternal Spirit-led life of Jesus. That is why Paul added to the fact that not only was he "crucified with Christ" and therefore "no longer" lived, "but (now) Christ lives in me."

Just as surely as the flu bug will affect us if it is in our bloodstream, the Spirit of Jesus (the Holy Spirit) will affect us and change us if He is in us. This happens on two foundational levels.

One of the roles of the Holy Spirit is to *produce spiritual fruit* in the lives of God's people. This is where we as Christ followers begin the spiritual process of exchanging our old character for Jesus' character qualities (see Galatians 5:22–23). These Spirit-manufactured qualities in the life of a Christian define what it truly means to exhibit "godliness" in our lives. Being "like" Christ is more than just merely trying to imitate Him; it has everything to do with Jesus living and working *through* us.

None of us can live the Christian life "fruitfully" in our own strength; it will lead to spiritual frustration and letdown every time. We simply do not as sin-marred creatures possess the natural power to live out the will of God in our lives. Faith, as seen through obedience and self-denial in the life of God's people, always begets God's power!

The second foundational level in which the Holy Spirit affects the life of the new believer in Christ is in the area of *serving within the Body of Christ* (the Church).

When the disciples of Jesus committed to Him in a relationship of trust and faith, the Lord then commissioned the work of His ministry to them. As Jesus served He trained His disciples to do likewise in order for them to be equipped in carrying on His ministry after His ascension into Heaven. When Jesus put His Spirit in them, they, in essence, became His hands, His feet, His voice, and channels of power to the world. As a result, when they spoke, the people heard Jesus; when they acted, the people experienced the power and glory of God. The same goes for our ministries today!

Therefore, we cannot possibly know God, cannot possibly know what He requires of our lives as His servants, cannot possibly please God and bring Him glory or even begin to fully understand our own fallen human nature if the Holy Spirit is not residing in us.

That said, even Christians who are endowed by the Holy Spirit struggle to embrace basic biblical principles. I remember having a conversation with another church leader who was quite adamant that a lot of the contentions and strife amongst God's people in the Church today, he said, is a "direct result of Christians who fail to live out Galatians 2:20." It was hard to argue otherwise. The Bible clearly commands believers to "submit to one another out of reverence for Christ." If God's people can't train themselves to live out in practical ways the spiritual truth that they have already died to self, then how can they truly live for Jesus' glory and progress in the Life they took on in exchange for theirs?

The exchanged life says, "I no longer live, but the life I now live, I live in Christ." We have been born anew spiritually and are living a life we could never have lived on our own if we'd *kept* our own and not relinquished it to Jesus!

Lou Johnson played for the Los Angeles Dodgers of Major League Baseball when they won the World Series in 1965. For thirty years Johnson tried to recover his World Series championship ring, which he'd lost to drug dealers in 1971. Then someone who knew him saw that his ring was being auctioned off on the Internet for $3,400. The man bought the ring before any bids were posted and promptly returned the long lost ring to its rightful owner: his distant friend Lou Johnson. Upon receiving his team's '65 championship ring back, the retired ballplayer shared that there was a part of him that felt as if he was "reborn."

Likewise, the humbling Good News of Calvary's Cross is that we who were once far from our Creator (in a position to be spiritually lost for eternity), "without hope and without God in the world" (Ephesians 2:12), were bought back (theologically speaking, *purchased or redeemed*) by Jesus Christ when He was crucified. It is only *when* we fully surrender to God's Son that we indeed inherit the goal of His sacrificial death on our behalf: eternal life. At that point, *we* become reborn and can know with certainty that God is now living on the inside of us.

However, dying to ourselves does not spell the end of our birth-inherited personalities or to the things that make us unique individually. It's not a call to end our hopes and dreams in life either; for God *wants* to give us the desires of our hearts. That said, even the aspirations and goals we have as we put our faith in Jesus may be altered to suit God's greater purpose for our lives. We need to die daily to that stubborn part of our being, "the self," precisely because it always aims to fight the will of God being done in our lives.

To *die* to ourselves as an ongoing element of our discipleship is a call to submit our whole lives to God's redemptive cultivating of them; it's what we ask of Him whenever we sing, "Have thine own way, Lord."

Finally, those who relinquish their life to Christ thereby exchanging their old life for His, is a life that should also be characterized by *trusting* in Him.

THE TRUSTING LIFE

When we die to ourselves upon coming to Christ in saving faith, we are at the same time admitting that we cannot trust our own hearts and wisdom to be the guiding forces of our lives. The apostle Paul in the same verse goes on to complete his line of thought by stating, "The life which I now live in the flesh I live by faith in the Son of God" (Galatians 2:20 NKJV).

Trusting in our own sin-altered judgment to get us through this world is the epitome of foolishness. There are days when I think I'm a pretty wise person.

The harsh reality, however, is that there are other days when I wonder how disappointed God must be in me! I can pinpoint most of the moments in my life when I am relying on my own human faculties to make important decisions. It's in those times when I most acutely sense that I fail to trust God's best for me.

Consequently, "without faith" we cannot possibly "please God" (Hebrews 11:6). The life of a disciple is to reflect a *changed* life. It's a process that has many cadences and yet the spiritual transformation the Bible refers to that should mark the life of a Christian can only come about by them trusting in the transcendent wisdom and power of God.

Perhaps at one time we believed we had vats upon vats of knowledge and a wealth of learning to go along with our claim that we had a good handle on what "life" was "all about." As we grow older, though, we find from all the life experience we've garnered that we *know* even less now than we originally thought we did in our younger days! As the clock of our lives keeps ticking onward, our thoughts of eternity will more frequently colour our perspective on life about as much as our inevitable and ever-looming meeting with Christ will contextualize all that we are and do as His disciples.

As we not only head towards the grave but headlong towards an always imminent Rapture (whichever comes first for us), it will be imperative for us as the Church to live the spiritual life more by faith than by sight. We can only own the kind of peace it takes to influence those around us who lack it if we are trusting in God to grant us that peace supernaturally. Who wouldn't want their lives changed by having the unshakeable peace of God lodged deep down within them? What a powerful witness a sensitive and peaceful Christian can be to this disordered and chaotic world.

In this present age, we who know Christ intimately are being shaped for eternal sinlessness and for life and communion with God when we finally get to our eternal home in Heaven. And while that is true, it still leaves us with another truth to contend with in the here and now: there is no perfection in any one of us yet, something I am very thankful for! Can you imagine having to talk to or work with someone who is absolutely perfected in their salvation? Though we will not know what it's like to be unable to sin (until we get to glory, Heaven), we'll always be able to see how our sinful nature as Christians on this side of eternity can be harmful to ourselves and to those around us whom we sin against.

If the Bible tells us anything, it's that the Holy Spirit is too powerful *not* to change our lives if we want that enough. Christlikeness is the desire and the goal of our faith, not an automatic spiritual given. There are Christians who believe in Jesus, and there are Christians who aim to live like they believe in Jesus! The more I come to know the Church and the unfortunate realities that sin in the lives of God's people can bring about in the Body of Christ, the more I must ask, *Have we forgot that as much as we're alive in Christ, we're supposed to be dead to self as well?*

Dietrich Bonhoeffer, a German pastor who was put to death by the Nazis during the Second World War, wrote, "When God calls a man, he bids him come and die."[42] Bonhoeffer lived like he believed his life was God's for the taking. Where is the persistent attitude in the Church today that our lives as Christians have been relinquished to Christ and are now His to live through? Where is the exchanged life? Where is the trusting life?

Church, we are parched in our spirituality today. We should be imploring God for the springs of Jesus' living water to well up into a revival and spiritual renewal in each of our lives more than we perhaps realize. The spiritual starting line for such realities in any individual Christian's life always begins with the prayerful consideration that if we have, *indeed,* been "crucified with Christ," are we living in such a way that reflects a redeemed Spirit-residing life? Is there outward as well as inward evidence and promptings of that fact? Is our life impacted and insulated by a supernatural peace that comes from having a full-blown trust in Jesus Christ?

It behooves us as the countdown draws nigh when we shall see our Saviour face to face to consider abandoning our whole lives to God. We "give it up" in terms of applauding and clapping for famous and iconic figures of our culture whenever they walk on a stage or down a red carpet. Yet we're a society at the same time that seems to have little to no taste for giving ourselves up and turning ourselves in to God Almighty, who is more than worthy of our praise and worship. May we in the Church get it right and covet the spiritual merits of not only believing in being born-again but in being *dead to self* by giving ourselves up to God, and that on a daily basis. This is a discipline that requires, above all, a conviction of our own sin; a little humility wouldn't hurt either.

CHAPTER 12

BIBLICAL ARGUMENTS FOR THE CONSUMPTION OF HUMBLE PIE

A Revived Hunger for Personal Humility

Have you ever wondered what it would be like to be famous? I'll bet that at different times in our lives thoughts of personal fame and the fortune that comes along with such a status has solicited the majority of us. There's something about self-advancement and personal notoriety that flag down our hearts by their hypnotic dalliance. There's just something about being recognized, honoured, and even being famous that is extremely enticing to human beings.

Our culture's appetite to grab the world's spotlight by the jugular has increased enormously in the last decade or two. Reality TV has made many people famous, sometimes for entirely dubious reasons!

As a Western culture especially, we are obsessed with our "fifteen minutes of fame." Words are powerful, and with technology the way it is now, one can express their unfiltered innermost thoughts (even if they are inappropriate) in 140 characters with just a click of the button (can you say "Twitter"?). People today will use any mode of media to steer the world's attention their way. The latest stab at notoriety (and let's be honest, at fortune, too) within our society can be seen in and through the many sordid "tell-all" books that are being written by the quasi-famous and famous alike. Though we may not like how it wears when it's caked on us, we sure love to read about someone else's dirt-stained life!

Speaking of books, I devoured a great one a while back entitled *The Call*, by Os Guinness. It's a profoundly blunt read that offers acres of insightful wisdom. The book's message centres on our culture's search for meaning, purpose, and success in a world largely deaf to the call of God upon its conscience. In regards to the fame-intoxicated self-absorbed society we live in, Guinness remarks,

> Formerly…heroism was linked to the honor of accomplishment. Honor was accorded to the person with some genuine achievement, whether in character, virtue, wisdom…Today, however, the media offers a shortcut to fame—instantly fabricated famousness with no need for the sweat, cost, and dedication of true greatness. The result is not the hero but the celebrity, the person famously described as "well known for being well-known."[43]

Could such a sentiment be any more relevant than it is today?

I could think of several people in the entertainment world right now or in the "sphere" of the famous that I'd like to ask, "And just why *are you* considered a celebrity?"

Many Christian leaders who enjoy a perceived "successful" and prominent ministry would probably concede that the *fame* card has periodically and no less tantalizingly surfaced to the top of the deck in terms of what motivates their leadership and what "could be" for their lives. The alluring pull of self-advancement is particularly enticing to spiritual leaders who possess a charismatic presence and wads of influence to boot.

By the same token, most Christian leaders would also admit to struggling with the level of accountability that comes with positions of spiritual authority. The ground of leadership authority, no matter what concourse of life it's exercised in, never appears firm; it always feels like it could give way to quick sand at any given moment. If, in fact, it is "lonely" at the top, it's got to be somewhat better at the bottom, wouldn't you think?

Like anyone else, well-intended, godly Christians struggle with the tension of remaining humble while entertaining personal ambitions at the same time.

However harmless ambitions can appear, they can go wrong in people's lives, even get ugly, really quick. What often goes missing in action, in terms of character, whenever ambitions control one's life (even Christians) is (drum roll please)…*humility!*

A truly humble person, it's been said, is hard to find. That is why people like Booker T. Washington stood out in this world. The renowned black author and teacher, who died in the early 1900s, was an outstanding example of such a person. He was ambitious, yet undeniably humble.

Shortly after he took over the presidency of the Tuskegee Institute in Alabama, he was walking in an exclusive section of town when he was stopped by a wealthy white woman. Not knowing the famous Mr. Washington by sight, she asked if he would like to earn a few dollars by chopping wood for her. Because he had no pressing business at the moment, Professor Washington smiled, rolled up his sleeves, and proceeded to do the humble chore she had requested. When he was finished, he carried the logs into the house and stacked them by the fireplace.

A little girl recognized him and later revealed his identity to the lady. The next morning the embarrassed woman went to see Mr. Washington in his office at the Institute and apologized profusely. "It's perfectly all right, Madam," he replied. "Occasionally I enjoy a little manual labor." She shook his hand warmly and assured him that his meek and gracious attitude had endeared him and his work to her heart. Not long afterward she showed her admiration by persuading some wealthy acquaintances to join her in donating thousands of dollars to the Tuskegee Institute.[44]

We could use more people like Booker T. Washington in the world today, *especially in the Church!* The founder of Radio Bible Class, M. R. De Haan, said, "Humility is something we should constantly pray for, yet never thank God that we have it."[45] It's like the old saying, "If you say you are humble, *you no longer are!*

The gospel's witness to Christ's humility and selflessness all too often convicts me to pray for a deeper knowledge of the Saviour, His heart's burden for the spiritually lost and His sacrificial nature and example of unconditional love for all people. Speaking from the perspective of a pastor, it's too easy for me at times to take my eyes off the fact that though ministry affords me the opportunity to develop my gifts (and my ambitions), serving Christ is primarily about serving *people* in humility; consequently, it can never be about self-advancement or about elevating one's stock in Christian culture.

Humility in a Christian's life *can* co-exist with one's authority, at least to the extent in which the one who holds some authority knows how to ground that responsibility and keep its power and influence under spiritual wraps by seeing it through the lens of a servant's as well as an *eternal* perspective.

In reality, we are people who are often prone to developing an inflated view of ourselves. The fact that we're "Christians" should change that tendency, but often it doesn't. Sadly, conceitedness is just as prevalent in the Church as it is in the "world." We all bump into Christians from time to time who come across as being really full of their selves. It's kind of like the title of the Mac Davis song

"O Lord, It's Hard to Be Humble." Some of us believers indeed find it *hard* to be humble before the Lord and can go a little overboard when we gaze into the spiritual mirror by admiring our reflection and looking at it longer than what we ought to!

In all seriousness, humility, it's been said, is not thinking any less of ourselves; it's just thinking of ourselves *less!* Humility (though some may think hilarity, not to mention irony) is playing a game of Twister (as a leadership team-building exercise) with people you are in conflict with where your shnoz could almost smooch a contrary fellow leader's backside that's pointed straight at you!

Humility is something that can pay spiritual dividends, not to mention may lead to respect and recognition over time. There are those amongst God's people who seem to spend a lot of precious energy chasing after authority and control in the Church, only to find it eluding them. By contrast, there are others in the Church (who are more humble) who seem to acquire authority without even so much as a hint of pursuing it.

Chasing after self-advancement and stalking ambition was something we never saw the One who has *all* authority doing. When we read about the ministry life of Jesus Christ, we don't have to strain to notice how adamantly the Lord deterred His listeners from actively seeking places of prominence and importance in society. The Lord taught people to seek humility in coveting the backstages of life instead. Desiring to be a "headliner" in the ranks of the world instead of being content with playing a part of the supporting cast can leave us discouraged and red-faced and even damage our witness. Any promotion is best left in someone else's hands and to *their* discretion.

Jesus put it like this:

> *"When someone invites you to a wedding feast, do not take the place of honor, for a person more distinguished than you may have been invited… But when you are invited, take the lowest place, so that when your host comes, he will say to you, 'Friend, move up to a better place'…For everyone who exalts himself will be humbled, and he who humbles himself will be exalted"* (Luke 14:8–11).

James had similar advice for the readers of his New Testament letter. "Humble yourselves before the Lord, and he will lift you up" (James 4:10). God alone is the greatest self-esteem booster and the greatest rewarder of our humility! One of the firstfruits of a spiritually revived Church should be a collective readjusted

Godward view of the self; a spiritual perspective that leads to a better grasp of Christian humility. Various times in the book of Proverbs we're told that "humility comes before honor" (Proverbs 15:33). On the "flipside," we're counselled that "Pride goes before destruction, a haughty spirit before a fall" (Proverbs 16:18).

This is what happened to Solomon's son Rehoboam as the heir to Israel's kingship. The newbie sire hastily rebuffed his people's requests for leniency in the areas of taxation and enforced labour rules (concessions his father, Solomon, refused to make for the nation). Far from resembling a man wearing a crown of humility, King Rehoboam leaves his inauguration *humbled.* After starting off celebrating his coronation with all twelve tribes at his feet, he leaves the event with *two!* The other ten tribes of Israel threw their weight behind Jeroboam (a possible rebellious subordinate of Solomon's administration) and crowned him king of Israel. The self-centred Rehoboam ended up a rebuked and reduced ruler, with his father's kingdom divided up. If it was respect the king was after, he managed to apprehend the opposite!

The Bible's perspective of humility teaches us to go out of our way to seek lowliness of character and to avoid attaining to the unrighteous levels of self back-patting. Simply put, the way for one to be raised up and recognized in life is not a self-made ladder; it is a God-willed and God-appointed one, with each rung on it being upward steps in humility (whether we're kings or subjects; leaders or lay people). We must all know our personal limitations as Christians and seek to live within the parameters of God's will, direction, and blessing.

In terms of our ambitions, then, one thing is rather clear. Christians should not strive to be someone whom they're not and focus more on the uniquely gifted person they *already* are.

One church leader in the United States shares,

> I believe that much of what God is doing in our lives is to sift out and rework our ambitions. Sometimes our ambitions are too grand for our gifts and we need them realistically downsized…when you observe a great preacher, don't envy…just thank God that there are those with exceptional gifts. And desire to use the gifts you've been given for God's glory.[46]

There are those popular leaders and personalities amongst God's people today whom it would seem are busy trying to build up their own earthly "kingdoms." Should it be "above" Christians to like how important their name looks on publications and to get carried away at how high their ministry stock has risen within their denomination's hierarchy?

When you really mull it over, ambitions can be just as irreligiously and selfishly driven with God's people at the wheel of them as they can be humbly driven and God glorifying.

Sometimes it's not necessarily church leaders who are guilty of self-promotion (despite their authority and popularity); it's the "supporters" they have backing and glad-handing them in the pews who want to elevate the gifts and abilities of a particular leader. More often than not, these situations can grow divisive legs and become a source of great conflict within the Body of Christ.

Some of God's people can be quite shrewd in their ability to make their leaders appear (and even feel) as if they're the greatest thing since the lapel mic or the Plexiglas pulpit! I feel nauseated anytime I hear a Christian refer to a more prominent Christian as being "powerful" or "heavily anointed." I have seen "ordinary" and out-of-the-spotlight preachers deliver profoundly effective sermons. By the same token, I've heard well-known and highly talked about "powerful" preachers and evangelists stumble over their theology on their way to delivering highly emotional yet quickly forgotten messages. Who's better? And what's really best?

The fourteenth century preacher named John Tauler no doubt struggled to show humility. Perhaps we would have too if we had been the premiere speaker in all of Europe at the time. Sizeable crowds would converge at his Strasburg Cathedral to hear him expound from the Scriptures. Tauler was a learned man and an eloquent orator. However, to one man's ears and eyes there must have been something lacking in the reputable speaker. A man no one seems to know much about, Nicholas of Basle, cared enough for Tauler to hold him accountable.

One day Nicholas went up to the preacher after another great sermon, saying to him, "John, get alone with God. Leave your crowded church, your admiring congregation, and your hold on this city…Go aside to your study, be alone, and you'll see what I mean." The following Sunday as Tauler stepped into the pulpit, he found that he could not speak; there were only tears. "Dear children, I cannot speak today for weeping," the mushy preacher announced. "Pray God for me that He may help me and then I will make amends to you," Tauler concluded. Nicholas of Basle saw that the preacher had become bigger than the God he preached; as a result, he had become a celebrity.

No leader is greater than his message, larger than his ministry gifts, or more important than the organization (church or other), he serves in. A telltale sign that a church might be in need of revival is the levels (or the depths) to which believers will quarrel with one another and get divided over which leader deserves the biggest gold star. The ungodly actions of rival ministers, competing spiritual gifts and ministry personalities hobble (and can eventually humble) the witness of the Church. These kinds of school-ground antics actually occurred in an ancient church the apostle Paul was associated with.

The Corinthian Christians of the first century possessed some spiritually horrendous issues, including immorality, pride, personal conflict, and the abuse of spiritual gifts. If we think the Church of Jesus Christ is in the roughest shape it's ever been, we need to go back in time and read the New Testament once again!

One of the problems facing the church in Corinth was that the believers there couldn't stop bickering over which teacher of the Scriptures should have been held in the highest regard and deemed the most authoritative. Their disputes and incessant loyalties were rising to epic levels of creature worship; yet like the saying goes, "Hero worship is really zero worship." If anything was lacking in Corinth, it was a good dose of *humility* amid the Body of Christ.

Paul implored the Corinthian flock to see that God used their preachers' teaching ministries to work *together* for their greater spiritual and common good. One of the main points the apostle rebuked the church in Corinth with was his insistence that those who were charged with teaching God's Word were merely *servants*. "What after all, is Apollos? And what is Paul? Only servants" (1 Corinthians 3:5–9).

Both Paul and Apollos were merely using their respective spiritual gifts to grow the Corinthian believers in their faith; there were no "best preacher" conversations or awards allowed.

Such a thought would have been preposterous to Paul. Under his pastoral guidance the Corinthian believers would not get anywhere near the paradox of servant-worship. Today, as evangelicals, especially, it appears that some of us may be bowing (unknowingly) at an idol known as the *cult of the speaker*. Certain personalities and ministry "CEO" types in the Church appear to be the ultimate spiritual authority, quoted more than the Bible itself and getting more air time than God Himself!

In the Gospels when the disciples of Jesus were arguing with each other over who would be the "greatest" in the Kingdom of God, you get the impression they weren't nearly expecting the response they got. In answer to their inquiry, Jesus promptly punctured the disciples' inflated (and highly misguided) ambitions to ascend to greatness in His heavenly Kingdom. The Lord did this by establishing the spiritual measuring tape for such a lofty aspiration: the greatest in His Kingdom would be "the servant of all" (Mark 9:35).

No matter what we accomplish for God and His Kingdom (and there have been spectacular things done for the Lord through His people), at the end of the day we are all merely His servants.

None of the "big name" ministry types out there (fill in your favourite) are greater than you and me simply because they're a famous commodity. Greatness in the Kingdom of God will always be reflective of the consistent, obedient and sacrificial nature in which one *serves,* and that in *humility.*

Furthermore, God doesn't revive His Church in order for His people to become "great" (for "greatness" is rare and difficult to define). Rather, I believe God revives His Church in order to increase their *faithfulness* to Him.

Was there a greater prophet than Jeremiah? Despite the relatively dismal turnaround in Israel as a result of his prophetic ministry, who could argue against how faithful to God and how humble in his person *and* ministry Jeremiah remained?

Likewise, Paul was saying to the Corinthians that all the teachers they admired and adhered so closely to (him being one of them) were just faithfully going about their divinely appointed tasks. The bottom line was that none of them were worthy of more recognition than the other.

Paul used a farming metaphor to make his point. He said he "planted" the initial "seed" (a church in Corinth was formed), but God also gifted Apollos and sent him along to teach them, or to "water" the soil of the hearts of the new Christians in Corinth. Paul said in effect: "Give all glory where it's due, because it is God who causes the spiritual growth in the lives of His people." Therefore, "neither he who plants nor he who waters is anything" (1 Corinthians 3:6–7).

It's not that *we* who serve God should be deemed as "nothing" in the eyes of those we minister to either. Paul was simply clarifying that it is God who is the *source* of the spiritual growth in our lives (we just play a part in that process). Without God's blessings upon our ministries, our efforts would be skin-deep and ultimately ineffective.

However, it's not like those who teach the Word of God shouldn't take any credit for the growth of God's people. God doesn't bypass His servants in order to be glorified. Though He gifts His people to perform certain tasks, He wants us to be encouraged and blessed by our labours for Him as well. We should credit faithful and willing servants in the Church for their work, because God does so in Heaven's servant ledger (Matthew 16:27; Ephesians 6:8).

Biblical Arguments for the Consumption of Humble Pie

Too many servants in the Church today are weary and are often taken for granted. The more humble of Christians, however, should never attempt to compensate for their lack of affirmation by using ambition to gain personal recognition. Yet when we have a revived view of godly humility in the Church and when we're renewed in the acceptance of our own unique identity and giftedness, it should affect the attitudes of not only those *whom* we serve but those who are *doing* the serving.

God glorifies Himself through the willing hearts and service of His people, and it is a joy to see Christians serve with the objective of pointing people back to Him, not their abilities. Some of God's people in history grasped the enormity of what recognized leadership and authority in the Church entailed. Some of them were brilliant thinkers who no less struggled to feel adequate. In humility they identified with Paul in how he counselled the church in Corinth about how God's people were to view their teachers.

Ambrose, a great figure of the fourth century Roman Catholic Church, was one of them. At one point he occupied the governor's seat of a region called Liguria in the Western Roman Empire. Ambrose was said to have led with such love and concern for his people that they even thought of him as a father figure. When the Bishop of Milan passed away a campaign mounted to have Ambrose take the position. Crowds of people would shout his name repeatedly, trying to persuade him to "bite," as it were.

However, Ambrose felt wholly unworthy as a mere servant of God to receive the high office the Church was offering him. He could never be found guilty of harbouring the *pride of life* sin pointed out in 1 John 2:16: "the boasting of what he [man] has and does." Ambrose responded by actually ducking out of Milan one night to avoid being swept up in the frenzy of fanfare. Eventually, however, he would accept, and his ministry in Liguria would turn out to be highly fruitful. Ambrose's ministry would influence the life of a once tormented young man so profoundly that today we know him as one of the greatest theologians of the Catholic faith: St. Augustine.

What Ambrose saw as his unworthiness to look at himself anymore highly than he ought to have was the precise spiritual point Paul was trying to convey to the church in Corinth. Their teachers (as gifted as they were) were not to be used to divide the Body of Christ. None of them deserved to be called *"the"* man.

Any spiritual benefit the believers in Corinth received from Paul himself or Apollos, for that matter, should have led them to praise God and glorify Him first and credit the teachers secondly.

Paul not only had issues with a lack of humility in the church at Corinth, the apostle also had to deal with a similar problem at the church in Philippi.

In Philippians 2, we can easily read "between the lines" and see that Paul had an obvious concern for the unity of the Philippian church. Somehow the harmony and oneness of the flock there was threatened as a direct result of some friction that stemmed from a lack of humility amongst its members. Paul in his letter to the Philippians pointed out that while he was imprisoned, some in the church were fostering less than pristine motives, "selfish ambition," as they preached Christ (Philippians 1:17).

Paul brilliantly ministered to the problems that faced the believers in Philippi by simply exhorting them to emulate the greatest example of humility from the most humble person ever to live—their Saviour, Jesus Christ. When we speak of the need for a revived personal humility in the Church, the Lord is the mould that will never be broken. Like footprints that stay forever embedded on the moon's surface for a lack of wind, Jesus' demonstration of humility will always remain untouched.

Philippians 2:5–11 is loaded with wisdom for the Church. The passage serves as a Christo-theological "drawing board" for God's people to go back to time and time again; dare I say it's the perfect precursor for praying for revival and renewal! In the Philippians 2 passage, we are challenged by Paul to possess the same "attitude" and vision for our lives that our Lord Himself had. Ultimately, living a selfless life of humility helps to temper our desire for the perks and laurels of personal ambition and notoriety; it also leads to blessings from God we couldn't otherwise experience.

Humility in the Body of Christ also promotes unity amongst brothers and sisters in Christ. Paul pleaded with the Philippians to be "like-minded, having the same love, being one in spirit and purpose" (Philippians 2:2). The Church was to have a common outlook on the *spiritual* life. What did Paul mean to be "like-minded?" Well, it doesn't mean that each Christian should cease from holding their own opinions or that everyone in the Church should agree on all matters all the time. (Like that's even remotely a possibility).

Paul was probably talking about the doctrine of the Church more than anything else, yet the greater principle of being unified as Christians is intended. Mutual Christlike love in the Body of Christ (a by-product of an inward humility) will always be a witness to God's love flowing through His people for those outside the Church to see. Today, if you were to ask the average person what characteristic most defines Christians, I wonder if "love" would even break the top ten!

Through personal ambitions that go awry we can slowly pry ourselves away from our jointedness with other believers. We can overlook the truth that ministry is team-oriented. Jesus called disciples to carry on His work, even sent them out two by two! In the same vein, Paul called for the church in Philippi to get away from their unhealthy spiritual differences and misguided ambitions, which could only segregate some believers while elevating others. There world was to see them standing unified, not divided, or worse, lying sprawled in defeat.

Unfortunately, the "buzz" on the secular street sometimes leaves us who are Christians feeling as though the Church is way off the intended mark in our pursuit of attracting and winning over the world for Jesus. I remember being on a chat board for one of my favourite professional sports teams when one contributor admitted to being depressed and having suicidal thoughts. I was startled by the desperate comment and became angry when someone responded to the person's plight by encouraging them to "make sure" they avoided the Church and anything "religious" as a means of counsel.

How can we as Christians rise above the tag that we've earned, in many ways, as being nothing but arrogant, hypocritical, and opportunistic?

One pastor in the United States had this to say about the need for Christians to operate in humble incognito for the good of its unity and witness:

> We [the church] must love without putting our acts of kindness on a pedestal; we must love without strings attached; we must not be concerned about being unnamed, rewarded or repaid; we must be a voice to the voiceless, be better listeners to those who need to be heard, and be more gentle with people.[47]

Basically, it's a call to a humble way of living our lives as people who are known to be followers of Christ. It all starts in the Church. If God's people fail to exercise humility of character inside the Body of Christ, it will inevitably show when we come into contact with those *outside* the Church.

This line of thought summarizes the spiritual case Paul was making to the Christians in the Philippian church. "Do nothing out of selfish ambition or vain conceit, but in humility consider others better than yourselves" (Philippians 2:3).

Paul's teaching (especially in Philippians 2) almost seems like a plague to the modern believer. We've forgotten how to be consistently selfless, how to be attractively sacrificial. Paul's exhortations to the church in Philippi cut totally against the hardened cultural grain of our Me-first, I-centred, every-man-for-himself world that is subtly influencing God's people.

When Jesus came on the scene, His culture considered a person who was gentle, "meek," and "lowly" in stature to be weak and cowardly. Meekness and humility were seen in a more negative light and yet Jesus gave them a spiritual facelift; now if we'd be godly, we had better be lowly and see ourselves as we truly are in light of who GOD is, *not others.*

Ambition in the Church will always be welcome; we need people of courage and creativity and those with enterprising passion to serve God and advance the gospel in the world. However, as Paul reiterates throughout his letters in the New Testament, Christians need to have a measured opinion of themselves.

A fellow told me that he was sitting in his church one Sunday, and as he often did, that morning he had grown bored with the pastor's message (he had "heard it many times before"). This man along with his wife happened to be sitting next to a person whom they knew felt the same way about their pastor's sermons and who tended to have a rebellious attitude about the church. The fellow said to me, "Ron, a year ago I would've gotten up from the service and left and not care about what others might have thought. But I stayed seated because I didn't want to be a bad example for the guy next to me, who needed me there more than I needed to leave."

This is the kind of mindset Christians need today!

In the Church, instead of always thinking, "What's in it for me? What can I get out of this?" we all need to be thinking more along the lines of "What can I do to help that person?" and "What will benefit these people spiritually?" Sometimes this is hard to do if we feel our service for the Kingdom has gone unnoticed or unaffirmed, only to see someone else get the recognition. Ambition and the pursuit of notoriety are sometimes the invention of their mother: *pride!*

The great devotional writer and pastor Andrew Murray wrote, "The humble man…can bear to hear others praised and himself forgotten…He has received the spirit of Jesus, who pleased not Himself."[48] Humility will always be easier to cultivate than ambition will be to corral once it's off course.

God's people should consider being ambitious and notorious for the greatest of godly reasons; we might even find ourselves *famous* in the process! In 1 Thessalonians 1, we can dig up and find the kind of ambition and even fame Christ followers ought to be pursuing.

Paul the Apostle let the church in Thessalonica know just how *famous* they were, "known everywhere" in the surrounding regions (1 Thessalonians 1:8). In the first century, the world was a small place, and for all the Thessalonian believers knew, the whole world was literally their "stage." Their witness for Jesus "rang out" (literally *echoed*) with such impressive force that they gained a reputation. It had nothing to do with misguided ambitions or a lack of humility. The Christians in Thessalonica had become famously known for their unwavering faith. What a commendation!

It can be difficult to live by the kind of biblical humility that calls us to turn away from the types of sinful actions and attitudes that have held us for a while. A Christlike humility can take a while to root itself in the life of a believer. However, without a determined attitude to live our lives *in humility*, we leave ourselves wide open to the possibility of actually living contrary to the manner and character in which Christ Himself lived. Paul said it best when he exhorted the early Christians in Philippi to be *shining stars*, not *superstars*, for the Kingdom (see Philippians 2:15).

I fear that we in the Church for far too long have been but a blurry reflection of Jesus to our world. We weren't saved to live as if our witness for Christ were *out* of focus. Those whom we meet (outside the faith) should be able to look at our lives and clearly see from meeting us what Jesus would be really like if they'd met Him. Our Christian lives are to present people with a crossroads where the unsaved must decide whether they will consider the Saviour simply by their having come into contact with us. Though amazingly gifted people with ambition are always welcome in the Church, it's a revived personal humility amongst Christians that's needed even more!

CHAPTER 13

When Heaven's Runaways Return Home: Malachi's Message

Reviving a Burden for Righteous Behaviour

It's no longer commonplace to hear people freely share that they live their life "by faith" and "seek God's Word" on matters of everyday living. A pastor friend of mine some years ago told me how awkward things became between him and his wife and the car salesman they were talking with after they told him they needed to pray about a certain vehicle they were considering to buy. The convicting vibe Christians tend to give off at times to unsuspecting non-believers must seem like God's people make a habit of spiritually hitchhiking: *our sore thumb of a witness will stick out enough to cause a lost soul to stop and give us an ear.*

We live in a day when trying to live out the gospel as Christians can seem extremely foreign to our secularized society. One marginalized political party in Canada has already proposed a ban on the public use of religious symbols. Our culture has become so distanced from the biblical worldview and so ignorant of spiritual things that there are those who actually feel science is disproving the reality of God and that our well-being as a human race is in capable *human* hands (all while Adam and Eve roll over in their graves!). Faith comes in many shapes and sizes, and there have been believers throughout history whose level of trust in God actually did turn worldly heads and spiritual tides.

About 300 years ago, a Puritan preacher named Cotton Mather greatly desired to see a spiritual revival come to the New England region, a movement of God that would impact his life, church, town, and ultimately his nation. By God's leading, he resolved to fast, pray, and seek God's heart for 490 straight days.

Some thought he was crazy, even mad. If we were his contemporaries, we might have been some of them! As it turned out, the 490th straight day in which Mather fasted, prayed, and sought God was the same day he passed away. However, on the very day he died God sent a wave of revival and renewal as well as a hunger for righteousness (the First Great Awakening) that would sweep through the entire Northeast United States. It would be led by someone named Jonathan Edwards, who would become a highly effective revivalist preacher in the Enlightenment era.

Throughout the ages, God's people have always longed (and prayed) for revival and for the blessings that such a spiritually powerful event entails for the Christian. In fact, prayers for revival on the part of God's people go back farther than we might think. Israel clearly prayed for the revival of their national identity and spiritual vitality when they were in exile.

Malachi, the last of the Old Testament prophets, was a man raised up at an interesting time in the history of his fellow people, Israel.

The book of Malachi shows us that he was a rather unique prophet in how he ministered to the nation. God works through each of His children in different ways, which was just as true for the prophets. God is a God of infinite variety (there are no two snowflakes the same, no two fingerprints, no two people the same). His plan for each life is *different*.

That is why Peter, at the end of John's Gospel, was bluntly rebuked by Jesus when the inquisitive disciple asked the Lord, "What about him?" (He was inquiring about John and what God's future plans for him might have been.) Jesus was quick on the draw with His comeback: "What is that to you? You must follow me" (John 21:20–22).

In the same way, God had a plan for Malachi's life and ministry, and his call would be unique among the prophets.

That being said, the prophets collectively *did* have a similar pattern about their ministry. They would be raised up and would often warn the people that what they were doing (their rebellious behaviour and lack of faith) was wrong and that God was ticked! The basic prophetic newsflash was this: *the people of God would be judged!* From that point, the prophets often invited the nation to repent, mourn for their sin, and then turn back to God.

When police cars turn up across the street from us and police officers knock on our neighbours' door, it's often a red flag that trouble's encroaching upon their home and lives. Likewise, when heavenly policemen in the form of God's prophets began to make their rounds in Israel, the people knew something ominous was up and they were about to be caught with their spiritual pants down. Hearts were going to be knocked on and arrested by the accountability of a holy God and His Word! Prophets were always raised up when the people of God or their king were turning *away* from Him, and not when the going was good or great spiritually within the nation.

Finally, the prophets would usually finish their prophecy by providing a picture of what was going to come in the future (speaking of what was ahead). They forth-told God's address to the people, but they also *foretold* events that were to happen. Most importantly, even though the prophets may not have known exactly how their words would have worked out, they could not refrain from speaking about the prophecies of Jesus and the coming of Messiah.

However, in the book of Malachi, the prophet doesn't seem to follow the same pattern of ministry the other prophets carried out.

Malachi didn't thunder forth like many of the Old Testament prophets, who would belt out, "Thus saith the Lord!" (As a preacher, I have often been tempted to bellow that myself!) Malachi's prophetic ministry involved him raising an accusation that the people of Israel had against the Lord, followed by the prophet responding back to them as God spoke through him. Malachi's ministry took on a sort of ancient "town hall" feel and flavour, with the tone of the conversations as well as the points made being as sharp as they could be subtle!

Malachi was raised up in the fifth century BC and spoke to the people about 100 years after they had returned from exile in Babylon. The people of God were once again in their own land and they had built a marvellous temple. Time had moved on, and the people of Israel were living with the expectation that God was going to send the Messiah and along with that justice and mercy in the land.

However, as much as it was a hopeful time, it was a sour time as well.

God's people have always managed to mess up a "good thing," and during the time of Malachi, it was no different! Hundreds of years had passed, and the promises that God made to bring forth the Messiah had not been fulfilled.

Our own lives can reflect the frustrations that come from holding great expectations of what we would like to see God do in them. We may have been praying about something or expecting something to come through for us, and after a while it still hasn't come to pass. We can begin to get turned off and think, "Maybe God has forgotten me." Somehow, even though God promises that He'll never leave us or forsake us (Hebrews 13:5)—He even has us written on the palms of His hands (Isaiah 49:16)—we can get to the point where we might feel God has ignored us or overlooked us.

If you've ever had those thoughts, you'll understand the feelings of the people of Israel in Malachi's day.

As a result, they began to once again turn away from God, something their forefathers did as covenant-breakers throughout the history of the nation (see Malachi 3:7).

The temple that had been rebuilt with great excitement under the leadership of Nehemiah and others by Malachi's time was left vacant and neglected. The rich began to oppress the poor, spiritual values became afterthoughts, and even the priests of Israel became utterly useless and corrupt. You get the sordid picture.

Malachi's name means "a messenger of mine," and the words of God that he spoke to the people of God were as judgmental and spiritually walloping as they were graciously hopeful. Basically, Malachi was charged with the task of relighting the lamp of faith in the nation. He was called to bring them to revival!

We often yearn for revivals in the Church whenever the times seem to grow darker spiritually and when we as God's people are being challenged to speak out for righteousness while we're fatigued in our faith.

When the people of God seem embattled and when we *feel* we are losing the ongoing war with the forces of evil, a revived spirituality always holds hope for us to carry on. It's at our spiritual low points that we experience the bang of God's vindicating power the most. It's the oasis of refreshment we can't help but prayerfully crawl towards when we're baking in the desert of a dried-out faith.

In order to be the bright lighthouses for God we're called to be in this spiritually flailing world, we as His people must collectively return to Him and ask for forgiveness where needed and for our reinstatement into Heaven's army of service. In the Bible, revival is always meant for *God's people* first and for their spiritual benefit as the Lord calls us back to Himself and to His Kingdom priorities.

We live in rapidly changing times where the world scarcely resembles the kind of place it was even twenty years ago. It's not hard to see that our society is moving farther and farther away from God, as evidenced by its spiritually suspect values and ever-loosening morals. The evolution of our increasingly God-averse world is unfolding in a very intentional manner as well.

I read about a school in the United States that had their nation's motto, "In God We Trust," painted on the wall of their gym—that is, until a parent complained. The school board promptly had the "offending" words painted over.

This might seem to be a minor issue, but add this to other situations where the Name of God or the expression of one's Christian faith is being muzzled or discarded, and the push-back from our secularized culture grows that much more! One Georgia man (a professing Christian) was recently let go from his job because he refused to wear a sticker that read "666" (the number of consecutive days the factory he worked in operated without having an accident).

The fired employee had no problem with wearing the "665" sticker the day before, nor would he have squawked at wearing the "667" day sticker the day after. The Bible specifically states that "666" is the symbolic number of the lawless one (the devil) (although the actual sequence of numbers is not evil in itself); in light of this, perhaps the fired employee's conscience and spiritual sensitivities should have been respected. It can be a dicey situation when the biblical views of Christians conflict with and overlap the wishes and laws of worldly systems and authority.

In fact more than ever before, theological heresy and unbridled blasphemy is becoming commonplace in the media and popular culture. It's hard to be lights for Jesus when so much darkness abounds and when the Church struggles to keep its flame of faith burning bright.

As I've discussed throughout this book, God's people of Israel were called to be a nation of spiritual light, to be a spotlight as well as flashlight of righteousness as a witness to nations encased in the darkest of pagan ritualistic practices around them. Yet all that seemed lost when Malachi was calling out God's people. Simply put, Israel had failed miserably in living out their vision statement!

Within Israel itself there existed God-naysayers and judgment-ho-hummers who defiantly began to rub off on the people, which eventually led to the nation's righteous commission (as being contenders for the one true God) to fall on plugged-up ears.

This can be just as true of our lives as contemporary Christians and as the twenty-first century Church. There are people who crowd into churches every week who have already bit down, in some spiritual manner, on the devil's shimmering bait and have bought into *the lie* about God. Even those who identify themselves as "Christians" can begin to listen to and believe in (if it were possible) "the lie" that maybe God doesn't care how we live as much as we've been told; maybe God isn't as powerful as we've first thought; maybe all that is written about Him isn't as accurate after all!

Israel in the time of Malachi weren't merely people who had come to be known as vision-busters and law-breakers; they developed full throttle into a nation that had come to believe in "the lie." God's people were hemorrhaging in their allegiance to Him, and scarily so, by adopting the hideous spiritual out-workings of the pagan people of Canaan.

Many in our modern-day Canaan-like world, though they may not be hostile to the Church, have blindly accepted either the satanic lie that God is not an option for their lives, not the God the Bible says He is, or the eternally tragic deception that He doesn't exist at all. The devil always gives the world multiple choices in terms of spirituality, but all of them are a great lie.

Malachi, if he were with us today, would come to us and say, "Remain faithful!" The prophet would plead with us, "God has been faithful! God *will* be faithful! Do not dishonour God!"

This is what our faithful God is calling on each one of us to do today as His people: *to believe in His promises; to obey and trust in His Word.* Unlike Israel in Malachi's day, we are not to believe in what the brainwaves of our twisted world have to say about God; we're not to believe in our own trying situations or in what our heartache is telling us about God. We are to believe *God!*

Jesus tirelessly punctuated His teaching by calling people to *"Have faith in God."* It is *as* we obey, *as* we remain faithful, and *as* we trust God that He, in return, will bless us…and revive us!

The headline in gaudy bold print that would have topped the front page of the Hebrew newspapers in the day of Malachi (had they existed) would possibly have read *"*Local Prophet Calls for Revival amongst the People of God!"

We know why ongoing gushes of revival and spiritual renewal are needed in our own lives and in the Church today, but as we delve deeper into the state of the nation of Israel in the time of Malachi, we'll see in greater detail why revival was needed in that nation.

At the very start of the Old Testament book we find Israel on a respirator, with its spiritual life draining out of it. Evidence to the fact that God's people had come to believe in the great lie about the Lord is captured poignantly in the opening lines of the book of Malachi. "'I have loved you,' says the LORD. 'But you ask, "How have you loved us?"'" (Malachi 1:2).

Israel became an ungrateful people towards their God. As you read through the entire book of Malachi it's easy to spot God's repeated heart response to His nation: He was guilty of nothing but being fair with them. Israel had no case they could make stick against their God. Trying to lay charges of unfaithfulness on Him would be a spiritual exercise impossible to justify, like attempting to pin Jello to a wall!

Israel's asking their God to explain how He had been "good" to them reminds me of how my own children at certain times can convince themselves that their mother and I "don't love" them. All it takes is Elaine or me gently reminding them of all the things we've done for them and continue to do for them for Cassidy and her brother, Dakota, to slump, feel ashamed, and come to their childlike senses!

The spiritual lesson behind Jesus' parable of the prodigal son holds a mirror to the spell of deception Israel seemed to be under in Malachi's day. The prodigal, remember, never had justifiable cause for feeling like his father was holding back any blessing from him. However, in his rebellion and during his runaway season of abject folly, the prodigal son realized just how wonderful he had it back home under his father's roof. The extent of his father's longsuffering love for his son would eventually be confirmed. The father welcomed back his contrite prodigal son with open arms (and a party!).

It may have been a case of spiritual immaturity showing up; it may have been a jack-in-the-box type of inward lust springing up that led the younger "prodigal" son to hastily depart from his father's home in order to sow his wild oats. Yet why did Israel feel they had to run away from their perfect, faithful God?

In basic terms, it was a result of *a lack of faith* on the part of God's people. What's new, right? The Spirit is always willing, but the flesh of humanity is more weak than we sometimes imagine it to be. Plain and simple, Israel became disrespectful towards God. "A son honors his father, and a servant his master. If I am a father, where is the honor due me? If I am a master, where is the respect due me?" (Malachi 1:6).

The people of God in Malachi's time didn't stop there, though. To their lack of faith and disrespectful attitude towards the Lord they added *corruption*. This was particularly stark and reprehensible within the priesthood of the nation. "For the lips of a priest ought to preserve knowledge, and from his mouth men should seek instruction—because he is the messenger of the LORD Almighty. But you have turned from the way and by your teaching have caused many to stumble" (Malachi 2:7–8).

Unfortunately, receiving spiritually deceptive counsel within the Church, even from the ranks of the *clergy*, is not too hard to fathom happening in our day and age. I have seen more than a few situations in mainstream denominations where God's ordained shepherds have sadly joined themselves (as well as their people) to a confluence of deceptive and syncretized theological teachings of mumbo-jumbo proportions.

What will become of our society, not to mention the Church and Christian witness, if those who are charged with bearing biblical truth no longer function as to preserve righteousness? It can only keep those who are spiritually lost locked in their sin while enabling our culture's distaste for repentance to go unchallenged and unaccounted for; inevitably, however, it will also draw the ire of God's judgment.

The religious "go-to" guys in Israel were so corrupt that they were no longer fit for being trusted with the spiritual leadership of the land! The priests who *should* have been promoting the praises of God and the sacrifices *to* God had actually led the people astray and in a different spiritual direction. They were unworthy shepherds! As the saying goes, "If gold rusts, what will iron do?" If the priests (who were in place to lead people to God) turned away from God, what would happen to the people?

The answer we attach to this question (in our day) is the same one that God made burn within His prophet Malachi. People who look for spiritual guidance generally follow suit in that they too become as unfaithful to God as those who are guiding them!

The priests of Israel delved into sorcery; they were unfaithful in marriage; they practiced mixed marriages (which led them to worship foreign gods and to idolatry). It wasn't just spiritually untidy in God's house; it was a ransacked all-out disaster zone, spiritually, in God's house! After all the Lord had done for His people, there was mass rebellion amongst them toward Him. A heavenly people had become runaways on the spiritual streets of no-name gods.

In chapter 3 of Malachi, we read of where Israel grew weary of obeying God. "You have said, 'It is futile to serve God. What did we gain by carrying out his requirements…?'" (Malachi 3:14). The nation at that point was back in its homeland, albeit a smaller version of its former self, and still existing in the shadow of the greater backyard of the Persian Empire. All the promises of the prophets (people like Haggai and Zechariah) who spoke of Israel's great and glorious future had come to nothing at that point. The Messiah was nowhere to be found, the temple remaining void of His filling presence. As a result, the people had basically resolved, "It is not worth it anymore to serve God. It's of no use!"

Bitterness about expectations of God that have not been met can tempt many to turn away from Him. As Christians we meet people all the time who point to such things as injustice, natural disasters, and famine as a justifiable soap box for spewing their own rejection of and anger towards God.

In Malachi we find the same kinds of bold justification coming from God's wayward people of Israel. They were trying to make it look like they had good reason for turning away from the Lord. "But now we call the arrogant blessed.

Certainly the evildoers prosper, and even those who challenge God escape" (Malachi 3:15). The people of Israel were calling what was good evil and what was evil good. Incredibly, they brought themselves to think that God could actually *bless*, as a reward, those who did wickedness.

More incredible than the thickness of Israel's rebellion towards the Lord was His desire to revive the people *despite* all the horrible things that were going on in the land and despite how His people were treating Him!

It's easy to give up on people (even God's people). When we don't see any outward changes in the spiritual course of people's lives, especially after we've invested a great deal of time, heart, and prayer helping them, we can get discouraged and drop the burden. It's also easy to read into the early passages of the Book of Malachi and predict that God is going to bring the hammer down on Israel and be done with them for good.

However, God didn't do what you and I might have done. As He already did some seventeen times before, God sent His people yet another prophet (Malachi) who would speak to them in attempting to turn Israel's heart back to the Lord. It was a commission whereby Malachi would be asked to be the kindling for God in order for Him to set the fires of revival and renewal to the nation's spirituality.

The prophets had the most unenviable task of any person in the land. They were often outnumbered by the mass of brooding darkness harboured within the people they prophesied to that would often close-in around them.

Yet all a prophet like Malachi could do was talk to the people. There were no sleight of hand, tricks, or smoke and mirrors at his disposal; there wasn't any bribe money to give out, and neither could Malachi physically force the people to follow God. Some of the prophets came thundering, some came reasoning, some even came weeping; all however, had the same message and sang from the same choir book: "Repent, and turn back to God. Be faithful to God, He is faithful to you! Allow Him to revive and renew you!"

That is Malachi's message. It's a journey into the longsuffering concern God had for Israel. The Lord's love towards His people in many ways was unreasonable. Why would God commit to such a group of people who would disobey Him time and time again? Why wouldn't He choose a nation who would be faithful to Him, who would appreciate the wisdom of His ways? Whenever Israel rebelled against God and turned away from Him, He went looking for them anyway, pursuing His people like He asked Hosea to pursue the adulterous Gomer. You read Isaiah, you read Jeremiah, and you hear the phrases "Come back," "Let's reason together," "Return to me."

Great and godly things *do* happen whenever Heaven's runaways return home! God would open His arms wide yet again if Israel turned from their sin and sought to be revived and renewed in Him.

Today, we as God's people have an unprecedented opportunity to be an eternal blessing to our fallen world. Every Bible-believing Christian has the awesome charge of being a counterwultural movement towards God. If we who have been "rescued" from the "dominion of darkness" and who've been "brought" into the "kingdom of the Son he [God] loves" (Colossians 1:13) would more consistently obey the Word of God, trust Him like we never have before, and believe that He will bring about His good promises, imagine how much more we could accomplish for God, as His Church, and how many more people could be reached with the gospel!

I heard of someone who had written in the front of his Bible, 'If of Christ there is only you, what would be the view?" In other words, if all there were on earth to represent Jesus were you, what would people see? It's a searching question that rises to the level of challenging us to be renewed in our spiritual fervour as end-time Christians.

If revivals *were* to happen in our lives and in our churches, their fruit would probably bring about similar spiritual reformations to those of Malachi's day. Instead of being cranky, disrespectful, and even caustic towards the Lord, the way Israel had become, we would once again have an attitude of thankfulness and generosity towards God.

Israel wasn't happy with the apparent lack of blessings coming their way, and they let their offerings speak for it! However, a revived people of God could no longer think of doing such a thing. "'Bring the whole tithe into the storehouse, that there may be food in my house. Test me in this,' says the LORD Almighty, 'and see if I will not throw open the floodgates of heaven and pour out so much blessing that you will not have room enough for it'" (Malachi 3:10).

Can you imagine God blessing our lives and ministries to the point where we wouldn't have nearly enough room for it? There are seasons as well as moments when we can experience bundles of blessings from Heaven. There are times when peace and joy well up in us inexplicably; times when our families, marriages, and relationships are strengthened. There are seasons when serving God is a breeze and when we feel privileged to be His ambassadors on earth. There are times when God drops bundles of financial resources and gifts on us. Then there are those beautiful moments in our lives when God seems to press in so intimately while we pray that we can almost touch His face, if it were possible. There are trying situations and circumstances in our lives in which we're keenly aware that God is carrying us and has our backs.

If we can take anything of great spiritual worth when exiting the rich book of Malachi, it's this: when revival hits our lives and fills our churches, we're going to see it and we're going to feel it in powerfully spiritual ways! There will be a return to a humble reverence for God and a fortified devotion towards Him. Spiritual backsliding will take a back seat! There will be a greater appreciation for God's holiness and an intense sorrow for one's sin. There will be sacrificial generosity towards mission and a refocused burden and openness to serve. We need this kind of spiritual turnabout in the Church today!

All of these changes were needed in the spiritual culture of Israel in Malachi's day. Thankfully, these changes finally came about! When we look into some of the final passages of Malachi 3, we find there a revived and renewed passion for God amongst Israel. "Then those who feared the LORD talked with each other, and the LORD listened and heard. A scroll of remembrance was written in his presence concerning those who feared the LORD and honored his name" (Malachi 3:16).

The message of Malachi, then, overall, is one of great encouragement. How could we see it otherwise? The prophet shows us that it doesn't matter how far away one *is* from the Lord or how long one *has been* away from Him. When we resolve to turn back to God in contrition of heart, He is there to forgive and to heal us. God's arms are always open to receive the penitent and brokenhearted; such people will never find them folded! We may live in a day of major disappointments and discouragement, but God will never let us down. Despite the satanic rumour mill, God is not only alive but He's a personal deity who created us to have communion with Him in order *to bless us!* His faithful love for us is endless.

If you are reading this and muddling through a godless, sin-filled lifestyle that hasn't worked out for you, take heart: *it wouldn't work out for any of us!* But when we live for God through faith in Jesus Christ, we'll find that He gives us a peace about our lives we never thought we could have.

The greatest blessing God has for us this side of Heaven is the opportunity He gives us to know Him and to make Him known. The greatest privilege He gives us then in *this* life can only be His commission to us to serve Him.

CHAPTER 14

CHRISTIANS OPEN THE GOSPELS ONLY TO FIND "HELP" WANTED
A Revived Zeal for Servanthood

The Screen Actors Guild Award winning and Oscar nominated film *The Help* is an adaptation of Kathryn Stockett's novel of the same title. The movie shed further light on the many struggles people of colour had to endure in the civil rights era of the early 1960s American South. The story takes place in Jackson, Mississippi, with a plot surrounding two black maids hired as "the help" to serve in the homes of white families. The maids' presence in these homes reveals various forms of racism black people had to endure during that time.

Eugenia "Skeeter" Phelan (a young white woman) returns home from school to her parent's plantation, seeking to become a writer. Her first project involves doing research on hints for homemaking. Eugenia discovers that her white friends (who have black servants) have certain discriminatory attitudes towards people of colour. She ends up putting the stories of two women, Minny and Aibileen, in her book. When it's eventually published it gives the two black women a voice whereby the many abuses they've had to endure are exposed. Though both Minny and Aibileen are fired from their jobs and falsely accused, they discover some dignity in the process.

Serving as the help for white families was trial-laced, yet Eugenia, it can be argued, *redeemed* the two black women by helping them to make a new life for themselves. Eugenia ended up sharing the royalties she made from the book with Minny and Aibileen, which in a sense revived and renewed the purpose and meaning of their lives.

In being cared for by Eugenia, the two black women got a glimpse of the kind of blessings that flow from sacrificial actions and when people of a selfless nature care enough to willingly serve the needs of others. Isn't this the very attitude Jesus called people to serve Him by? Eugenia, by virtue of her benevolent gestures, actually modelled the type of servant's heart that pleases God. Eugenia displayed the kind of righteous character qualities our Lord expected of those who were the first to follow Him.

It was only by living sacrificially that His disciples could trump the selfishness that was engraved in the lives of so many leaders in Jesus' day. In the Gospels we recall the accounts where Jesus commissioned the twelve to be *His* help in serving His Kingdom's ministry priorities. He equipped and empowered the disciples He chose to serve as He did: *humbly*. The Lord was keenly aware of the tendency humans have to exact unfair treatment over those whom they have authority.

In the movie *The Help*, black servants were made to feel less than human by their white employers. In the Gospels, the Roman rulers were the onerous authority putting people under their imperial thumbs. However, Jesus' disciples were to have an intentionally different outlook on what it meant to lead, serve, and help others. It was a Kingdom value that was to act as a heavenly serum, providing the necessary antidote for the self-serving attitude many authoritative figures within their culture clung to. The Lord stated,

> *"You know that the rulers of the Gentiles lord it over them, and their high officials exercise authority over them. Not so with you. Instead, whoever wants to become great among you must be your servant, and whoever wants to be first must be your slave—just as the Son of Man did not come to be served, but to serve, and to give his life as a ransom for many"* (Matthew 20:25–28).

Oh that more Christians today could claim with integrity that that is their rallying cry when it comes to serving others and to the stewardship of their time, talents, and treasures!

Though Jesus never lorded the commissioning of His disciples *over them* in the same way that the Romans lorded their authority over the Jews, He nonetheless had certain expectations of His followers when it came to serving in His Kingdom.

The original twelve disciples of Christ had to take on the mindset of being enslaved to their fellow brothers' and sisters' needs in such a way that was fitting for their bondservant status as followers of the Lord.

However, as we look at the Church today, particularly in North America, and see how many Christians are actively involved in one or more ministries, the numbers are not encouraging. With the amount of options for experiencing a faith community increasing (cyber-church, house churches, pub-based meetings), it's hard to know how many believers are actually engaged in ongoing accountable structured ministries in the Body of Christ.

Sometimes it seems as though God's people have turned the tables on Jesus somewhat, having certain expectations of their own that need to be met in order for them to serve in the Body of Christ. What a foreign idea this is to the Gospel accounts that have Jesus teaching His disciples to become slaves one to another! Christians are not to discriminate as to what areas of need in the Church are worthy of their service and which are not. For Jesus, a need (whatever it was) was a need to be served, not to be complained about. A ministry opportunity spoke of the potential for God's Name to be exalted and glorified in the world, irrespective of one's title, age, experience, or credentials to serve it.

In his book *Jesus Hero of Thy Soul: Impressions of the Saviour's Touch,* Jim McGuiggan writes of a story told in a war about a soldier who lay dying. A preacher, who was in the same battalion as the mortally wounded soldier, came to attend to him. The preacher wasted no time in asking if he could help the man in any way. "I'm cold," the dying man told him. The minister then took off his overcoat and placed it over the fading solider. After that, the dying man complained that his neck was hurting, and so the minister took off his suit coat and put it under the man's head to serve as a pillow. Then a few moments later, as the soldier's voice began to grow softer and weaker, he whispered, "I'd sure like a cigarette." The preacher then reached into the man's pocket and pulling out a pack, put one into the soldier's mouth, and lit it.

When the minister took out his Bible, the dying soldier made a final request. "Mister, if you've got anything in that Bible of yours that makes you act like this, read it to me." There's a lesson here for us as Jesus' disciples, isn't there?

People who don't know the Lord as their Saviour may not be impressed by our knowledge of God's Word, yet most people (whether they are dying or not) will be impacted and possibly even led to the Lord through our Christlike service and testimony. The Lord had a passionate heart for meeting the needs of those whom He encountered, and we are most like Christ when we do likewise.

This is why people all around the world love Jesus! The word many people associate Jesus with and describe Him by (outside of "Saviour") is *"servant."* Though many people have yet to bow a knee to the Lord in worship, they nonetheless still respect Him as someone who was humble and even great. The Bible tells us that Jesus is a friend (not a foe) of sinners and that while we were still in our sin and separated from God, Jesus died for us (Romans 5:8).

What is there *not* to love about Jesus? People we come into contact with may be wary of organized religion, and even wary of Christianity, yet we'd be hard-pressed to find anyone who will be angry about Jesus Himself.

Most of the people in the Bible who didn't like Jesus were those who were jealous of His popularity with the common folk of His day. The power-trippers and agenda-pushers of Jesus' time saw Him as a threat, while the poor, the outcast, and those viewed as the "dregs" of society felt an irresistible spiritually magnetic pull towards the Lord.

Jesus was the sort of person anyone would have wanted as a friend: kind, wise, strong, and full of mercy. However, what separated Jesus from all others was the sacrificial and selfless nature of His life and ministry. Another way of stating this is that Jesus was the perfect example of what it means to *be* a servant.

I get the feeling sometimes that the disciples' association with Jesus must have periodically gone to their heads. While the disciples were going back and forth over which of them would rise, like cream, to the top of Heaven's pecking order (who would be classified as the "greatest" in the Kingdom of God), Jesus flummoxed them by telling them that it was actually the "least" among them who would be considered the greatest.

No doubt it was one of those "Huh?" moments the twelve disciples were probably used to experiencing whenever Jesus inverted their flawed human ideas of what it meant to be "great" in the eyes of God. The disciples would later experience their Master administering an act of service that would leave no further question as to how God defined greatness in His Kingdom.

Every one of the Lord's followers would have to submit to Jesus' washing of their feet (a duty reserved for a lowly house servant). It was an event that must have seemed surreal to the logic of the disciples: *Rabbi Jesus acting like someone He wasn't!* The followers of Christ viewed His washing of their feet to be an act of service totally inappropriate for Jesus to perform (as seen by Peter's indignation), a menial task that was so thoroughly "beneath" Him. The Bible states, however, that the Lord performed the lowly act of service to leave them an "example" that they should follow in doing for others as He had done for them (John 13:14–15).

Amy Carmichael, an Irish missionary of the early 1900s, was ministering in the Dohnavur Fellowship in India when a Christian woman came to the fellowship wanting to help with the babies that were taken in. The woman was immediately asked by Carmichael to wash the floor of the nursery. The woman said that due to the caste she belonged to (a social status that dictated one's relationships, marriage, and work), such labour was "too humiliating" for her to carry out.

Without delay, Carmichael picked up a bucket of soapy water and on her knees proceeded to wash the floor. While washing, Carmichael resolved that "Housework, like any other job, is God's work. Whatever we do becomes a good and holy task if we do it for God."[49]

Amy Carmichael lived in the light of Jesus' teaching on servanthood for a disciple to be readily willing to serve, even in the most humble of ways. The Lord wanted His disciples to take His approach in their attitude towards servanthood, to be a people who are not above serving the needs of others but are available to serve in challenging situations they didn't plan for.

Though we are a busy people who know we should be serving God, the obstacle that often prevents this from happening are the conditions we attach to our services: *we want to serve on our own terms.* We have all been guilty at times of reserving, too tightly, our right to choose when, where, and how we are going to serve God in the Body of Christ.

Yet no matter how we slice the servanthood call, serving God doesn't always amount to the servant being fulfilled by their service, nor does the service we're being asked to perform always come at a convenient time. Serving God is often a spontaneous event and means serving people and making sure that *their* needs are fulfilled when that need arises. That being said, Christians are good at turning simple commands into complicated spiritual ideals at times.

When Jesus calls us to serve Him, He simply asks us to remain flexible to His Kingdom priorities. We should know by now that the Lord makes a habit of keeping us on our spiritual toes by calling us to the unexpected in serving Him. Christians should be a people who are both bendable and amendable in their attitudes towards serving God, people who He can rely on who will do what He asks them to do, people who will go where He wants them to go and serve who He desires that they serve. The poor, the oppressed, the outcasts, and other *untouchables* of our time are all targeted by the Lord for us to serve. Though needs may pop up when we're tired and running on empty, our resources of time, talents and treasures are yet to remain accessible for the furtherance of the Kingdom of God and the glory of God.

We'll find it an exercise in endless frustration to search the Gospels for proof that the Lord calls us to predictable and comfortable service in terms of our role in His Kingdom on earth. This is why we find serving in certain areas of the Church a daunting task.

By nature, we don't like being stretched, something that doesn't exactly change when we become Christians! After some years of serving in the ministry, I've noticed amongst God's people some who act like they've "earned the right" to serve in whatever capacity they want to and to avoid whatever areas of ministry they'd rather *not serve in.*

Yes, we should be serving according to our giftedness; after all, God has wired us to serve in specific areas of ministry and to serve in them effectively. However, there are times when something in the Church simply needs to be done, and someone has to step up and do it (for Jesus), regardless if it's their strong suit gift-wise. What if Jesus said to His disciples, "Hey guys, I was going to wash your feet to give you an example of humble servanthood, but then I thought, 'Wait a minute! Something like that is not in my heavenly CV; it's not divine work—you know what I mean?' Sorry! I guess I'll leave that for some lesser lights to do." Thankfully, Jesus had the perfect perspective on the topic of servanthood, a godly one! Our Lord willfully took upon Himself a servant's nature (Philippians 2:7). For the Lord, a servant served where serving needed to be done! One-off opportunities to serve God *outside* our church walls that cross our paths from time to time are just as important as the sustained weeks or months of committed service *in* the Church.

Many of us Christians have a backwards view of what it means to serve God, that is, what matters is *us* first; what God may want is often relegated to second place. We need revived hearts and a renewed zeal for the kind of *help* Jesus is calling us to. There will always be Christians who think they should serve for what *they* can get out of it, when really, serving God is serving for what effect it will have on *others*. I like to teach (it is one of my spiritual gifts), and I value how I'm often stretched spiritually whenever I study for a sermon. However, I get even more joy from realizing that there are people who appreciate my teaching ability.

There are times, though, when I choose to serve in an area of ministry where I don't have expertise. What does it mean when my service to God in an area of ministry I could "take" or "leave" bears fruit I never could have imagined?

God still has use for us and can bless us in our service for Him even when we feel our giftedness is not being used. We are not really servants (in a fully sacrificial sense) if we are always reserving our right to cherry-pick what we've determined is best for us to do in the Church.

God expects us to be available to meet the Heaven-couriered assignments of servanthood He specifically sends our way. Even if they fall into our laps at an inopportune time, are not what we were looking for, or appear too difficult to accomplish, they all come from Him, and they all confront us with a choice: *will we be the help God is asking us to be, or not?*

Perhaps the greatest opportunity that the disciples of Christ had to live out what it meant to be a servant of God is recorded in Matthew 14. If we are to grasp anything of biblical theology, it's that God always acts "on purpose." As we probe the Matthew 14 account of the feeding of the five thousand, we find some incredible spiritual lessons pertaining to Christlike servanthood.

Jesus obviously wanted to teach the disciples that serving God would not always seem straightforward to them or be viewed as advantageous. Different needs would come across their paths, whether they went sniffing them out or not. I find it very interesting that the Lord often encountered the needs of people while He was actually *withdrawing* from them. Even when He was on the down-low, our Lord was still in great demand! Jesus could have been on His way to some solitary place for rest and prayer, and yet people would still pursue Him like a pack of hounds chasing their prey. The cries of a hands-open world were no respecters of our Lord's personal spiritual needs, a reality that can be just as true of our own lives.

Most of us who put in some good hours throughout the week serving God in the Church can get annoyed at the ill-timed phone call, the unplanned visit, and the seemingly unreasonable demands within the Body of Christ that often shadow its leaders. Some of us in pastoral ministry know exactly how we can interpret those times: *people are being inconsiderate of our family time!* We're available all day, but when we get home we'd rather *not* be available! When we're tired, when we're trudging through seasons of discouragement and feeling mentally crowded, any spontaneous request for us to serve others even in the smallest of ways can appear too tall an order to ask of us.

Jesus, however, had the kind of perspective that all great servants share: *He rolled with it!* Though the Lord definitely had barriers built around His life and ministry to protect private times of reflection and rest, let's not overlook how vastly generous His "open door" policy was.

Matthew tells us the miraculous feeding of the five thousand came on the heels of John the Baptist's execution at the hands of Herod the king. John was a very popular figure in Israel, someone who was looked upon as a great hope for the nation. Possessing a pointed prophetic voice, John's role was to till and even off the soil "pathway" of people's hearts, readying them for the seeds of Jesus' ministry to be planted in.

John the Baptist did this by calling people back to God through repentance. His message resembled a big convicting stick that would be spared on no one (including tax collectors and Roman soldiers) in calling their sin what it was (see Luke 3:11–15). John had his share of "followers," just as Jesus did. However, by the time Matthew 14 rolled around, the refreshing hope of John's commanding presence and reviving ministry was cruelly snuffed out.

To whom did the people begin to look to for renewed hope and leadership in the land of Israel after John's death? They looked to the One whom John pointed them to—*Jesus!* After hearing what had happened to John the Baptist, Jesus went into acute grieving mode and "withdrew" from everyone "by boat privately" (Matthew 14:13). Sometimes we need to be alone by ourselves when we're mourning, and Jesus, in His humanity, was no different. The Lord needed to gather Himself and refocus on His ministry objectives as the Son of God. I'm sure He looked forward to the moments when He could just lose Himself in His Father's cupping presence and be comforted via prayer. But like best laid plans… *they didn't work out that way for Jesus either!*

When the Lord moved out to be alone, thousands of people, Matthew says, moved along with Him, only to move *in* on Him. "When Jesus landed and saw a large crowd, he had compassion on them and healed their sick" (Matthew 14:14). This verse is crucial for us to personalize if we're going to grasp the kind of servanthood Jesus is calling us to as His disciples. The Lord always responded appropriately to great need, didn't He?

As the preeminent Good Shepherd of God, our Lord just couldn't bring Himself to say "No" to the thousands of need-strapped sheep who, Matthew wrote, were suddenly flowing in and blanketing the ground around Jesus. The desperate people wanted to be where Jesus was; they knew the hope and the help they required was completely embodied in Christ. The whole scene depicted an incredible movement of faith towards the Son of God. In response, Jesus' default reaction to the spiritually seeking was to take them under His wing. They weren't viewed as being an inconvenient "doorbell" to Him but rather as a wide open door to bring glory to God.

Mark, when he recounted this event in his own Gospel, wrote that the Lord had compassion on the thousands of people swarming Him because they appeared to Him as "sheep without a shepherd" (Mark 6:34).

Jesus was the greatest pastor ever to live, and He discerned ministry needs perfectly.

However, even while showing compassion to the crowd, Jesus was quite possibly mentally tired and emotionally wrung-out. The Saviour was in *retreat* mode while the sea of people washing up on the shores of His respite time were in *entreat* mode. The Lord was grieving while the thousands around Him were merely hungry. Whose need would make the most noise and win out? Even the Saviour of the world needed a time out! Amazingly though, by all accounts the Lord never interpreted the emergence of the thousands of people as an unwelcomed hiccup to His rightful agenda of seeking peace and quiet.

Rather, Jesus knew that the people needed *Him* more than He needed to send them away. For the Lord, there was a time to resist the wants and demands of others (even their genuine needs) in order to secure prayerful solitude as much as there was a time to allow the pressures of ministry to crash in on and overtake His personal itinerary and spiritual priorities. Both realities could be blessed and used of God.

Jesus could have used someone to minister to Him for a change, and yet HE went to work ministering to others by putting their needs ahead of His own. He went about that, Matthew wrote, until "evening approached." Most scholars agree that it would have been late afternoon, just prior to sunset, when this great impromptu healing service took place that saw Jesus lay hands on the infirmed among the masses.

In a comical turn of events, it seems as though Jesus' disciples thought the Lord was losing track of time and didn't even realize where He was. They say to Him, "This is a remote place, and it's already getting late. Send the crowds away, so they can go to the villages and buy themselves some food" (Matthew 14:15).

When we really think about it, however, why would these people have wanted to go anywhere else? The massive and equally famished congregation had all they wanted and needed right there with them—in Jesus. Maybe the crowd paid little attention to the fact that the sun was setting, and yet, as the day wore on, the appetite of the people no doubt increased. Jesus had a miracle in mind, and so it's not like He was going to say, "That's all for today, folks; besides, the sun is going down fast, and your stomachs, well…they're giving off deafening growls! It's time we'd all move on!"

Instead, the Lord responded to His disciples' advice to send the people away by recognizing the situation at hand. It was a prime opportunity to teach His followers (and the five thousand plus along with them) something of how the

God of the *possible* could address the *impossible* dilemma facing them if they'd just be willing to serve right then and there and trust Him with the results.

Jesus knew that there is no better moment to teach about serving God than when one is confronted with a great need. With that intention in mind, Jesus broadsided His disciples by replying, "They don't need to go away. You give them something to eat" (Matthew 14:16). In Jesus' mind, His disciples were "the help" He enlisted to make an eternal difference in the corner of their first century world—no one else, no exceptions!

When we read of our Lord's take on the unique situation facing His disciples at that moment, it's actually *the disciples* who are made to sound more realistic and practical, not Jesus. It's the disciples who seem to have the voice of reason! In their estimation of the situation, they're in the right, and God, well, He's not thinking clearly this time. We can almost hear the kind of case they were trying to build. "Jesus, it's late! Haven't you noticed? These people aren't the only ones here who are hungry and who've got to find a place to bunk in for the night!" In present day terms, the disciples' protests might sound something like, "Jesus, we hear that Burger King closes at 7 tonight! The nearest motel is miles and miles from here. Their vacancies might be all taken up before we even pull into the parking lot! No dice! Let's just head out now."

With things looking like there would be no fortuitous turn in the situation, Jesus' disciples found themselves in what they believed to be a problem impossible to solve. When confronted with great need and a call to serve that need with little to give, it's the *disciples* who actually sounded rational; it's Jesus who sounded irrational and even ridiculous with His directive "You give them something to eat."

However, just as we often do at the drop of a God-appointed test, the disciples too were walking strictly by *sight* at a time when they had no choice but to walk by *faith*.

By sight, they were right! The Gospel says there were roughly "five thousand" people present there at that moment. But keep in mind that if there were "about five thousand men," then there were probably close to about five thousand *women*, too! And if there were five thousand men and five thousand women present, there were probably five thousand or more children there as well. We know by the history of the culture that entire families would follow the Lord and sit and listen to Him. In reality, then, there were quite likely fifteen thousand people present at this event. To the common sense person, trying to do something about the collective hunger of so many people with hardly any resources from which to do so would amount to a tadpole in a jar's chance of becoming a frog. (It won't happen!)

Predictably, the disciples were adamant that they did not have the ability to meet and serve such a calibre of need. Their skepticism must have been growing like well watered weeds in the noonday sun. I have always envisaged Peter boldly accosting Jesus and with hands on hips and an "I know better" tone to his voice appealing, "That's all well and good, for You, Lord, but look at what we're working with!" The disciples did indeed speak up about the situation. "We have here only five loaves of bread and two fish." The cash on hand was not even remotely close to the cost to buy enough food needed to supply the unexpected army of worshippers with enough sustenance.

So often, individual churches and other Christian organizations find themselves in the same boat. Certain needs within the community are there for the serving, but churches and para-church ministries are gasping on a respirator of indifference. This indifference can be seen in the deficits of both time and financial investments on the part of God's people. All too often, we're more apt to help a ministry by loosening our wallets than loosening our rigorous hold on our time. Some causes simply ask us to sacrifice funds, but oftentimes ministries within the Church ask us to hand our own selves over as well.

Many needs around us will stay unmet and God robbed of glory if Christians are more interested in merely attending a church service than they are actually *being* the Church and actively seeking to serve as God's people. Too many spectators in the Body of Christ are watching and letting the participants wear out.

This common dilemma concerning servanthood within church life is illustrated in a television commercial where a mother hosting a birthday party for her child attempts to make balloon "animals" for all the children in attendance. Trying to manipulate the first balloon into the shape of a dog becomes such an energy-depleting workout that she appears totally overwhelmed, this just as the second child waiting in line steps up to receive *his* balloon! The giving of our time, strength and giftedness when serving in the Church can leave us feeling like the mother in the commercial: everyone wants programs up and running and expects them to produce, while the few who *are* serving and making the ministry work are either wearing down or worn out. There just doesn't seem to be enough servant resources in the Church sometimes to cover the necessary ground of ministry.

We can very easily become overwhelmed by the great need we see around us in society. We can get discouraged by the inadequacy we feel to meet more of the kinds of needs we're confronted with on a daily basis. Maybe our well-rehearsed knee-jerk response to God whenever He seems to call us to serve Him "outside the box" is to automatically reject any notion of it. When there is teaching to be done, we might say, "God, what am I to do? Go and get a theological degree?" When there's money that needs to be given, we might say, "God, what am I supposed to do, go and get a better job?" When there's a need for a friendship and a listening ear, we might say, "God, what do I look like? I'm not a psychologist!"

Yet God is calling us to not look the other way or despise the constant dripping of need around us, simply because *He* doesn't do that. Jesus is calling His Church in these last desperate days on earth before He returns to turn up the heat on our service, to do something about the needs around us, to roll up our sleeves and be *the help* He desires for us to be as His instruments of grace.

So if our resources, like those of the disciples, seem all too small sometimes to serve the great hunger of ministry needs around us, what point was Jesus driving home? The Lord was saying that when it comes to serving Him, in whatever capacity it might be, it's not really about how much we *have* to give; it's about trusting what God can do with *what* we have to give in terms of our time, talents, and treasures. An underlying principle, then, in the passage of the miraculous feeding is that our limited resources, when they are placed in Jesus' hands, suddenly become adequate. God's in charge of the results of our service; we're on the hook for the amount of effort we put into serving! To put that another way: God simply wants us to be willing; it's *His* job to multiply our resources and to bring about miracles.

That's why we shouldn't always measure a need or a challenge by our mere human ability to meet and serve it. However meagre our time, talents, or treasures may appear to us, when they're at Jesus' disposal they can become powerful tools by which we can make a difference in any situation.

Jesus saw a great need. He could have said, "You know, people, I've been through a lot, and you are *a lot* of people!" He could have responded in many ways, and yet He didn't spurn the need at hand. The disciples would have needed much more money than what Judas would have had on him in order to meet the food demands of all the people. Their report back to the Lord sounded like Mother Hubbard on her last food stamp, and yet Jesus wasn't concerned.

We have no trouble identifying with the disciples' doubts, with feeling unable to meet and serve such a giant need. In fact, we stand here as if with our own five loaves of bread and our two measly fish, as individual churches and Christians facing needy communities, cities, and world. And yet it changes not

Jesus' commission to God's people: "You give them something to eat"; "You meet that need"; "You be that voice of hope"; "You go with that person;" "You make time for them;" "You are the help I've summoned!"

Jesus didn't have to get with reality; the followers had to get with God's program *and* power! The needs of people will always be great; that's a given. But God's provision through His people will be enough if we all do our part and are willing to serve, even if it means being stretched in our limitations. No one on the field that day taking in the miracle of Jesus who saw thousands upon thousands of people needing to be fed would have predicted leftovers, especially the disciples. However, there were ample amounts of food still uneaten that day at the end of the world's largest picnic: *"twelve"* baskets full.

Before I was married I roomed with two other guys I knew from Bible college. It never failed in that no matter what they or I made for supper, after I got home from a night class nothing was left! These two overgrown boys—not five or ten, just two—ate us all out of the house! Not a crumb or a mouse-sized morsel was left for the tasting after they were through with the food. Someone was losing weight in the home, and it wasn't them! I could have used a few miracles involving the instant production of food back then.

A deeper spiritual meaning to the leftover food after the thousands had filled their bellies speaks of the overflow that comes from God's grace to people whenever we make ourselves available to Him. When we serve others we too in a real spiritual sense benefit from our own service.

John, in his Gospel account of the miraculous feeding, makes note of a very important detail that Matthew leaves out in his. The servant heart of Jesus brought such glory to God that those among the crowds thought He was the prophet who was to come into the world (see Deuteronomy 18:15).

The beneficiaries of both the healings and the feeding recognized God was at work in Jesus, and if we who are disciples avail ourselves to the cause of Christ, others around us may well recognize God's touch through our helpful hands and credit Him for it. That, plain and simple, is our ultimate hope as God's people when we serve Him as His Church!

A note was once spotted on someone's desk in the White House that read, "The secret nature of my job does not permit me to know what I am doing." How strange it must be to serve in that kind of environment! The same, however, cannot be said of a Christian's service to God. We, as servants of Christ, are not called to a secret service. We are called to a sacred service! Our motto should be: "The sacredness of my job permits me to know that God knows what *He's* doing."

Jesus knew the job He had as the Son of God and why the Father sent Him. He said, "The Son of Man did not come to be served, but to serve, and to give his life as a ransom for many" (Matthew 20:28). As Christians we must make Jesus' attitude towards servanthood our calling card wherever we encounter or uncover need, even the seemingly impossible to meet kinds of needs. We underestimate how maturation in the faith is uniquely tied to the extent of one's commitment to serve in the Body of Christ and the spiritual stretching and sacrifice ministry requires of us.

Craig Groeschel of LifeChurch.tv offers his perspective on the topic of serving God and how it relates to spiritual growth in a Christian's life:

> If someone only attends weekend church services, their spiritual growth will be limited. If the same person starts using their gifts to serve, participates in biblical community, and begins to live missionally, their growth trajectory will likely skyrocket. To help believers become more like Christ, we concentrate on…A service-oriented culture that transforms people from spiritual consumers to spiritual contributors.[50]

People who are spiritually lost and distant from God don't care to hear a sermon in the Church as much as they'd like to see one applied *by* Christians. If we're going to serve anyone or any cause in this world, what better a call to service than the one to serve the living God that comes with the opportunity of being able to make an eternal difference in the lives of people today.

Serving God is part of how we acquire a happy and more fulfilled life as Christians. Owen Strachen and Douglas Sweeney in *Jonathan Edwards on the Good Life*, The Essential Edwards Collection, share,

> Too many Christians fail to taste the profound satisfaction offered them in the gospel…They know that God wants them to be happy, but they have not realized that joy comes not primarily from having one's desires met by God, but by serving God and doing what He desires… One does not become happy by liberating oneself from duty; one becomes happy by obeying and following the plans of the Lord.[51]

Pastor and author Charles Stanley notes as well,

The wise person faces the reality that God both deserves and demands the right to everything that we are…the authority and right to express His life through us—through our lips, eyes, hands, feet, body, thoughts, emotions—in any way He so chooses. We are not merely to be reflections of the way Christ *was*…we are to *be* living, walking expressions of the life of Christ in the world today.[52]

Nowhere in the Gospels did Jesus call and appoint some of His disciples to be exclusive soakers of ministry fruit or to be lifelong eyeballers of ministry work; *all hands* were expected to be put upon "the plow" (Luke 9:62). If we're going to sing God's praises in our churches, how then can we not be compelled to serve Him as well, to be "the help" He saved us to be? The Christian life is more than just telling about Jesus; it's about serving like Jesus too. We have much ministry work yet to do, and with decreasing numbers of servants and resources at our disposal, we have much to answer for as well.

CHAPTER 15

EVERYBODY WANTS TO RULE THE WORLD, BUT ONLY ONE CAN CHANGE IT

A Revived View of Our Role in Seeing Jesus' Kingdom Come

Whenever I recall the story of Samantha Smith's short, impactful life, I am both inspired and left with a sense of sadness. Samantha was a young girl from Manchester, Maine, who was light years ahead of most kids her age in her burden for the world she lived in that was at risk of nuclear war. The year was 1982, and the two superpowers of the earth (Russia and the United States) gave every indication by their war-hawkish rhetoric that they were edging closer to the possibility of an unthinkable showdown: a war with nuclear weapons. As was the case with so many people throughout the world at the time, such terrifying prospects were indeed unthinkable to Samantha Smith, and it scared her.

Samantha's mother encouraged her to write a letter to the then Soviet leader Yuri Andropov, stating her concerns. The determined ten-year-old girl did just that. There's a particular line in her letter that caused a lump to swell up in my throat the first time I read it. "I would like to know why you want to conquer the world or at least our country. God made the world for us to live together in peace and not to fight."

It was only after Samantha sent a subsequent letter that she was personally responded to by the Soviet leader himself. Andropov assured the young girl that his country's intention was to never start a nuclear war or use their weapons but to actually eliminate their stockpiles of them. Samantha Smith was issued an invitation to visit the Soviet Union, which she eventually did with her family. Tragically, this young ambassador for world peace, who captured the attention and the hearts of so many, lost her life along with her father in a 1985 plane crash.

How amazing it is to consider that ten-year-old Samantha was able to identify a sin-nature-rooted problem within humanity so simply and succinctly. She keenly believed that God made the world and that it was meant to be inhabited in peace. Samantha Smith, even from a child's perspective, could tell that the powers that be in God's creation threatened its well-being because of their desire to rule this world irrespective of their Creator's will.

How did this all start? In the Garden of Eden, the devil, by using his tactics of deception, commenced to counteract God's work in the world. The satanic objective was to get creation to fall, causing humans to fight against each other over who was to blame for the spiritually set-in-stone consequences to follow. We as a human race are still pointing fingers at each other for the global mess that ensued after the fall of humanity.

In fact, political powers and personalities throughout our world's history (some of them quite evil in nature and philosophy) have always sought to gain the upper military hand in order to rule. That, for one example, is exactly what happened in terms of the terrorizing reign and rule of Adolf Hitler in the Second World War.

The Garden of Eden "no-no" accomplished by Adam and Eve got the ball known as our common and unavoidable inheritance at birth of a sinful human nature *rolling*. Sin's potential to destroy humanity right away picked up steam through the offspring of the first couple (Adam and Eve): Cain would end up murdering his brother Abel. Sin's existence and momentum in the hearts and lives of human beings kept rolling along. We read of the drama between Jacob and Esau not long after the scandal of Cain and Abel. We know the rest of the story throughout our world's history: dysfunctional and broken homes, marriages, relationships, and nations, and I haven't even gotten to all the really bad stuff yet!

Veteran recording artist and New Jersey rocker Bruce Springsteen has always strived with his music to paint realistic scenarios of hard-luck living as the voice of blue-collar angst rock n roll. His critically acclaimed album *Wrecking Ball* carries with it that exact message on a lyrically angry level.

Springsteen still doesn't see much hope for the everyday person. Instead, he sees the oppressed in our society being oppressed even more, as much as injustice is being justified even more. One review of the album states,

It's an impressive vision of musical Americana, but it's as much an idealized construct as the bicycle-safe small-town streets of Ronald Reagan's "Morning in America." In both cases, we're presented with a set of signifiers meant to trigger emotional associations that will help us believe in the righteousness of the view being presented.[53]

Protest music has been around a long time; the existence of high ideals over how the world should be run has been around even longer! Some of our world's ideas to promote peace and equality are God-honouring and Bible centred, while others come via the mouths of preachy far-reaching ideologues irrespective of God's Word. One of the first so-called "protest" songs I had ever heard was the Beatles' *Revolution,* which includes the line "You say you want a revolution, well, you know, we all want to change the world." The words of the song seemed as cool and heavy to me as the opening guitar riff of the song!

The 1960s youth culture was primed and ready for change. In fact, *a lot* within the fabric of society during the 1960s was changing. Some things were getting longer (young people's hair), while others items (girls' skirts) were getting shorter! Their political views, philosophy of life, and how they related to the "establishment" dictated which "side" they took.

Many a young person felt they knew what needed to be altered within the troubled womb of the world in order for peace and harmony to be birthed. Though the youth may not have wanted to actually rule the world, they did desire to be heard and to influence change. A primary outlet for their views was the decade's pop and rock music.

Worldwide, the youth generation of the 1960s seemed restless with the status quo and disillusioned with their previous generation's traditions while eagerly seeking to adapt to a changing landscape culturally. In the summer of 1969 Moscow even reported that the Soviet youth were vandalizing phone booths in order to use its electrical pieces to convert acoustic guitars into electric ones.

Reams of bands, songs, and concept albums in the 1960s brought many among the rebelliously discontented and "flower-powered" hippie culture under the doctrine of their "take back your freedom" anthem. With the Vietnam War as a galvanized example of human devaluation, there was a thumping plea for world peace and societal reform, including individual liberties and the call for transparency and accountability amongst governing officials.

History tells us that in the big scheme of influential things all the protestations of the young people throughout the decade of the 1960s and into the early 1970s didn't quite yield the result they were hoping for: *to change the minds and the ways of the world's movers and shakers.* Many of the socially disgruntled within the hippie generation of over forty-plus years ago may have had a lot of good ideas about world change and even a humble spirit to match it, but they lacked the right means to see it happen. Even if at times they nursed a somewhat misguided message (tune in, turn on, and drop out), and campaigned for social reform irrespective of biblical values, the hippie culture grasped what the new society they were endeavouring to see might look like.

At one point during the three-day "Woodstock" music festival in August of 1969, where over 400,000 people gathered at a farm in upstate New York, concert officials announced that food was available for everyone, but they had to make sure *everyone* received some. The record-breaking crowd had to "feed each other" and be good to each other as "brothers." One official, taking in all that was going on, eventually concluded, "We must be in Heaven, man!"

To some people, that is their definition of a changed world: an imaginable heaven-like experience involving mutual sacrifice, a sharing community, and kindness to one's neighbour. Come to think of it, isn't that what the Church of Jesus Christ is called to lead the way in?

Why is it, then, that the predominant hype within culture is that the betterment of the human race must come from *within* the human race? We have tried to rule and to change our world to bring about hope and peace, yet as long as we've tried, we've never even been able to deliver optimism! God's left us to our pettiness and depravity in trying to rule ourselves; He knows it never has and never will work.

From a biblical viewpoint, the world doesn't need cosmetically empty and deceptive philosophies from its leaders or quasi-spiritual ideals being fed to its already spiritually confused inhabitants. Rather, the world needs to be *redeemed* through the witness and ministry of the Church and by the consequential spreading of God's transformative Kingdom amongst it.

If this is to happen on a greater and deeper spiritual level, God's people will need a revived ability to take their role in the world as bearers of truth and light more seriously than ever before. In case the big, bad devil has convinced us otherwise, we need to remember that our presence in this world as Christians is still as vital to its spiritual welfare as it ever has been.

We are more than mere sinners saved by grace. We are agents of change! God has made us into a new creation, and we are now conduits of His power on earth. As the deceptive smoke of Hell continues to thicken and cover the world in these end-times, God's people must remain fervent and resolute in their work to see Jesus' Kingdom values—and the spiritual transformation that comes from that—furthered in the world. There is a coming world ruler and new order (as evidenced by the biblical prophecies about the antichrist) that our sitting duck of a world must be made aware of. Being able to effectively combat the devil's wiles with biblical clarity and gospel urgency will be paramount. Acknowledging the supremacy of God, not only in our individual lives and homes but in our nations as well, will be of the utmost importance.

Pat Buchanan, a conservative political personality and commentator, in his book *Suicide of a Superpower* laments that his homeland (America), which once identified itself as a union of people living beneath the sovereign rule of God, is no longer considered a game-changer and world-influencer and could even fail to be relevant twenty-five years out. The "'One Nation under God, indivisible' of the Pledge of Allegiance is passing away. In a few decades, that America will be gone forever. In its place will arise a country unrecognizable to our parents."[54] Yes, in many regards, as goes the spiritual attuning of governance and leadership *in* the nations of the world, so goes the spiritual welfare of the world *itself*.

We all would like for our world leaders to step up and be men and women who govern from a godly standpoint, who like the late Samantha Smith will recognize that our Creator holds the central meaning and purpose to our existence as a human race, and *no one else*. All the wishful hoping and baseless, aimless faith of a desperate, lost humanity will get them nowhere.

However, a revived and spiritually renewed Church that puts a consistent emphasis on prayer for world governments and embattled political leaders, though it may not drastically change the tide of history right away, will help in fostering spiritual traction by which God's voice and Christian witness can permeate further. Judging by how current developments in the news reveal mounting civil anarchy, social unrest, and unprecedented financial and political instability, we need the merciful hand of God to radically bring about a spiritual shift in the hearts of people throughout the world.

We need His mercy, especially in light of the Bible's revelation that "When [God] is angry, the earth trembles" so much so that "the nations cannot endure his wrath" (Jeremiah 10:10). We can't look around at the shape our earthly abode is in and not accept that God is terribly angry about it. He is holy, and so much of what "flies" in this world is causing Him great grief and sadness and, as a consequence, is provoking His judgment.

Yet God sent His Kingdom-Ruler and world-Redeemer in Jesus Christ; now it's His disciples (that started with the original twelve) who are charged with turning the world upside down in pointing it back to God, who will yet renew it and reign in it (see Revelation 21:1–4).

Unfortunately, the Church's message today seems too simple and weak for many to put their hope in, too narrow-minded and old-fashioned to impact and transform the day. Largely gone are the days when political leaders pursued godly ministers for biblical accountability and counsel. Equally gone, it seems, are the days when political leaders openly talked about needing God's guidance as they governed.

Abraham Lincoln once remarked to his governing party in the midst of a crisis, "The times are dark, the spirits of ruin are abroad in all their power–but the mercy of God alone can still save us." Don't you wish we had more godly standout leaders like that today running nations, men and women who recognize the need for God's gracious intervention and favour in this troubled world? How refreshing it would be!

How refreshing it would be, as well, to see every church thoroughly sold out for praying for the leaders of the world (even those we might despise). The apostle Paul encouraged that practise in his own day for the good of the Church's witness to the Roman Empire (see 1 Timothy 2:1–2). Even Jesus taught the Jews to "Render therefore to Caesar the things that are Caesar's" (Matthew 22:21 NKJV). The Lord knew there was a human authority the Father had established in the world and that that authority could only be impacted by the Kingdom of God if the people of God respected it as such, even if they didn't always agree with it.

Many of the Jews who adhered to Jesus' ministry expected Him to rule the world (at least what was known of it by virtue of the Roman Empire's geographical dominance). Although He did, indeed, *ultimately* rule, His purpose in coming to the world was to redeem it. In other words, from the perspective of Heaven the world didn't need some conquering cowboy of divine dispatching to come in and obliterate the irreverent, villainous Romans. They weren't the real, ultimate, enemy, only a microcosm of the source.

The real enemy causing the unrest within Israel was a more personal one; it was the sin of God's own people as well as that of the entire Gentile world. "For all have sinned and fall short of the glory of God" (Romans 3:23). Jewish and Roman citizen alike were under the same spiritual accounting and consequences of God's Word. Jesus was not going to give any other message or accomplish anything else on earth other than that which communicated humanity's need to be redeemed from the bondage of its sin. It was the new spiritual grid that the entire world needed to see the authority and power of the Christ through.

In short, the world needs to live in peace with God first if it's to have any chance of experiencing harmony (as well as an enduring peace) within its nations.

There have been some very good and valiant attempts to make our world a "better place" to live in. However, all our machinations to attain such an exalted goal will ultimately fall way short of their potential without the message of the world's Redeemer (Jesus Christ) at the centre. This is why an image of Jesus Christ on the cover of *Life*'s reissued *100 People Who Changed The World* seems out of place. Considering the biblical fact that our planet was created with the preincarnate Son of God's full involvement, Jesus should never be lumped in with other "world changers" that include the likes of Einstein and Ghandi, not to mention Oprah Winfrey. (Mere mortals!) Christ is not one of many world changers; He's the world's Creator, Saviour, and Ruler, as well as its Ultimate Changer! God, through His Son, is not only ruling the world but effectively changing it through Him as well. The incarnation of Christ and the subsequent sending of the Holy Spirit was always meant to transform the world by the redemption and empowerment of one disciple at a time.

Unfortunately, our religiously pessimistic world is largely no longer considering the Church for answers to what ails the human condition. Rather, it is searching in vain for enduring peace and long-lasting hope under every shallow promise its world leaders issue to them. Imagine the spiritual transformation that could come about in communities wherever the Church of Jesus Christ is situated as a result of revived and reinvigorated Christians reaching out? Imagine God's people all over the world filled with an urgency of mission as was the case at the first Christmas.

One of my favourite songs during the Christmas holiday season is "It's the Most Wonderful Time of the Year." Whenever I hear the tune it just makes me feel good inside, even though it really has nothing to do with the biblical message of Christmas.

If you've ever paid close attention to the lyrics of the song, you know that the songwriter doesn't give us the *true* reason why Christmas is the "most wonderful time" of the year. It's a classic case within culture of creation's indifference to their Creator by supplanting God (in Christ) as the foundational centrepiece for their happiness and blessing with human-focused, frivolous activity.

Quite like how the people of the world strive to see positive change happen around the globe while bypassing the all-powerful Change Agent, even Christmas songs can reflect a world celebrating the trimmings of the season while avoiding the inspiration *for* that season!

Christians for over sixteen hundred years have celebrated the timeless account of the first Christmas: the *birth of Christ in Bethlehem* (foretold in the Old Testament and realized in the Gospels of the New Testament). It is the "most wonderful time" of the year because we celebrate the Saviour of the world's advent and humble birth on our planet Earth. *God came to be with us in order to be one of us, in order to redeem us!*

The first Christmas song ever written *and sung* is the one often referred to in Bibles by its Latin title, the "Magnificat." Upon hearing of her blessed position as the channel of God's blessing to His people (and the world), Mary spontaneously broke out in divinely inspired song; they're words that will forever grace the pages of Luke 1. "And Mary said: 'My soul glorifies the Lord and my spirit rejoices in God my Savior…His mercy extends to those who fear him, from generation to generation'" (Luke 1:46–50). The song is a form of Jewish psalm that is strikingly similar to the song attributed to Hannah in 1 Samuel 2.

I've always wondered what the words coming from the mouths of God's messengers sounded like to their recipients on the hillsides of Bethlehem's pasture lands. One thing we don't have to ponder, however, is the *effect* the angels' heaven-born message concerning the birth of the Saviour had on the privileged shepherds who were God's intended and isolated congregation that night.

The pronouncement of the angels that the Saviour had come made the shepherds the very first evangelists in the Gospels. These men of the sheep pen quite literally overnight became preaching pioneers of their time and era. Before there was a Wesley, Spurgeon, or Graham, there were…*the shepherds!* Ordinary men, because of the joy set before them, unabashedly announced the coming of the Heavenly Ruler (Christ) and by virtue of that became heralds for world change.

God's promise of salvation in His Son, Jesus Christ (a name that means "Saving Messiah"), extends each Christmastime to all, that those who believe may receive the true "reason" for a season that is truly the most wonderful time of the year. The gospel message should be a daily soul-burden for those of us who call Jesus "Lord" and who worship Him as Saviour. When was the last time we channelled our inner shepherd-evangelists and ran to tell someone about Jesus with a zeal such as theirs? When was the last time we, as Jesus' disciples, not only acknowledged but acted on the reality that our feet (like that of the shepherds) are shod with the readiness that comes from the gospel of peace?

Some Christians hang on for their dear *redeemed* lives to the excuse that "evangelism" is not their spiritual "gift." But try telling that to the shepherds, who weren't exactly known for their social skills, or for their learnedness either!

God purposes to revive His people as often as spiritually necessary in order to turn them from idle and passive possessors of the good news into portable evangelistic amplifiers of it. Indeed, it seems at times like everybody would like to take a stab at ruling the world, some for noble reasons; some purely for the sake of power and personal agenda.

The only way our tired and torn planet will realize the hope and change it so haphazardly lunges at is for an "all-in" revived church to provide it. Though what constitutes "good and acceptable" change in the world today is highly debatable, the kind of transformation the Kingdom of God on earth is bringing (however unpopular or even unwanted aspects of it may be) is spiritually non-negotiable.

God invites those who want to rule the world to allow His Son, Jesus Christ, to reign in them first, for one day they will reign *with* Him. In that way, they not only become world-changers now but will be new-world rulers for all eternity (see Luke 19:10–27; 2 Timothy 2:12; Revelation 2:26, 20:4).

CHAPTER 16

WHY DON'T THEY WANT MY JESUS OR MY CHRISTIANITY?

A Revived Revelation of the Person of Jesus

An eighty-nine-year-old evangelical broadcaster and preacher from Oakland, California, named Harold Camping predicted the return of Jesus Christ to the earth on Saturday, May 21, 2011, to rapture His Church. It was a spectacle that surprisingly grew more legs than prophecies of that nature should. One man nearly drained his life savings to spend on a transit-ad campaign in order to warn people that the world as they knew it would end that Saturday in May.

Camping's prediction may have duped a good number of his "followers," but as we might expect, atheists weren't biting. In fact, they used the event to mock the whole idea of a biblical "rapture." Many atheists and agnostics alike actually blew up balloons made to look like human forms, which were then released into the sky as the evening of May 21 approached. Other groups partied throughout the night and celebrated with signs the fact that Camping's prediction didn't come true.

It's not the first time (and I'll be surprised if it's the last) that someone claiming to be of an evangelical persuasion predicted Jesus' return and the end of the world. It's not the first time Camping made a prediction of such apocalyptic proportions either. In 1994, he predicted a similar return of Jesus, and like his most recent pronouncement, the prophecy in '94 failed to be fulfilled as well. For some inexplicable reason the controversial preacher seems to be wholly inept at accurately pinpointing the return of Christ! *Ya think?*

What is it about some Christians who feel they have to deplete any respect for biblical prophecy some non-believing people may still have left? Though

Camping's second prediction concerning the rapture may have made a lot of people laugh the next day, its major consequence is seen in that the non-event (and other ill-advised prophecies and predictions like Camping's) only served to reinforce how a lot of people view evangelicals.

The most important questions we must answer as people who do refer to ourselves as "evangelical Christians" are these: *Are we really living out our faith in a biblical manner, and are we communicating the person of Jesus in the same way?* As people who genuinely believe Christ *will* once again emerge on the world's stage at a time known only to God, I fear that we are giving the world every reason to doubt our scriptural exegesis and, even worse, our sincerity.

The Bible is clear in that no one can know the time or date of Jesus' return (Matthew 24:36). The only clues Jesus gives us are located in the end-time passages we have in the Gospels. Though there are other supporting "timeline" Scriptures in biblical books such as Daniel, Ezekiel, Isaiah, and Revelation (to name just a few), we can only know for certain that Jesus will come "like a thief in the night" (when people are least expecting Him to) (1 Thessalonians 5:2). How people like Harold Camping could possibly justify coming up with solid dates for Christ's return when Jesus Himself told us not to mark our calendars, I'll never know!

We're a world, nonetheless, that's still obsessed with predictions, prophecies, and yes, even with the idea of *Armageddon*. Many Christians seem to want to hear biblical teaching and preaching on such subjects exclusively. On the opposite side of the spiritual spectrum, there are Christians who remain uncomfortable with anything that sounds remotely charismatic *or* eschatological coming from the pulpit.

What we desperately need, however, is a revived, biblically accurate knowledge of the Person and ministry of Jesus in our churches today!

There will always be people in and around the Church (a lot like the frenetic curious of Jesus' day) who tag behind the Lord for pure entertainment value. Attracted purely to His magnetic chutzpah, they have little spiritual stomach for much else from Him. They are *fans* of His, first, but have no clue of what's required or what it means to enter into His "follower" club. In the Gospels there were those amongst the crowds clinging to Jesus who enjoyed His spine-tingling show-stopping displays of supernatural power, perhaps more than anything else He had to offer or say. These types of people still frequent our churches today; they drop out at the hearing of a sermon on challenging spiritual topics: sin, repentance, forgiveness, serving, or tithing. Take your pick!

Why Don't They Want My Jesus *or* My Christianity?

During my devotions I came across a recurring theme in the Gospel of John, in terms of the spiritual dynamics that existed amongst the "seeker" crowd around Jesus. What struck me was the tension that existed between people asking the Lord for a "sign" that He was the embodiment of God's "Kingdom" to come and their lack of faith when presented with difficult teachings from Him afterwards. Some people after witnessing Jesus perform a miracle, for instance, would seem to exhibit an initial faith in Him, resulting in their decision to carry on following Him.

The inevitable moment would arise, however, when the Lord would stop and teach those who were hanging out with Him (the immediate twelve, as well as stragglers within His sermon's earshot) for the sole reason of purging the uncommitted extraneous element mixed within those who were following Him. If Jesus simply desired loyalists en masse so that He could boast to the Pharisees (in Facebook-speak), "Look how many people *like* me!" all He had to do was perform acts of wonder and seal the allegiance of seekers that way.

However, it is clear from all four Gospels (especially the one authored by John) that Jesus was more interested in increasing membership *in Heaven* than He was in appearing to be someone who could draw a crowd or pack out a synagogue. He left such shallow aspirations to the flighty Pharisees.

When the Iraq War commenced on March 20, 2003, the headlines in newspapers the following morning referred to the pre-emptive military strike by the coalition forces by the evocative phrase "Shock and Awe!" The words in bold print described the strategic military offensive against the then Iraqi leader Saddam Hussein and his imperial guard.

Though the spectacle of the aerial attack was indeed both shocking and awesome to behold, Jesus is the original holder of all things *shocking* and *awesome*. The Lord had tons of "awe" value in His ministry possession as well as endless amounts of "shock" value in His divine arsenal.

In John 6:35, Jesus pronounced that He is "the bread of life." It was a simple enough statement, yet a telling one. The Old Testament radar of any self-respecting Jewish person would have picked up on such a figurative term involving bread. Within Israel, bread was a symbol of God's providential care and blessing. The Jews might have thought that Jesus, by attaching the term "bread of life" to His persona, was sounding as flaky as a piece of manna itself! Didn't this Galilean carpenter's son know how intimating that He was somehow from the same divine flour that brought their Hebrew ancestors bread-like wafers to eat while they were wandering in the desert would taste in the mouths of His Jewish listeners?

If Jesus' pronouncement in John 6 wasn't awesome sounding (as well as intriguing) enough, the Lord proceeded to dovetail His cryptic statement "I am the bread of life" with a shocking sequel: "Unless you eat the flesh of the Son of Man and drink his blood, you have no life in you" (John 6:53).

This statement was taken to heart by the early Church. Tradition shows us that upon someone's deathbed, the request was made to receive communion (symbolically, the body and blood of Christ). In some people's theological understanding, that is *the* way they can be sure they have "life" in them. Yet an all-important question remains about why the Saviour chose such a graphic, head-turning statement to convey a vital spiritual truth about Himself? Why *did* Jesus express that one must identity with Him in such a way?

The foremost message of true biblical Christianity is that Jesus is *Lord of all, or not at all,* the one "mediator" between God and us. To word the truth we as evangelicals believe about Jesus another way: He is the spiritual "credit card" we are not to leave our earthly home (by dying) without.

To the casual Gentile listening to Jesus' words that day, "Unless you eat the flesh of the Son of Man and drink his blood, you have no life in you," the Lord probably sounded as if He was encouraging a sort of instituted cannibalism as a form of worship. Such a deduction would have made cultural sense given that many religious rituals involving human sacrifices took place in many of the pagan temples of the first century. It shouldn't come as a surprise to us, then, that this was often the Romans' perception of the worship practices of the first Christians. Despite such misunderstandings, all that Jesus was trying to communicate by His stunning words in John 6 can be clarified, explained, and even put into cultural context for us today.

The Lord, as He so often did, utilized a method of communication called hyperbole to communicate a vital truth about His place in God's redemption plan for humankind. In John 6, Jesus was actually saying something to the effect of "Listen up, people! Spiritually speaking, only I can be the sustenance for your lives. So unless you're willing to feed and drink of Me in that way, your souls will shrink up and die." As spiritually and religiously exclusive as such an interpretation comes across, Jesus meant what He said. Salvation isn't something anyone should assume he or she already has; it's not some spiritual fad or option to be snagged when it's attractive, convenient, or earthly advantageous for one to do so either.

If the Gospels clarify anything about the Lord, it's that He could never be mistaken for some religious one-trick pony. When people in the first century thought it was enough to get into the Jesus' boat and sail (follow) with Him based solely upon a miracle He did in His ministry (though Jesus did seem to encourage such motives), John would warn the readers of his Gospel to be sure that that spiritual boat wasn't filled with holes. John was concerned for those whom Jesus cautioned, "Do not work for food that spoils" (John 6:27).

In other words, salvation is something to be received in the One who *is* the Bread, not in what they might get out of the Bread to satisfy them and keep them hooked. If people missed that crucial point in the spiritual crosshairs of His ministry, they missed everything, even if they were physically blessed by the Lord in some unimaginable manner (e.g., the feeding of the five thousand).

For John, any potential disciple needed to know that there was more to who the Lord was and more to His message than some mind-bending magic-man. Most people gobble up the sensational and pine for the spectacular in terms of leadership; it's something that keeps them coming back for more! Style, in many respects, still trumps substance and even spiritual solidity when it comes to the sort of people we'll elect and follow as leaders.

Along this line of thought, John's Gospel shows us that to be in possession of a pebble's worth of truth in terms of Jesus' person and mission (for example, latching on to Jesus' miraculous power but not His claims to divinity) isn't nearly enough. The spiritual truth embodied in and substantiated by Jesus Christ throughout His ministry could never be interpreted or accepted as faddish or harmless. If we are to believe Jesus, we have to own everything He did and said: the good and the downright unpopular, as well as the shocking and awesome, an example of which we find in John 6.

Jesus' words still aim to rock the boat of anyone's spiritual ideal who is simply satisfied with coasting on the waters of spiritual intrigue or, worse, ignorance in respect to Him.

The Gospels were written at a time of heightened Roman persecution towards the fledgling movement of Jesus' followers in order to hearten and affirm the earliest Christians that they had (in a "faith" sense) bet on the right horse! The first couple of centuries following the Church's inception were often characterized by the top-down cruelty of the Roman Empire. Prior to the time of Constantine's reign, non-conformists to Caesar's lordship would not be tolerated. The early disciples needed encouragement to keep-on-keeping-on in the faith. They needed a written go-to document reminding them of all the things Jesus said and did to pad their resolve to obey Him and to give the Christians exposed to Roman hostility hope to endure in their unfettered allegiance to Him.

The Lord was always willing to say whatever was needed in order to weed out the serious followers from those of the fair-weather contingent. In the Gospels we never spot our Lord being discouraged over the fact that people decided to defect from Him. Jesus used various shock and awe statements such as the one in John 6 to *intentionally* separate those who were going along with Him for the wrong reasons from those He was purposing to shape for ministry, those whom He knew would stick with Him and eventually shine for the Kingdom of Heaven.

Nothing changed when the Gospel accounts were eventually taught by the apostles. Committed worshippers in the early Church began to surface and separate from the more casual stock, while those who found Jesus' teachings to be distasteful when preached by the leaders of the Church hit the road.

It can be said today that Christianity isn't for "sissies," just as the foundational beginnings of our faith, in the form of our Lord's teachings, wasn't for the faint of heart and spiritual "wimps" of His day. Those among the Lord's synthetic followership in the first century were no different in their spiritual tendencies from many of the Jesus part-timers today: they too were religiously skeptical, fickle to a fault, and would go on-and-off the "Praise the Lord!" bandwagon frequently. Something about Jesus that's not easily spotted as the Gospels are read is how frequently He left many people disappointed who were only looking for Him to pull some spiritual rabbit out of a hat. Just as Jesus marvelled many with His profoundly unique words, He also disappointed many by them as well.

John 6 was one of those moments in which Jesus scaled down His travelling salvation show on purpose. Many of our Lord's larger than life's lessons and calls for a radical commitment to Him had to have sounded like a dirge to some who were hoping to stick with Him. The more Jesus poured on the hard teachings, the more those who were restlessly undecided about Him must have seen the daylight of unbelief between them and the Lord increase. Every bit of challenge on an eternal plain issued from the spiritual lectern of Jesus signaled another nail in the coffin of someone's messianic musings of Him. Many of those who initially preened over Christ like groupies of some religious supernova saw their head-over-heels honeymoon of interest in the Son of God come to a grinding halt.

When people turn from Jesus by rejecting the Holy Spirit's nudge on their hearts, that's one thing; when it happens as a result of a tarnished and unreliable testimony on the part of God's people, that's another thing. Harold Camping with his string of scripturally irresponsible predictions regarding Jesus' return to this earth mentioned earlier in this chapter is not the only example of Christians shedding a negative light on their faith and perhaps on the Object of it (Jesus Christ), but it's a prime one. However, it's never a negative thing to speak boldly, yet tactfully, for Jesus and to utter spiritual truth in such a manner that will cause non-believing people to raise their eyebrows for the right reasons; it's not always a bad thing to test a friendship using biblical standards and our devotion to Jesus as subjects. Non-believing people must know that as much as a relationship with Jesus isn't based on rules, it's not based on adaptable and shifting values either. By determining to commit to Jesus Christ, one is, in a sense, "asking for it." Christianity, from a Bible-believing standpoint, is not an easy, fluffy religion of convenience and piety that asks nothing of us outside the doors of our local parish. Rather, going with and *sticking* with Jesus, the Bible tells us, means entering into the costly process of discipleship as well (see Luke 9:23–25).

Numerous people have told me that they'd have faith in Jesus and go to church if He would only do "one thing" for them. The difficulty with rational faith, however, is that it's based on variables we can touch, see, and understand; it's based on outward things that attract us and justify our beliefs. This was *not* the kind of faith Jesus was calling for people to have. If we're to be in discipleship with the Saviour, we're to not only believe the incredible and see the invisible, but we have to accomplish the impossible through Him as well.

No doubt the Cross of Christ is often viewed as an offense to the spiritually lost. It's a stumbling block to many within the Jewish nation who can't fathom fitting the crucifixion and the spiritual rationale for it into the framework of their understanding of the Messiah's ministry. Jesus warned His followers that to remain offended by His teaching could put them in the precarious position of turning away from Him. The Lord's disciples were not to see themselves as being scandalized by their close association with Him. That is, those who committed to Christ were to be less concerned about what others erroneously thought of their Master and more concerned about what He had to say *about* the human spiritual predicament in relation to the Kingdom of God.

Jesus is the most misunderstood figure in human history. Has there ever been another person who has attracted as many opinions about himself as the Son of God? Numerous biblical academics within Canada have become increasingly intolerant of the Bible's orthodox message, which teaches that Jesus Christ is God's Son, the third Person of the Holy Trinity, and the only means by which redemption and salvation can come about (see John 3:16, 14:6; Romans 8:18–21). A few years ago, *Maclean's* magazine featured an eye-popping expose on the historical Jesus of Nazareth, entitled "The Jesus Problem." A spattering of views from New Testament scholars revealed an unbridled skepticism towards the accuracy of the traditional Gospel narratives that show Jesus as the Son of God. Gone for many within modern academia is the belief that the biblical Jesus is God's central address to us as a human race.

One "leading Canadian voice in progressive Christianity" added her two cents by stating,

> Jesus' moral teaching is not outstanding...His words are dead to many people. The world has changed. The words don't make sense any more... Why do we need a 'revolutionary' voice from two millennia ago to guide us? We have fabulous ideas of our own, that are constantly weakened by having to tie them back to Jesus and Scripture.[55]

The Bible's teaching that the Lord is the exclusive centre of God's address to us as well as His redemptive plan for us seems to fly over but never quite land on the hearts of some people who, it could be said, are genuinely hungry for the significance of the spiritual in their lives.

Over the years there have been high-profile celebrities who've made it their life's passion to seek out a higher spiritual "reality," only to falter by trying to fit the teachings of Jesus into other spiritually misguided moulds.

The late former Beatle George Harrison was among those who couldn't quite see Jesus for who He truly is. Harrison, when referring to Jesus' baptism at the hands of John, once commented, "That was when he received his mantra."[56] A mantra traditionally is understood to be a word or group of words used for chanting while in a meditative-like trance that is believed to possess the capability of bringing about spiritual transformation. It is a ritual used within certain eastern religions such as Hinduism and Buddhism.

Author Steve Turner, in *The Gospel According to the Beatles,* elaborating on George Harrison's discombobulated spiritual view of the Son of God, explains that the former Beatle believed, "When Christ said, 'The kingdom of God is within,' he was recommending deep meditation techniques. His death and resurrection were proof that he was fully realized because a fully realized person can move outside of the physical body with ease."[57] Further, Harrison was said to be okay with Jesus but not with identifying Him with either the Church or the Christian faith. Turner states, "Despite this appreciation for Jesus, he maintained a beef against Christianity and the established church."[58] Unfortunately, when someone divorces the Person of Jesus from the people of Jesus (the Body of Christ), it will never lead them to the truth about Jesus!

Some would argue that either the Church (especially in the West) has lost the attracting spiritual essence of Christ's ministry or the people who like what Jesus had to say but don't believe in the Church haven't really considered that the Lord Himself empowers Christians to represent Him on earth. My guess is that both of these are correct to a large extent; in fact, they essentially influence each other. Christians often have failed to be spiritually magnetic to the lost, and yet there are those amongst the unsaved in our world who just flat out want nothing to do with what they believe is a man-made institution (the Church). The Gospels require a practical reference point from which people can accept its teaching and spiritual impact. In other words, the unsaved need to see the gospel activated amongst Christians if they're going to even consider it.

In truth, the Holy Spirit *can and does* use the lives of God's people to convict the spiritually lost of their need for Jesus Christ. On that optimal plane the Church has both greatly excelled and miserably failed. Many people, however, have allowed the shortcomings of the Church to colour their overall impression of Jesus; it's a reality.

Sadly, some people who don't know exactly what to make of Christianity or the Church still convince themselves that the God Christians espouse as worthy to be praised and obeyed is too high and mighty for them to come to.

Charles Colson, the late former assistant to President Richard Nixon, shared an encounter he had shortly after he became a follower of Christ while in prison for his involvement in the Watergate-related convictions. During a conversation with a wealthy industrialist, Jim Fuller, Fuller divulged his admiration for Colson's "unusual kind of strength."

Immediately Colson sensed an open door to express to the rather hard-nose businessman that he too could have the kind of strength Colson had from having a relationship with Jesus Christ. Colson recalled how in an unpredictably furious manner Fuller barked back at him. "'Don't ever talk to me about Jesus Christ,' he shouted, slamming his fist on the coffee table so hard the cups rattled…'I'm sorry,' he quickly retreated. 'It's just that I can't be a hypocrite. I don't believe…I can't say I do if I don't…if I were to seek God, I'd want to get my own life in order first.'"[59]

It was often difficult for people to come to Jesus, because He knew the hearts of men. John 6:64 tells us that the Lord "had known from the beginning which of them did not believe and who would betray him." There are people who love the darkness way too much to come to Christ in faith. However, there are also those who, though they are respectful towards religious people and biblical teachings, may see the bar of God's acceptance of them as being too elevated to get over.

At other times Christians are the ones guilty of raising that bar too high, where even God must be thinking, "It's no wonder sinners feel they can't come to Me!" Jesus never mounted up spiritual rules and regulations as if they were religious scaffolding, to the point where the spiritually lost were meant to experience a fear of heights for how high they'd have to climb in order to reach the summit of God's acceptance of them. As truth-bearers Christians must resist turning what are spiritually surmountable barriers (in the lives of the unsaved) into religiously insurmountable walls.

The Church must always remember that it is far easier for those of us who are born-again to feel justified as *we* are than for the unsaved seeker or skeptic to feel qualified to come to Jesus as *they* are! So let's not prevent anyone from coming to the Saviour by shocking them. Rather, through our humble sharing, may we allow the pure Person of Jesus to motivate and even *awe* the unsaved into embracing Him as their Saviour. Perhaps we as Christians should be praying more along the lines for the Lord to reveal Himself to *us* so that we'll be more equipped to represent Him to others. That's what we're supposed to be about as advertisers (evangelizers) of Jesus; it's also what qualifies so many of us as being *evangelical* as Christians.

CHAPTER 17

ODE TO THE TASK OF SHINY, HAPPY "GOOD NEWS" PEOPLE

A Revived Understanding of What It Means To Be Evangelical

As I have reiterated throughout this book, I believe the Church is in need of a revived and renewed spiritual vision for living a radical, gospel-centric Christian life in order to meet the challenges of its faith and ministry in these end-times and last days. Christians need to be leading exemplary lives of righteousness amidst a flaunting culture that's unabashedly checkered with an in-your-face *unrighteousness*. Ironically, as "aliens and strangers" on earth and yet citizens of Heaven, the Church of Jesus Christ must strive to be *the* most humble and real of all people our world has to offer. God calls us to this not only for our own spiritual development and good but for the good of those *outside the faith* who are observing Christians.

Our spiritual ancestors (Israel) were told by their prophetic leaders that God had no time for religious observation that was synthetic at its core and led astray others who were locked in spiritual darkness and dying for His truth. Long before Jesus called the Pharisees out for being "blind [spiritual] guides" (Matthew 15:14), the Lord warned His revival-needy people through Isaiah to stop their acting jobs and masquerading as worshippers and start acting like the real McCoy!

> "You were wearied by all your ways, but you would not say, 'It is hopeless.'... Whom have you so dreaded and feared that you have been false to me...?...I will expose your righteousness and your works, and they will not benefit you. When you cry out for help, let your collection of idols save you!" (Isaiah 57:10–13).

When we as Christians come across the numerous stories and statistics out there that reflect an ungodly and very carnal witness within the worldwide Church of Jesus Christ, it's hard not to feel like the most formidable spiritual opponent we face in evangelizing the world is ourselves! I wonder whether we're as convicted and concerned as we should be about our collective testimony.

How many of us as Christians are actually living entirely misleading lives of faith? How many of us who profess Jesus Christ are causing the unsaved to stumble on the chunks of rubble falling from our vaunted yet cracking and crumbling morals and ethics? How many of us would even consider whether we have become spiritually calcified due to a hardened hypocrisy and legalism burrowed deep within us? How many of us are personally taking the responsibility upon our spiritual shoulders to give some people's opinions of evangelical Christians a makeover? Depending on who you talk to, different people have different viewpoints of "evangelical Christians." But just how did we get to the point we're at today, where the term "evangelical" has become such a provocative and even scorned term in culture?

Evangelicalism, which came to prominence in the eighteenth century U.K. within the Protestant Church, is a theological stream of Christian faith that has become somewhat controversial in our culture today. Its bold, unwavering view of the historical biblical Jesus and its refusal to adjust its doctrine to the world's changing social values and perceived needs is rubbing our world the wrong "religious" way.

So just what does it mean to be evangelical as a Christian? It means we believe that the main thrust of the gospel can be found, for instance, in a passage such as John 14:6. There, Jesus minces no words in regards to His true identity and why He came to the world: "I am the way and the truth and the life. No one comes to the Father except through me." The evangelical Christian believes the Bible to be telling the truth that Jesus is the exclusive way in which one can know God personally and gain eternal security in Heaven. As well, many evangelical churches believe their central purpose in ministry is to seek conversions among the spiritually lost (who without Christ would die in their sins), to fulfill the Great Commission (Matthew 28:18–20).

As I discussed in the previous chapter, oftentimes Jesus sought to thin out the crowd of His superficial admirers who were trying to claim a spot on His roster of known followers, something our Lord wasn't going to make easy for them to do. However, as the revival-starved Church today, we occasionally (and unfortunately) accomplish our own thinning out of potential Christ followers.

Oftentimes this happens as a result of Christians failing to consistently strive for godliness in how they interact with the world. There are opportunities for Kingdom good and eternal impact that we as God's people often let get away; even worse, we sometimes flunk in being the kind of loving people we should be and are *expected* to be.

An Ontario public school board's decision to ban distribution of Gideon Bibles to its young students unleashed a torrent of threatening, rude calls and hateful emails from professing Christians directed at the board's trustees. Some of the responses to the ruling from "evangelicals" were regrettably inappropriate and downright spiritually irresponsible. Some of the messages to the Bluewater District School Board expressed racist sentiments and even questioned the trustees' patriotism. Board chairwoman Jan Johnstone admits the vitriolic responses—some even urging trustees to "watch" their "backs"—were unnerving. "People do crazy things," Johnstone said. "They see Christianity as a fundamental part of their Canadian identity." The invective of some within the Church, indeed, pressed on a sore spot!

Was it Christians' prerogative to respond to the decision of the school board? Absolutely! That being said, it wasn't at all profitable to commit a spiritual double standard in the process. Communicating on the one hand that the school board has no reason to treat the spirituality of committed Christians and years of fruitful privilege in such dismissive ways while advocating at the same time a chuck-your-godliness-at-the-door type of protest sends the worst of conflicted and highly hypocritical messages. We can ill afford as God's people to hastily erode any capital the unsaved may give us in being willing to "hear us out" on issues of faith. When will we ever learn as humans that our mouths are quite often faster runners than our brains?

Unfortunately, some evangelicals think they can just say anything about God in the hopes of stirring up controversy and forcing the resultant attention to be put on the Christian faith as a whole. Sometimes, however, this strategy backfires! We hear biblically buttered yet undeniably inaccurate statements being made all the time from "outspoken" evangelical church leaders, media personalities, and even politicians. Case in point: an evangelical candidate in the 2012 U.S. national elections was quoted as insensitively connecting pregnancies resulting from the event of rape to God's will. Though the candidate in question may have been theologically misunderstood, his words nevertheless were interpreted as being theologically butchered. When God's people (especially those who are in the public eye) fail to take time to pray and to think through their theology (being careful of its accurate transmission) before making statements of faith, they can end up repelling and alienating the public rather than drawing them in. No wonder so many people are weary of evangelical Christians and mock our perceived "brand" of Christianity! We need to be ever-cognizant of practising a biblically honouring evangelical witness that only an individual introspective heart-cleansing revival and spiritual renewal can bring to the Church. Instead of WWJD, perhaps we need to consider HWJR: "How would Jesus respond?"

In the face of what appears to be a growing (and fashionable) bullying of the Christian faith within culture today, God's people need to do better than to allow unfavourable circumstances and unsavory opponents to press the buttons of their sinful natures as they push back. The only response to gospel-opposition that's both spiritually productive and godly is the one that stays clear away from the degradation of our testimony.

Despite any shortcomings on the part of God's people, despite the reality of aging and decreasing numbers of churches, most recognized pollsters report that the Christian faith is still the world's largest religion. Should we take that to mean, then, that we are still living in a predominantly Christian time after all? The accurate answer is: no. Though Bibles, church buildings, worshippers and crosses still polka-dot the globe, we've actually been living in a post-Christian world for a while now. Canada is evolving into a very socially liberal country, where the issue and place of religious faith and observance, though still important in the lives of millions, is not factoring as much into the values expressed or the moral decisions made within government and society. Christianity is no longer the standard and authority within everyday culture. Such days passed long ago.

What are we as evangelical Christians to say about what other religions teach about Jesus and how one is to achieve salvation? How are we to deal with the argument that there are truths present in other religions and that God can use any faith background to bring a person to His Son? These are questions that we as believers may feel we shouldn't have to deal with. We preach Jesus, and people just have to grasp that and "get saved."

However, what often exacerbates the efforts of God's people as they go about evangelizing their communities is that Christianity is now deemed just one faith option (and an antiquated one at that) on the many speckled shelf of religious ideologies for the choosing. The inescapable reality glaring at Christians in the twenty-first century is that we worship Jesus Christ amongst a crowded and complicated religiously pluralistic society. The growing number of faith backgrounds and religious belief systems pressing in on the margins of what were

Ode to the Task of Shiny, Happy "Good News" People

once spiritually heterogeneous neighbourhoods and cities are what now make up the Christian's *new* and *normal* "harvest" field.

In Canada, as well as in other multicultural countries throughout the world, it's possible for us to come into contact with multiple religious ideologies each day. It's hard enough to share our faith with those who speak our religious "language" (those who hold some knowledge of either the Bible, Jesus, or the Christian faith); harder still is the challenge of dialoguing about God and salvation issues with those of a faith that is totally *foreign* to us. Traditional missionary work has gone overseas and has returned back to our shores here in the Western Church.

The million dollar question people of no specific faith background continue to challenge Christians with remains *How can Jesus be the only way?* There will always be people of an atheistic persuasion who don't believe in a particular "way" to attain salvation simply because they don't believe that they, or anyone else, are in *need* of one! I know of some critical thinkers who, while not necessarily hostile to the gospel message, observe the lives of some Christians and judge that the churchgoers are no better off than they are! Where are all the Christians that "shine like stars" in a "crooked and depraved generation" (Philippians 2:15) when we need them?

Many of the more gospel-hardened and ready-to-mock-at-all-times kinds of non-believers we dialogue with also question the value and difference Jesus makes in our lives. "Wasn't He crucified?" they insist. "How can God die?" they ask. Psalm 22 frames the struggle Christians face evangelistically. The psalm is messianic in its literary nature because it prefigures the suffering of Jesus Christ. Purporting Jesus Christ as Almighty God, while knowing He also made Himself vulnerable (even unto death) as Psalm 22 prophesies, leaves evangelical Christians, for sure, with some explaining to do.

At the scene of the crucifixion Jesus looked the furthest thing from bearing the attributes of Almighty God, let alone the great, majestic hope of Israel and the Saviour of the world. Many people seeking to understand the biblical message of evangelicals (and indeed the entire Christian Church) on a purely rational level struggle to grasp how God could allow Himself to be man-handled the way Jesus was, only to come off as looking ultimately powerless and fraudulent as so many of His enemies suspected He was.

It would have been easy at the scene of Calvary to walk away from a dead Jesus thinking everything He did and promised was somehow a hoax to end all other hoaxes. The theological significance of the Cross of Christ seems to contribute to a spiritual tension between faith and unbelief for many among the unsaved who view the end result of the crucifixion (the death of Jesus) as cognitively irreconcilable with the Bible's claim that He is God and also humanity's *judge*. There are non-believers who will readily accept the idea and possibility of a resurrection of the human dead more than they can swallow the apparent mortality of God.

Unbelief often mocks faith because faith continues to believe and trust when there is no apparent evidence to support it and when the evidence is perceived to have weakened. Can we as Christians (evangelical or otherwise) prove that the resurrection of Jesus Christ happened? Can we really prove that Jesus died for sinners? Despite how simplistically and convincingly we may be able to explain away our spiritual experience, the unsaved are left with the choice to either believe God's Word at face value or not.

Those we evangelize will not come to Christ by mentally banking what we tell them about our Lord; nor can they afford to just keep it in their Bibles up on a mantle. Without the Holy Spirit's assistance, it's impossible for one to come to a *saving* belief.

However, it is surprising to me still how some atheists, for example, are willing to give religious people their due for the genuine beliefs they hold to and the commitment they've made to a life of faith. Some atheists even "get" why such a large amount of our world's population remain religiously oriented and are even willing to laud the merits of faith for its contributions to society (though they refuse to actually, um, *believe* themselves!).

Author Alain de Botton, an atheist, shares,

> Religion understands we need guidance, that we can't get through this life without help…The vulnerability and fragility of being human are right at the centre of religious analysis. Obviously there's a supernatural component as well, the reassurance about the next life. There's reassurance about marriage, relationships and children…there's an emphasis on wisdom…about finding peace in a noisy world…But religion is only secondarily about a book.[60]

The reality that God-deniers could, on the one hand, allow themselves to appreciate the seemingly useful rationale behind religious beliefs while on the other hand be left cold and spiritually unhinged by them baffles me. Atheists will always be around, and yet since the time Jesus called followers and demonstrated His divinity and the power of God's Kingdom through His ministry, millions upon millions of people have gone to their graves confidently entrusting their eternal souls to Christ by faith.

In an ancient tomb located below a modern condominium building in Jerusalem, archaeologists have found ossuaries (bone boxes for the dead) bearing engravings that could represent the earliest archaeological evidence of Christians ever found. The tomb has been dated to before AD 70. According to the excavators, if its engravings are indeed early Christians, they were most likely made by some of Jesus' earliest followers.

One of the limestone ossuaries bears an inscription in Greek that includes a reference to "Divine Jehovah" raising someone up. A second ossuary has an image that appears to be a large fish with a stick figure in its mouth. It would seem that the image represents the biblical account of Jonah, who was swallowed by a large fish and then released. It's believed that both the inscription and the image of the fish represent the Christian belief in the resurrection of the dead.

In brass terms, this is the certain faith and eternal hope of evangelical Christians. The faith we as Bible-believing evangelicals preach, teach, and view as spiritually vital and life-changing (and would even give up our lives for) isn't about *good ideas* for today's world; neither is it about adaptable religious practices and doctrine that can be amended for the sake of political correctness and social acceptability.

The faith of all Bible-believing Christians rests upon and centres around a Risen Saviour. We don't believe in keeping our image of Jesus as One who never got out of the manger. We certainly don't believe the best image of Him is the one picturing His crucifixion, either, for that was not the *end* of Him. We believe He was raised from the dead and has gone back into Heaven, from whence He will return once again. We believe, as evangelicals, that the pre-incarnate Christ (as the third Person of the Trinity) came down off His glorious throne in Heaven to this earth in the flesh as Jesus Christ (God with us) in order to seek and save a spiritually lost humanity and has left a body of people (the Church) to do the same through His name and power.

Part of what it means to be "evangelical" is to keep the theological hand-in-glove messages of Christ-crucified and Christ-Risen urgent and fresh in our preaching and everyday witness. The spiritual efficacy of both the crucifixion and Resurrection of Jesus not only changes lives; it's what secures "eternal life" for all those who would come to the Lord. A world in need of God's grace and mercy in Christ must see consistent attractive spiritual fruit from our belief in Who Jesus Christ is if they're ever going to give Him a piece of their time, let alone all of their hearts! It may take seeking a personal revival in our own lives as disciples of Jesus who have been called to make *other* disciples for that specific burden to spread up into an evangelistic inferno within us once again. After all, the only reason the Church still inhabits the world is because our work of evangelism is not completed as yet (see Matthew 24:14). No matter how increasingly our culture sneers and gnashes at the biblical message of Christianity, God's people must continue to relate to, serve, and pray for our sphere of influence as evangelizers of the gospel's "Good News."

Despite these noble challenges, evangelicals have become fodder for icy, insidious, ridicule, and jagged-edged personal insult. For many people, when they hear the word *"evangelical"* they immediately think: fundamentalism, legalism, the Religious right, the Christian coalition, and other negatively laced connotations and labels. Those of us who are evangelical in our expression of the Christian faith are being told that *we* are what's wrong with society today; we're intolerant, narrow-minded, prehistoric, and homophobic. As evidenced by comments continuously being made within television network commentary and the realm of social media, there are those who just seem to get their "jollies" from staking out and jumping on any sound bite that reeks as remotely *judgmental* coming from recognized evangelical figures within the public eye.

We must concede (as pointed out in the previous chapter) that sometimes evangelical Christians (and God's people in general) are their own worst enemies. Like anyone else we can act and speak like boneheaded magnets that attract base kinds of insults and character assassination on account of our own lack of biblical scruples and deficit in spiritual maturity.

I often find myself having to skip over certain comments in the editorial sections of anti-Church, anti-Christian news publications these days as well as those posted on the Internet from the progressively left populace. It's not hard to sleuth out how demonized evangelicals have actually become in our increasingly secularized culture whenever they weigh in on any given social issue of our day.

It grieves me to read of the rather blunt and over-the-top disrespect many people have for evangelical Christians, charging us with being too caught up in the *Leave It to Beaver* era and thus totally out of touch with the realities of the twenty-first century. Though that may be true of *some* evangelicals, it doesn't make traditional Christian values wrong. Wasn't our world a much less socially complicated and problematic place when the best of traditional Judeo-Christian values were uncontested as the standard for living life? Yet I'm often appalled anew by what I read on newsstands, in bookstores, and on the Internet that appears to be a brave piercing hatred of the Church, newly contorted views of spirituality, and out-and-out blasphemy directed towards God. If we're familiar with our New Testament, however, we shouldn't be at all surprised by this.

Paul's ominous words of warning in some of his letters to the early Church serve as a modern-day "heads-up" for us as they relate to the state of the "last" days world (the time in which we presently live). Even if the apostle had one eye specifically on his time, his prophecies nonetheless are as relevant today as they were to his first century audience. Paul wrote that those who would inhabit the earth in the end-times would be demonstratively "proud, abusive...unholy... brutal" and even "treacherous" (2 Timothy 3:1–4).

I believe we can all agree that not only has Paul's prophecy materialized but the reality of it is now permeating and filling world governments, our educational system, and our courts, at a great rate and with greater spiritual consequences. With a mission field like this facing us who are evangelical Christians, sometimes it's too easy to hang the head in despair of how people can possibly come to know Jesus Christ today. As a result, numerous Christians in the world may end up not only thinking it but actually living out the attitude that wonders why they should even bother attempting to "preach Christ."

As worldwide persecution of Christians begins to swell beyond the point of what it already has, the test of our commitment to evangelize as the Church will truly be put to a harsh test. Will we continue to live as a commissioned people with an unquenchable burden to communicate the love of Christ to the spiritually lost? Or will we sit on the gospel in the hopes that it will somehow hatch and give birth to the salvation of souls without our direct (and expected) agency? The Father can certainly work to bring people to His Son without us, but He chooses to work *with* us and *through* us as well!

Evangelicals (as well as other branches of the Christian Church) purport that a passage such as John 14:6 is absolute truth—for all times, nations, and people— and that all other claims to the contrary are false and deceptive, persecution be darned! Evangelicals believe (and rightly so) the Bible's teaching that faith really is an eternal life-and-death matter!

However, for many people (including a great number of Christians) the issue of "faith" is a deeply private matter. The question is: *should* it be?

Some believers feel the best kind of Christian to be is the one who says little and who just lives the way *Christ* did. Sometimes you hear an unsaved person say such things as: "I know a person who is a good Christian, and they have a strong faith. But they don't feel they have to talk about it." Should we resolve, then, that

that is the highest form of Christianity? Should we adopt the old St. Francis of Assisi quote, "At all times preach the gospel; if necessary, use words"?

WHY BOTHER WITH EVANGELIZING?
If sharing our faith in Jesus Christ as "evangelicals" is such a controversial issue today and if we're going to face hardship over it, should we evangelize at all?

I want to suggest that there are good reasons for telling others about Jesus Christ. First, it's *commanded* of us by Jesus Himself.

If you were to do a study of the word *go* in the Bible, you will find that it is mentioned 1, 514 times. In the New Testament it is listed 233 times. In Matthew's Gospel the word *go* appears 54 times. Jesus in all four Gospels tells His followers to "Go!" He didn't mean for them to "get lost" (although He may have felt like that on some occasions). Rather, Jesus told His disciples, for instance, to "Go...to the lost sheep of Israel" (Matthew 10:6). He also told them to "Go... and invite...anyone you find" (Matthew 22:9) and to "Go back and report to John what you hear and see" (Matthew 11:4). Ultimately, Jesus commissioned His twelve disciples to "Go into all the world" to make *disciples of* the nations (Mark 16:15).

Secondly, as evangelicals we should tell people about Jesus because they *desperately need to hear the good news about Him.*

We tell people for instance about sales we see in stores. For an example, we might tell someone that Wal-Mart has lowered their prices on yard pools. (I don't know this for sure, so don't run out!) If we were in a desert place completely surrounded by sand and we happened to stumble upon an oasis, it would be terrible of us not to tell others wandering around with the hot sun beating down on them about the good news that we have found a watering hole!

The Bible tells us that Jesus is the only One who can satisfy the thirst of the human heart and soul. It's not a product or a formula we need (we've been there and done that); it's not "more of this" or "more of that" that we need either. The Bible says we need a *person;* we need an object of faith: God's Son, Jesus Christ. We all want our needs in life met; our hungers fed, our itches scratched, and our parched ambitions hydrated. We're always pushing the limits in order to find self-satisfaction, only to find that it's elusive.

Sometimes desperate people get way off course and fill the potholes of emotional and physical need by inappropriate and even excessive means. Sadly, many people who chase after such vices end up finding that the very outlets they thought would satisfy their deepest cravings in life left them utterly *unsatisfied* and further disillusioned with life. Jesus Christ is the only One who can spiritually ground what we perceive as our life-needs and the only One who can truly satisfy the core longings of our intricately fragile lives.

Thirdly, evangelicals need to share about Christ *because we ourselves have been touched by the good news about Him.*

Jesus will always make a difference in our lives. God's chief aim, after all, is to redeem us! This ought to float the boat of our desire as evangelical Christians to pass on that message. For some of us, when we experienced the birth of our first child, job number one was to pick up the phone and tell somebody! The night my daughter Cassidy was born, I remember wanting to call just about everybody I could think of (regardless of time zones)! The thing about news is that it tends to travel with record-breaking speed. Some people (we usually call them gossips) want to be the first person to tell others about something they found out, even if the information is classified and hasn't been clarified. However, knowing the good news about the truth of our great Saviour *should* motivate us to put a voice to our faith.

I'm not suggesting that bringing Christianity and Jesus to the lunch tables and water coolers of our workplaces is easy, or even wise. We need wisdom to discern if we're among pearl-chomping swine or not. Raising spiritual issues and discussing biblical content can be potentially hazardous to our relationships with those we spend eight or more hours a day with. Any encounter we may have with non-believing people in which we choose not to hide our faith-light "under a bushel" possesses a unique element and level of discomfort and social risk. In fact, the thought of letting their spiritual "cat" out of the proverbial "bag" in talking about Jesus turns some Christians into spiritual statues *(they become paralyzed).*

On the other side of the spectrum, some Christians are so "on fire" for God that they want to tell everybody about it; they don't want to miss a single opportunity. Some evangelicals I know make a habit of going spiritually overboard whenever they witness for Christ. They're so concerned for people's sin and their souls that they end up speeding past the yellow light of sensitivity on their way to hitting a brick wall of resistance. The old saying is that if we charge around with a Bible like "a bull in a china shop," someone may not get saved, but people may very well get hurt, in the process.

Sometimes, Christians just don't know how to get that spiritual "foot" in the door. It's hard for some evangelicals especially to form relationships with the unsaved because of an underlying guilt in doing so; like they're "setting people up" so that they can "lead them to the Lord."

When we read accounts about Jesus we see how a lot of people actually *wanted* to be around Him. Jesus attracted others to Himself simply because He was refreshing. The Lord didn't run around with a rolled up section of the Torah, smacking people on their heads, giving them a rabbinic "what-for." He wasn't what I would call a microwaving evangelist, either, who pressed hard for salvation decisions. Incredibly, Jesus didn't even come across overtly religious or spiritually pushy! He simply served people. When the Lord found a willing heart, spotted a searching soul, or noticed a crack of a door's opening to minister to someone and impart something of spiritual truth, the Saviour took advantage of it.

Just as Jesus did, those of us who are evangelical Christians also need to care about the whole person, not just the spiritual aspect. We should want to befriend unsaved people because they need a friend like us, and not *just* because we have *another* friend (Jesus) we want to introduce them to. The bottom line is that if we're doing things Jesus' way, we'll help people to see *the Way* that much more!

It's always God's responsibility to convict people of spiritual truth, because only He *can*. We have another responsibility: to be faithful in ministering to non-believing people *by* the truth. We are mere witnesses for Christ (persuaders); we have no power beyond that. The apostle Paul made this point very clear when he stated, "Since, then, we know what it is to fear the Lord, we try to persuade men" (2 Corinthians 5:11).

A missionary pastor I once heard speak told of some despised but very brave lepers in India who would daily line themselves up in the marketplace, just far enough from people to persuade the unsaved to turn to the Lord. "We may have leprosy," they'd cry out, "but all of you have a worse leprosy…Repent and come to Jesus!"

It's one thing to proclaim Jesus; it's another thing to hold out a changed and empowered life (despite circumstances) as a case study for people. Suffering lepers may be the last people we'd expect to be praising God openly, but they're also the most convincing, wouldn't you think?

Evangelicals must aim high but shoot low when pointing to examples of how God can change a life by putting more emphasis on the merits of how one is inwardly transformed by the presence of Christ in their lives than externally made over. Most people I know who've come to know the Lord still have difficult circumstances dogging them. On the outside things look untouched by God, yet it's how they choose to *handle* their circumstances that really hits the mark and testifies to the glory of God.

Ode to the Task of Shiny, Happy "Good News" People

The greatest advertisement for the gospel, then, is what I call a life that's been "gospelized." If evangelicals had more of a reputation for being radically changed people than annoyingly *strange* people, imagine how much more those who are spiritually lost would have to take us seriously. Wouldn't it be great if our Christian lives actually functioned more like spiritually irresistible highways to Heaven, as opposed to byways that take the unsaved off and away from the narrow road that leads to the Saviour!

Shouldn't those who are spiritually lost be more intrigued by the uniqueness of our worldview than find it so repugnant, dismissing it so quickly? That being said, though, I wonder sometimes if the world today only wants to see that which is plain and uninspiring and even ugly in Bible-believing Christians. It's like asking what scenario is worse: to possess an incredible beauty of face and yet be invisible to onlookers or to be extremely unattractive and yet be unable to avoid onlooking eyes that despise our mug? In other words, as the Church it's hard to win with the world sometimes. We're conveniently ignored as often as we're centred out. When we do something profoundly good, the world seems desensitized and almost oblivious to it by virtue of its expectations of us. When we as Christians mess up, however, the world goes out of its way to tell us we're horrible "hypocrites."

Whenever Christians truly live like Jesus by obeying the Great Commission as well as the Great Commandment, such a prospect can spiritually inspire a watching world; it can also be a demonstration of godliness too ultra-convicting for many in our world to consider internalizing. The world will always be more appreciative of biblical character if it's accompanied by cultural sensitivity. Yet running into spiritually repulsive evangelicals who give the impression that they're actually programmed sermons and theological libraries all rolled up in a human body will do no service to the person who really just needs to see Jesus in us.

Despite the stark evangelistic challenges inherent within our religiously pluralistic society, our "great" commission must always supersede our comfort and complacency as Christians. We're to be shiny, happy, "good news" people who authentically speak into a harried and spooked culture with the truth and eternal relevance of Jesus Christ, as well as with the Holy Spirit at our backs!

In light of the cultural realities swirling around us in these last days, where the lost seemed to be getting even *more* lost, the Church of Jesus Christ should be lifting their voices in harmonized unison: "O Lord, revive Your Church so that we may truly be the people You want us to be and do what we believe You are calling us to do!"

CHAPTER 18

MUTED DISCIPLES AND THE SCREAMING SOCIAL MENAGERIE
A Revived Spiritual Voice in Culture

When the Church is absolutely different from the world, she invariably attracts it. It is then that the world is made to listen to her message, though it may hate it at first.[61]

I came across an article in a major news publication with the headline "A Snapshot of Modern Screaming Times." The article expressed how the eerily dramatic and traumatic looking 1895 painting *The Scream* by Edvard Munch mirrors the social angst of our time. The columnist writes,

> We love art because it takes life and reflects it back, in this case flinging it in our faces…We are embarking on an era of austerity, much of it imposed by a wrong-headed ideology that at least in Europe will end in blood, and we'll be living on biscuits and sawdust. We fear for our children, we are worried about money…and our own government appears to dislike us. We are all quietly screaming.[62]

If you're familiar with the image of Munch's *Scream,* you'll recall how with a swirly, swooping brush technique, using a spectrum of colours, the artist painted an abstract looking man on a bridge with his hands held up to his ears while his "O" shaped mouth, is, well, screaming.

When we look outside our front doors we don't seem to see "Mr. Rogers' neighbourhood" anymore; neither can we spot the familiarities and predictability of the Wizard of Oz's "Kansas." Though we may not hear packs of people literally screaming around us, the reality is, many well-intentioned people have seen any thoughts or hopes they might've had of experiencing the "good life" sail away from them on a boat of eternal illusion. The screams of society's downtrodden echo in various forms, and just because we might not hear them doesn't mean they're not there.

Take for instance the ebbing away of the institution (and sacredness) of marriage. Today, death is not what is causing the majority of married people to part ways with their spouses.

I was taken aback recently (though perhaps I shouldn't have been) at seeing a report in the paper announcing the divorces of two couples. One celebrity couple called it quits after just one year of a marriage, which apparently fizzled rather rapidly. However, the other couple in the report were divorcing after *seventy-seven* years of marriage (the husband was ninety-nine, his wife, ninety-seven)!

News headlines reflect that there's an unprecedented global lack of confidence in the times. Everything from the job market to family and social concerns to political drama seems brittle and about to fall apart at any minute. We don't trust people as easily as we used to in our society; our acceptance of hardship ever dipping, our suspicions ever mounting. Our world really is a menagerie of screaming social concerns and debilitating frustrations.

We're wary of white collars and blue collars alike; we're wary of our leaders and the phoniness, cronyism and entitlements that fuel our elections and government policies; we're wary of those whose hands are held out and empty as much as we're wary of those who have plenty; we're wary of those whom we need to help and wary of those who are supposed to be helping *us;* we're wary of our food and we're wary of our freedoms.

We're fed up and sick to death of greedy, heartless financiers (as seen by the recent "Occupy" movement) who seem to have abandoned common-sense principles and brought us nearer to the cliff of the unthinkable: another era of great depression and perhaps worse. We are fatigued over all the moral relativism that is slowly turning us into a society that will lack a conscience.

According to a national 2009 survey of nearly 1,000 doctors conducted by the Massachusetts General Hospital, many physicians don't adhere to the standards of medical societies and accreditation groups. These groups have long required doctors to be open and honest with their patients. However, the results of the survey showed that nearly one-fifth of doctors said that they hadn't fully disclosed their mistakes over the past year in order to avoid a lawsuit.[63] The survey confirms our society's growing distrust of all things related to big-business, profit-driven entities, professionals, and sadly, of people in general.

As we look out at our world we can indeed see the figure in Edvard Munch's painting indelibly fixed on it; it's the spitting image of the times in which we live. There is so much unrest and angst all around us, so much restless screaming going on in the world.

Most of us see ourselves as the little guy who hopes the bigger boy on the block will be good to us. All this to state the obvious: our world is in dire need of God's help. It's funny how we'll go to well-meaning yet fallible doctors to assist us in maintaining our health but we'll overlook God in seeking to mend our torn and tattered world when it's *He* who created it and knows how to redeem it! Make no mistake, humankind, in some ways consciously, while in others subconsciously, is screaming out in panic for some "jaws of life" to extract it from the perilous spiral it's in.

THE SCREAM IS REAL
Whenever I think of the current state of the world, Paul's words in Romans 8 come to mind. "For the creation was subjected to frustration, not by its own choice, but by the will of the one who subjected it, in hope that the creation itself will be liberated from its bondage to decay and brought into the glorious freedom of the children of God" (Romans 8:20–21).

The Church is supposed to be a visible, audible redemptive force that shouts hope back over the screams of its hurting society. But sometimes it seems like there's nary a whisper coming from the house of God (the Church) to counsel and bind up the ills and wounds of the world. I've always wondered, for example, why it took someone like Bob Geldof to organize an unprecedented and grandiose event like the July 1985 *Live Aid* concerts to raise funds for world poverty. Where were the visionaries, social-gospel advocates, and rising ministry "stars" of Christ's Church at the time to spearhead an event of a similar nature?

It sometimes seems like the Church has become more reactionary and copycat-ish on the world's stage than original, pioneering, and proactive. Our scared and screaming world may be missing out on more of a fuller gospel response from Christians (the promise of the dawning of a new day yet to come) on account of God's people having become too spiritually uninspired, in-grown and consequently unconscious to its mandate: to be like voices "calling in the desert." No republic or culture has ever been able to sustain morality and righteousness without the existence *(and voice)* of biblical religion.

As these "last days" wind down and ultimately lead to the cessation of the Church age, any ministry opportunities that present themselves to God's people must be met by putting the Church's resources and efforts where our Lord's burdens are. Being disciples in spiritually dirty and dangerous times requires that we get over our addiction to institutionalizing and commercializing ourselves.

Jesus expects us, as the people of God, to be enough of a socially conscious heavenly noise that our collective spiritually preserving voice will rise above the noise pollution of our society's blaring fears and be heard. However, the Church, in many ways, is seemingly being drowned out and even muted by the obstinate rebelliousness and granite-like indifference of a world gone spiritually spastic.

AN INTENTIONALLY MUTED CHURCH OR INTENTIONALLY QUIET CHRISTIANS?

Sometimes our Christian voice is muted because the world doesn't want to listen. Gone is the halcyon era of a Christianity that was believed to have the inscrutable power to inform and transform our lives for the spiritual better.

The increase of teen suicides as a result of bullying in our schools has become a focal point for governing officials and law makers. Unfortunately, faith-based groups (the Church, as well as other Christian organizations) are given very little consideration as a remediable tool or are discarded from the conversation altogether. A heart-change is needed in order for students who often compensate for low self-esteem issues and even deep inner pain and fear to come out of their bondage of dominating others. Yet despite all the spiritual and moral rot needing to be addressed and combated within our society, Christians and the Church as a whole are largely viewed as judgmental and discriminatory. They are therefore overlooked and even muted in their relevance and usefulness to their culture.

Another case in point: here in Canada, one of our members of Parliament has asked Parliament to debate the issue as to whether a child in the womb should be considered a human being or not. It would appear, however, that pro-choice advocates are refusing to discuss the subject in an organized and mature way. MP Stephen Woodworth, citing the fact that "Canadian law provides no human rights protection whatsoever for children before the moment of complete birth," called for a "respectful dialogue" within government.[64] His motion was defeated, 203–91.

At least there's *some* light shining on this controversially dense and uber-delicate subject that many in our world would rather see put in a room of silence with the door shut tight and the lights turned out. The Church seems to hit the proverbial "glass ceiling" on these types of sensitive social issues. We've made great strides and have come a long way, but we can always do so much more.

At the same time, the muting of the Church's influential voice within the context of our screaming society may also be a case of Christians choosing not to speak up, even failing to present a united front. Quite often there is not enough of a verbal protest and collective burden amongst God's people surfacing at the times it should. Oftentimes the social issues that matter to God are defended by scads of splintered voices within the Church instead of an army of God in full-volume going on the offensive.

Then there are times when even one seemingly inconsequential voice for God can be too loud for a world oriented away from Him to tolerate.

Just ask a certain TV and radio personality on a Toronto sports station (a devout Catholic) who stated on Twitter that he "completely and wholeheartedly" supported "the traditional and true meaning of marriage." The radio host said he was simply responding in kind to a certain hockey agent's comments on Twitter who had also publically taken a stand against same-sex marriage. The next day the radio host was fired, even though, according to part 1 of the Canadian Charter of Rights and Freedoms, expressing one's religious beliefs and opinions is not a crime. To sum it all up, an individual who took a stand for what he believed was truth suddenly lost his job.

Christians are often treated as though they should crawl back to their saintly hovels and never reappear again! In fact, the legal threats of many socially progressive lobbyist groups are very real; they're not the paper tigers we in the Church make them out to be. Their rhetoric can give way to the sharp bite of legislation on any social level. In fact, those who purport socially liberal and politically correct agendas within society can roar enough to cause even the most well-intended of the righteous to stand down and be ushered out of the public forum (in short, *muted*).

Recently, the Supreme Court of Canada, in a 9–0 ruling, rejected a case that claimed the province of Quebec's controversial school course requiring students to learn the basic tenets of other religions was a violation of freedom of religion. The court decided that keeping a child from learning about other religious belief systems "amounts to a rejection of the multicultural reality of Canadian society."[65] I found it disappointing and sad that the case was brought forward not by a hefty group of displeased Christians or even by a certain denomination but by one Quebec couple who wasn't comfortable with their young children being exposed to the potentially confusing and conflicting spiritual details inherent within other religious faiths. The parents felt that their freedom to exclusively teach their children their own religious values was being encroached upon, even if the required school course wouldn't rise to the levels of actually indoctrinating children. The question remains, however, as to where more of an objection was in terms of representation from the Church.

Why, as Christianity is being pushed to the thin margins of culture, are we as the Church not pressing more to create a Christian option (e.g., after-school clubs, open events) in our schools? Why shouldn't traditional biblical values and the social benefits of them be allowed to make a comeback in our educational system? Besides, a vast number of people in Canada still consider themselves "Christians" of some flavour.

Why must Christian students be forced to learn how other cultures express worship to the God of their understanding when any encouragement to express their own faith (in the same environment) has all but flat-lined? Doesn't this sound even a smidgen like a bold-faced double standard? Is it a case of the Christian faith being pushed down and levelled off to match the merits of other faiths so as to not "offend"? Or is our society slowly but intentionally running around muzzling anything that barks like Christianity?

Don't hear me wrong. I am not advocating that we establish a "Christian society" by force, forgetting that Christ and His message thrived in the first century, not through political manipulation, but through Spirit-filled witness and ministry. Too often, however, the Church appears to be spiritually zigging when it ought to be zagging, ebbing when it ought to be flowing, and seemingly muted at a socially opportune moment when it ought to be heard. During the Reformation era of the Church, Protestants were often too preoccupied with the distracting exercises of self-preservation and theological instruction to get involved in distinct forms of social action. We seem to have a similar problem in the Church today! What will it take for us to come out of our churchy closets more and to discover our spiritual voices and their eternal capacity to affect righteous change in our culture?

NEEDED: AUDIBLY AUDACIOUS CHRISTIANS!
Throughout history, revivals in the Church have prompted a kind of audacious faith in God's people that launched a brave voice for biblical consciousness in society. Could it be that we need the powerful spiritual fruit of revivals to happen today in the hearts and assemblies of Christians so we can do likewise? The sirens of flawed secular ideologies and values screaming out in these end-times simply

cannot be allowed to duct tape the mouths of God's children, who are to offer up biblical choruses of healing as a response to the world's attempt to redeem the day.

The problem is that we as believers (more so in the West) have become rather acclimated to a Christian culture and lifestyle that keeps us comfortably walled-in. Consequently, we can develop tone-deafness towards the pitch of cries coming from people all around us who don't have the hope of Jesus implanted in their lives. We can become socially aloof and indifferent to taking action when our predictable spiritual life and sterilized Christianity keeps us bottled up in its clinical contentment.

If we become evangelistically dull as a Church, we will most certainly lose our sense of urgency and God's timing to speak up for Him. Staying cocooned in the spiritually numbing confines of our Christian home-base will only further feed our fear of dipping our collective toes in the murky waters of culture (something Jesus desires we do in order to be where He desires us to be). We can wait too long to hold the hand of our world's pain and share our faith with a world blind to the kind of cure it needs.

An uninspired, indifferent, and inward Church of Jesus Christ is one that has gone from being prayerfully able and strategically mobilized to being muted and invariably invisible evangelistically. There can be no other explanation for this occurrence than to point the necessary finger at the imperative need for God's people globally to be revived and spiritually renewed in its heart for the call of Christ.

We are living *(and witnessing)* in a culture that markets the ever-reinvented fragrance of spiritual relativity. In spite of this reality, one's freedom of religion still carries the potential for some influential grip in society. We who are in the North American Church will not win every argument we purport in terms of biblical truth; in all likelihood, we won't lose our lives for it either.

That being said, Christians may still invite pernicious criticism and acrimonious insults from various social "watchdogs" who chase after everything they deem discriminatory coming from the mouths of God's people.

Despite these surging realities surrounding Christians today, our secular culture still doesn't seem to know what's good for it. Any anti-biblical sentiments and anti-Christian ideals and protestations coming from a chippy society must be treated tactfully yet assertively on the part of God's people. The world still needs a steady streaming spiritually counter-balancing voice of biblical accountability and truth as a push-back.

This is why I appreciate the Roman Catholic Church's leadership in their biblical treatment of certain social issues. Despite the fact that the Catholic Church is largely perceived as being morally challenged and therefore neutralized as a spiritual authority due to the numerous sexual abuse scandals amongst its clergy, who could argue against the fact that they are still the predominant "Christian" voice of biblical accountability in our world today?

In fact, the Vatican has once again spoken out against the "powerful political and cultural currents" that are seeking to legalize gay marriage in the United States. Pope Benedict XVI weighed in on the issue by publically opposing homosexual marriage. The pontiff was quoted as saying, "Sexual differences cannot be dismissed as irrelevant to the definition of marriage…[traditional] marriage and the family has to be defended from every possible misrepresentation of their true nature."[66]

The Roman Catholic Church correctly teaches that while homosexual tendencies and temptations are *not* sinful in and of themselves, acts of homosexuality are, and that the traditional family of a mother and father is still the best environment for children to grow up in.

Where are the big name movers and shakers in the evangelical Church of Jesus Christ today who are willing to put their faith and ministries on the secular shooting-line, as it were, for the sake of defending the biblical worldview in the secular realm? Too many of our Christian books are about self-help or leadership-help; not enough of them are about helping our society to see (through the bifocals of an uncompromising gospel of Christ) how thoroughly infirm it really is.

We as the Church can't just kick the can of social action, especially as it involves defending biblical truth, down the road for a future generation of disciples, hoping they'll be more up to the task and the world more open to their message. The Bible teaches God's people to both defend and contend for the faith (see Philippians 1:16; Jude 1:3). A viable future witness for Jesus in our world (no matter how much longer we have until He returns) depends on our faithful execution of the Great Commission in the here and now!

THE RISKY BUSINESS OF SPEAKING UP (AND OUT) FOR TRUTH
Whenever I read biblical accounts of people who took righteous stands for truth, I'm reminded of how profoundly harrowing such a proposition is.

I personally love the book of Esther in the Old Testament because the heroine appears to have been not only a no-nonsense woman of faith but a risk-taker!

We'd all like to be more like her, wouldn't we? Just like us today, Esther knew full well that there were elements within her society that sought to destroy life, purport injustice, and covet power.

For a biblical book that doesn't actually have the word *God* written in it, the book of Esther provides one of the greatest examples of how God sovereignly positions His people to not only speak justice into the world but to preserve life. Esther, by all accounts, was a dynamic woman of God who put actions of faith ahead of spiritual rhetoric. She'd be classified as a rarity today in how she risked it all for her people (Israel). Esther could do so because she believed in the power and goodness of her God to rescue them.

The account of Esther begins in 483 BC, some thirty-seven years before Nehemiah returned to Jerusalem to rebuild the city walls. By this point some Jews were still in exile and held captive under the rule of King Xerxes of Persia, whose army defeated the Babylonians, thus becoming the superpower of the day.

God's chosen person (Esther) to deliver His people from certain annihilation (as a result of a sinister plot cooked up by Haman) gets a hearing with the king. There at his throne Esther clarifies to Xerxes that it was actually her cousin, Mordecai (a Jew), who found out about a plot to kill the king, which saved his life. In the wake of Esther's revelation, Xerxes, in a twist of irony, enlists, of all people, Haman to robe Mordecai and lead him around town in a carriage in order to honour him publicly. Then, at a banquet Esther gives (with hidden motives) for Haman and the king, she notifies Xerxes of Haman's plot to have all the Jews in his kingdom killed, of which the king's life-saver, Mordecai, was one. Indignant, the Persian king blows his regal top and decides to have Haman hanged on the very gallows that Haman himself had built to put his enemy Mordecai to death.

In a very real sense, we who are God's people today are twenty-first century versions of the fifth century BC Esther. And our world is crying out and pleading for rescue today, for justice, liberty, peace, and harmony. The Church of Jesus Christ has been elected by Him to be spiritual trailblazers and risk-takers in bringing about His eternal Kingdom of peace and righteousness on earth whereby a weary humanity can escape into it.

If you are a Christian, God has given you a ministry; you have official Heaven-sanctioned credentials (not to mention *a calling*) to serve God. Each individual believer makes up the greater spiritual anatomy of Christ's "Body" (the Church) and plays a special, required, and unique role *in* that Body.

People are perishing eternally without Jesus; it's a prospect most evangelical Christians grasp without question. However, taking our role as ambassadors for Christ seriously enough to speak gospel truth into our noisy and spiritually mangled society is a biblical expectation many believers today find too unnerving a venture. Though there are indeed inherent risks involved with representing Jesus Christ to a fallen world, they are indispensable prerequisites of our discipleship.

Oftentimes it's rather plain to see that ministering in the Kingdom of God can be costly (spiritually, emotionally and physically). Any one of us who takes the "call of Christ" to heart realizes the Lord meant every word He spoke when referring to His commission to us: "I am sending you out like sheep among wolves" (Matthew 10:16). Our world is a spiritual jungle; we never know what dangers await us as we make our way through it, for Jesus' sake, with the gospel as our only means of protection and weapon. Our "commission" to minister for Jesus calls us to "take up" our "cross" (Matthew 16:24), to "count the cost" (Luke 14:28 NKJV) of what it means to identify with a God whom our society wants to mute.

When Queen Esther made a decision to lay her life on the line in the hopes of saving her fellow Jews, she was alone and as vulnerable as a sheep amongst a den of wolves within King Xerxes' kingdom. Esther had opportunity to either speak into the screaming plots and ploys of Haman and others (who desired to wipe the Jewish people off the streets of Persia) or to sit on her voice as a muted instrument of God; either option would come with its topping of risk-related consequences.

Esther was in a precarious position, to say the least! The most inspirational line of the Old Testament book that bears her name is one that reflects her ultimate choice to risk her life in asking for a hearing with the king on behalf of her people: "I will go to the king, even though it is against the law. And if I perish, I perish" (Esther 4:16).

Have you ever pondered what you are willing to die for? Sure, all of us reading this would willingly die to save the lives of our loved ones. But here's the real question: are we willing to risk, willing to give up *everything*, including the very breathe we breath, for Jesus? Are you selfless enough, trusting enough, as a disciple of Jesus to bid adieu to your career, your house, to put certain acquaintances or friendships on hiatus? Are you flexible enough to let your comforts, privileges, or security go if an opportunity to do something life-changing and eternally altering were to fall on your lap as if dropped down from Heaven?

How big of an imposition would it seem if God specifically directed us to serve some need or crisis within our church family or community that could use our biblical worldview and gospel touch? Would we have the perspective that God was butting in the line of our complacency when we'd rather He overlook us? Would we feel bothered or blessed, perturbed or privileged?

I wonder if Esther initially battled such feelings as she contemplated walking the long carpet that led to the throne of Xerxes. Her response to the crisis within Persia had everything to do with her people's survival.

Spiritually revived and rekindled Christians who are awakened to see with wide-open eyes of faith opportunities for ministry in these last days will be internally mobilized to project healing truth straight into the macabre social upheaval screaming all around them. These are Christians who with the spirit of the prophet Isaiah will declare, if not enthusiastically, *decidedly,* "Here am I. Send me!" (Isaiah 6:8).

The Church sends missionaries into the heart of darkness for Christ, sends them to minister in spiritually and politically oppressed and dangerous continents where people are gasping for the breath of human significance and a better life. Many of God's people are willing to leave their homes and families for long periods of time; they give up a good North American standard of living to live and work in deserts, disease-infected primitive villages, and remote areas of the world; in some areas, Christians readily (and knowingly) put their lives on the line.

The Church goes into all the world putting their faith in action because they realize that if they didn't go people would die *without* salvation. The Lord holds the suffering planet He created in His sovereign, loving hands, and He empowers His people (the Church) to work through and be heard amidst it.

ARE WE ANSWERING OUR WORLD'S SCREAMS?

What exactly are you, as Joe or Jane Christian, doing today for the cause of Christ in your corner of the world? Are the screams of a petrified culture overdubbing your required response as a child of God? Which social issue crashing in upon and morally devastating our society are you praying about or actively ministering to? How far would you be willing to flex your faith as a disciple of Jesus facing an ever-nearing Rapture of the Church, to sacrifice more than what you may be accustomed to (with your time, talents, and treasures), for the furtherance of the Kingdom of God in your community?

A sports program on television showcased the unique extent to which a football fan was willing to sacrifice in order to see his team play live. At a time when tickets to see a sporting event were much more affordable and when the giving of one's blood was financially rewarded, a Green Bay Packers fan was willing to donate as much of his red stuff as possible in order to purchase season's tickets to all their home games at the fabled Lambeau Field. We might think that such a sacrifice is commendable; he gave the gift of life in terms of his blood, even if he profited by it in being able to see a little live pigskin being played!

When we think of sacrifices, however, our Lord should always be foremost in our hearts and minds. His ultimate sacrifice at Calvary and the blood that fell from His body until He died is symbolic of a new covenant God was making with us. That is, we are now His people (in Christ), and He is our God; Jesus died for us, we now live for Him in return. He's called us to live out a great *(compulsory)* Commission, not an *optional* one; neither is it a call that affords us the autonomy to be selective in our hearing of it. Rather, our Lord has spoken clearly and plainly that we as His disciples are to speak His life-changing, hope-springing words into the screaming social menagerie of our world, and not to settle with being drowned out (muted) by it!

Though we who know the Lord cannot possibly claim to be hearing-impaired when it comes to the gospel's call, we *could* honestly claim to have an impairment of another sort! Statistic after statistic shows we are more immoral and consequently more unholy as God's people today than we'd like to think. Church, we're in need of a heart-altering revival! We've seemingly dropped off sharply in our commitments to the Word of God (to the very heart of God Himself); as a result, we've nearly tanked in our burden for the cause of Christ! What will we have to respond with to a terrified world with nothing spiritually solid to hold on to if the current trend of a decreasing faithfulness to biblical principles and standards continues in the Church?

The late Christian writer Michael Spencer wrote with a prophetic undertone, "Within two generations, evangelicalism will be a house deserted of its occupants…massive majorities of evangelicals can't articulate the Gospel with any coherence."[67] Perhaps this could explain why *Newsweek* magazine's front cover headline for its 2009 Easter issue read "The Decline and Fall of Christian America."

In Europe, it appears that interests in secular culture have taken over a lot of people's attentiveness to religious things. The late Pope Paul II described Europe as embracing a "culture of death." Pope Benedict XVI followed that spiritual prognosis up by referring to the EU as a "desert of godlessness."[68] In Canada, though having an affiliation with a church still seems to be important to many people, roughly only 10 percent of people go to a church for a religious activity or an event once or twice a week.[69]

One thing that isn't dwindling down, however, is the many-headed (and increasingly sprouting) social concerns and needs of our time. Most of them involve some form of controversy, and all require a response from the people of God.

A few years ago I was invited by a Christian-based organization to participate in a peaceful demonstration. I was asked if I'd join others in holding up signs that communicated a biblically centred pro-life message. I didn't hesitate to say yes, mostly because I felt it was the right thing to do.

As I held up the sign I had chosen, I was thoroughly convinced that its message was a correct one, both morally and biblically, even if those who passed by me thought otherwise. It's hard to see a person's heart when all they're communicating is a cold message on a piece of cardboard.

I thought of all the preborn babies in their mothers' wombs who might never breathe the air of their birth days on earth. Respecting someone's "freedom of choice" doesn't mean that we should dissolve our own freedom and mandate as God's people to speak up about that choice; "life," in every respect, depends on it.

Roughly 50 million abortions have been performed in the United States since the ruling of Roe v. Wade. Abortions precipitated by a cultural preference for males in China and India have killed an estimated 163 million Asian females over the past few decades.[70] In countries such as these, endeavouring to be a righteous voice for life must seem like too small a spiritual punch to many Christians where the Church does not enjoy a privileged position in society.

However, nothing we do for the Lord is worthless and wasted; we always have to trust that an all-present, all-knowing, and all-powerful God will somehow work through our finite efforts. When our hearts as God's people are so spiritually workable that they become vessels for His burdens to dissolve into, our evangelistic hunger and resolve to clearly represent the person of Christ to the unsaved especially will intensify and give way to action.

SILENCE IN THE CHURCH IS NEVER GOLDEN!
Just as our world's ignorance of God's Word and its spiritual disregard for its own fallen nature won't save it, the spiritual complacency inhabiting God's people about the escalating darkness within the social issues of our day won't redeem it either. A revived Church not only becomes more cognizant about the destructive

effects of its own sin; it leads to humility and authenticity as a witness to a sin-soaked culture. The greatest sermon is not the one spoken as much as it is the one genuinely applied and lived out in the lives of Christians.

Rarely do the unsaved realize that *sin* (not their failures, mistakes, or wrong choices, necessarily) is the underlying spiritual culprit explaining why we sometimes hurt ourselves and others as human beings. In general, that's why we don't see waves of people turning from darkness and sin towards the Lord these days. The devil aces most of his attempts to blindfold the faculties of everyday people in order to prevent them from believing in the scope of their own spiritual fallenness. As a consequence, our world conveniently misdiagnosis sin, calling it wrongdoing instead. "We may be *this* and we may be *that*," the world says, "but we're not sinners." The fruit of this spiritual misdiagnosis is plaguing and destroying lives; it's the reason our culture so aptly resembles Edvard Munch's *Scream*.

It's into this arcade of wall-to-wall heartache of slaughtered hopes and deceptive and anemic spirituality that God thrusts His people and bids them to speak into. How humbling it is to be in a position, as Christ followers, to leave the thumbprint of our Lord on a life, a community, or on a nation that's been reduced to a shell of what God intended it to be.

The rewards we'll receive in Heaven for having rolled up our servant-sleeves in the present are gravy; it's the impact of seeing lives changed as a result of God working through our ministries *in this life* that should motivate us to serve Him. What's more worthwhile a burden as a Christian: to grieve and mourn over the shape of people's spiritual lives (or the spiritual landscape of a country) or to go beyond that in seeking the resources needed at the throne of God to do something about it? Many heroes in the hallowed halls of biblical faith experienced both.

Nehemiah was one such person. Author Alan Redpath says, "You can never lighten a burden unless you have felt the pressure of it in your own soul… Nehemiah was called to build a wall, but first he had to weep over its ruins." Nehemiah knew that a burden alone never gets one very far. Tears are sometimes *not* enough! The welfare of his homeland (Jerusalem) could only be improved if he and his fellow Israelites were convicted that they needed all the spiritual resources they could glean from God (which included repentance and the longing for spiritual renewal) in order for the construction of the city's walls and the reinstitution of the nation and its worship in the land to be successful.

Sometimes God brings about an encounter, a burden, or a faith-sized ministry possibility He wants us to specifically serve. Some of those opportunities blare at us; sometimes they're more subtle and we need to decide what, if anything we are going to do with them. If we believe in God-appointed moments of ministry, we should accept the fact that He sovereignly puts His people in certain places at spiritually advantageous times where they can not only become aware of a need but be in a good position to do something *about* that need.

Some ministry opportunities that swerve into the lanes of our hurried lives, though they're obvious enough, don't appear to be all that crucial to be met immediately. However, we can never tell when perhaps our sacrifice of time and words could have made a difference (even an eternal one).

In his autobiography *Just As I Am,* Billy Graham recalled a time when he was talking with President John F. Kennedy at a national prayer breakfast in 1963. Graham had the flu, and after a short walk with Kennedy, he wanted to return to his hotel. The president seemed troubled and wanted Graham to ride back to the White House with him and chat further. Graham told the president that he had a fever, was weak, and wanted to rest, and that maybe it could wait for another time. On that note, Graham and the president decided to part ways. They would never meet again. Not long afterward, Kennedy was assassinated.

Graham would later say that the long look on the president's face, how he hesitated to say goodbye, and his request to talk further with Graham that day have haunted him. "What was on his mind? Should I have gone with him?" he's thought since. It was a moment and a need he could "never recover."[71]

Billy Graham's experience points to the reality that when God brings a life-sized need before us (even if we're concerned with our own affairs), we may be the only one God has tagged who'll be in the right position, at the right time, with the right voice, to speak into that inward yet screaming need.

As difficult a prospect it is to wrap our minds around, the greatest regrets we will have in Heaven may be the opportunities for ministry God presented us with that we met by either overlooking them or ignoring them. The world is screaming for help, and whether it aims to dismiss or muffle the voice of the Church or whether God's people choose to remain quiet when it comes to the social menagerie of problems and desperation all around us, silence on behalf of God's people isn't anywhere near golden.

CHAPTER 19

Tiny Seeds Are All We Need: Becoming Beacons of Ministry

A Revived Burden for Personal Evangelism

In the movie based on the Dr. Seuss children's tale *The Lorax*, there's a scene where a young boy, Ted Wiggins, is encouraged to seek out the reclusive "Once-ler," who happens to have the last remaining Truffala tree seed in his possession. The Once-ler's greed was responsible for depleting an entire forest of Truffala trees. Years before, the tufts of the trees were used by the then enterprising Once-ler to build his empire of manufacturing Thneed scarves. The twelve year old Ted goes on an eco-restoration trip and visits the Once-ler with an ulterior motive to try to impress a girl he took a shining to (Audrey), who wished to see a real Truffala tree. Ted promised Audrey he'd get a tree to plant in the segregated, artificial, walled-in town of Thneed-Ville, which had been without real trees for years and whose citizens were being manipulated into buying "fresh air" from one Mr. O'Hare.

As the Once-ler places the last existing seed in Ted's hands, he says to the young boy, "It's more than a seed (that you hold); it's what it can become." Near the end of the movie the townsfolk of Thneed-Ville give birth to euphoric song after years of disappointment as they come to realize that they could benefit from the value of having real trees as a part of their environment and cultural experience. "Let it grow! Let it grow! You can't reap what you don't sow!" they sing.

When we think about it, shouldn't that actually be *our* burden and rallying cry as Christians for a more beefed-up evangelistic effort to characterize the Church of Jesus Christ in these last days?

We want to reap a harvest of newborn believers, but that inevitably means we must actually *sow* the seeds of biblical truth in the hearts of the spiritually lost *first*. The question is, how many of us Christians are actively doing this on a consistent basis, or are even mindful that we should be? That the Western Church is faltering in the number of conversions within congregations doesn't change the fact that the Body of Christ is gifted and commissioned *to* grow! Though many Bible-believing, Bible-teaching, churches are excelling in their efforts of evangelism, many have either put that mandate on the back burner of their "mission statement" or altogether stopped preaching and practising personal and corporate outreach.

Reaching out to people with the gospel is not all we do as the Church, but it is a big part of *what* we do! Some Christians feel as though they only have a "tiny seed" to offer the world in terms of their evangelistic efforts, and yet in the words of the Once-ler, "It's all we really need!" Our measly seed of witness (whether it be truth said in love, a kind word, or a timely deed) is all we really need, because of *what it can become* in the lives of others around us who do not know Jesus as their Saviour.

If we even lead one person to the Lord in our lifetime, we will have multiplied our one seed! Some of us evangelicals are so influenced by the bulky expectations of other "more spiritual" believers around us that we have to swing for "the fences" in terms of sharing our faith and getting people to respond to the gospel and have to have large numbers of people praying for salvation in outreach events to justify our efforts and the money we've earmarked for evangelism in our church budget.

That being said, we *do* have an aim and a goal in our ministry as God's people: to *know* Christ and to *make Him known;* it's a responsibility that each and every believer in the Body of Christ has. It's plausible that if we don't reach out with the gospel today, the Church will be almost extinct within one generation. It doesn't help that developing a lifestyle of evangelism and letting our "light" shine into the lives of others around us is something that numerous Christians can be hesitant about.

It's normal perhaps for the child of God living in a postmodern, post-Christian age to feel that they might be scoffed at or won't really know what to say when they're trying to articulate their faith with people. More than ever before Christians have an audience (in the twenty-first century) that is entirely fascinated with the spiritual. However, even if we are living in a world more desirous of understanding the inner life than ever before, that doesn't necessarily mean it's a world more open than ever before to receiving the gospel of Jesus Christ! Nonetheless, there remains much spiritual territory to be taken for our Lord!

THE IMPORTANCE OF *PRAYER* EVANGELISM

One way in which we can reach out to our neighbours is known as prayer evangelism. It's through prayer that "outreach" to people with the gospel's message (even our hardened next-door neighbour) begins. It's as we pray for others that God, in turn, gives us more opportunities in their lives. In this way we become *beacons of ministry* that shine the love of Jesus into the lives of those who are estranged from God: a parent or sibling, a co-worker, or even a lifelong friend.

We can become beacons of ministry by asking God to allow our lives to be godly influences to those around us, and especially to those who are spiritually lost. We are to shine God's light into other people's lives, not for us to look good but in order to lead others to the Saviour! It's as we pray for people we are spiritually burdened for that God will pry open an avenue from which we can influence their lives.

Jesus showed His first disciples how this can work. In Luke 9 the Lord had already sent out the twelve disciples with instructions to evangelize communities they visited. In Luke 10, the Lord does the same with seventy-two others (an average to small-sized church!). He sends them out "two by two"; that's thirty-six groups of two people each who then went into towns (uninvited) to prepare the way for Jesus' coming to them. The Lord was sending "ambassadors" for Himself even then!

Note that these disciples weren't going to people who were necessarily religious. The objective for these double-manned clusters of evangelistic disciples was to go into these towns and villages in order to befriend entire households. In basic terms, their main task was to tell people about Jesus (all He was saying and doing) and encourage them to "believe the hype"! The evangelistic efforts of the disciples would be the matchboard from which the people of the villages could strike their spiritual curiosity on while paving the way for Jesus to eventually minister to them.

In a vastly similar way this is the kind of spiritual ground-tilling we are called to do in the lives of the unsaved.

How we do that is a question the Church has been trying to formulate, perfect, and even market. Could it be that we as Christians have complicated Jesus' instructions a bit too much? Have we made a pharisaical dinosaur of the

Great Commission by constructing extraneous rules and principles around it that only serve to intimidate us and broaden what was supposed to be a simple action plan for Christian evangelism?

How we accomplish the Church's "commission" of Matthew 28, I believe, is by copying what Jesus' disciples did. Sounds too easy and uninspiring, right? That's because it is that easy (but also inspiring). Jesus knew our problem would never be that there might be a shortage of people who need God, for the "harvest" of souls is always "plentiful"; the problem Jesus foresaw, even then, was a deficit in the number of willing "workers"; they'd be "few." When it comes to reaching people for Jesus we are simply to "Ask the Lord of the harvest…to send out workers into his harvest field" (Matthew 9:37–38).

As we read through the Gospels we might think that, a lot like today, there was very little interest in the things of God back in Jesus' time, for the Lord Himself met up against opposition to His own message quite frequently. Oftentimes Jesus found little faith in people, and the writers of the Gospels made sure we got the ensuing underlying evangelistic point.

On a wide scale, the kinds of response Jesus' ministry received from Israel's spiritual leaders He encountered were telling. The religious elite who thought they knew better let the Saviour know it with truculence and pugnacity. However, what we can't overlook was the response that came from whom you and I might call the "average Joe." They were the ones on the "lower rungs" of society who knew they needed God's help; even more, they innately grasped the truth that they needed a *Saviour*.

A good number of the common people (many of whom we would classify today as living in poverty) accepted Jesus and what He was teaching about the human condition and the Kingdom of God. Could this be why Jesus said "the harvest is plentiful"? It may seem at times, from our tainted and pessimistic western Christian vantage point, as though nobody wants to hear the gospel anymore. However, Jesus didn't want His disciples to be impressed or discouraged by what the world was saying. The Lord wanted His followers to listen to Him because only He knows the hearts of people. Consequently, they were to remain focused on making "disciples of all nations."

Though it's hard to penetrate our communities and culture as a whole, taking Jesus' words as a general truth means there's a "harvest" staring back at us every time we look out our front window. Despite all the resistance to the gospel within our culture today, ultimately I believe people want God's blessing in their lives. St. Augustine, one of the early fathers of the Church whose theology basically forged the doctrine of the Catholic Church, said these spiritually iconic words in the fourth century: "You have made us for yourself, O God—and our hearts are restless until they find their rest in you."

Jesus knew this to be true about people in His day. He knows that we were created for God; to be in communion with Him and to worship Him "in spirit and in truth." There are restless people all around us today who are seeking elusive answers to life's biggest problems in all the wrong places. God's people must be that light in the darkness (as the first disciples were to be) that helps searching men and women find their way to God. The very same need for spiritual illumination and clarity existed within people when the Lord Himself walked upon the earth.

Jesus sent His original disciples out "two by two," for He knew they were going amongst people who wouldn't exactly be overjoyed at their appearing. For that good reason none of the disciples were to go their evangelistic assignments alone. There were potentially pockets of hostility that they could've unknowingly walked right into; a reality that Christian missionaries face today in some regions around of the world. Jesus instructed His commissioned disciples as they went about their evangelistic travels to "not greet anyone on the road" (Luke 10:4). There would be an element of real danger involved in talking about Jesus for the first people ever to follow and minister for the Lord.

Nothing has really changed in that way either. A few thousand years later, Christians still face some reaction or challenge to their goodwill. Sometimes believers are taken advantage of (financially or physically); sometimes they're killed for their vulnerability and faithful witness. Whatever the circumstances, the devil knows when God's people are treading on his territory, so to speak.

I read of one Christian couple who felt a burden to go to a certain shopping mall that had the dubious reputation of attracting the most crime and calls to the police in the city in which it is situated. After some months a few young people caught on to what the Christian couple were up to and expressed to them that they had "beat them to it." The young people were actually praying that Satan would "curse each store" instead! As it turned out, after the Christmas season was over the praying couple found out that there was less criminal activity and overall disturbance reported by the officials of the mall! This occurrence made more than a few of the non-Christians "curious."[72]

The biblical truth in circumstances such as these where God's people endeavour to prayerfully create spiritual furrows in order to plant seeds of gospel truth in the hearts of people somehow alerts the devil in his relentless seeking to unearth those very seeds and lay waste to them. Christians can truly be encouraged and take to heart that greater is the Lord who is in us (God's people) than he (the devil) who is in the world (1 John 4:4). The great bout with evil in our world has already been won (by our victorious Saviour); it's the individual rounds that we as the people of God must presently fight against Satan in the power and Name of Jesus!

Though the danger in representing Jesus to their first century world was very real, it would not halt the Lord's redemptive agenda, not then, and not today.

The first thing the commissioned followers of Jesus were to do when they came to a town where they intended to stay was to bless the people *of* that town. Good reception or not, the followers were to begin by blessing people as they met them.

ASK GOD TO BLESS THOSE WHO DON'T KNOW HIM.
I used to walk with another fellow from a Christian organization through the town of Minden where our start-up team planted Highland Lakes Community Church. We were known as "Paul and Barnabas" (though I'm still not sure who was who)! We would walk through the town as often as we could together, and we'd greet people and pray for God to bless Minden. We were, in a very real sense, praying for God's favoured peace to be upon them so that the people of the town would see their need for the Saviour.

In Luke 10:5, Jesus said to the disciples, "When you enter a house, first say, 'Peace to this house.'" The word *peace* comes from the Hebrew word *shalom*. In the Greek language (which Luke wrote his Gospel in), "peace" is the word *eirene*, and it means "to bestow favour." We who desire to see revival hit the lives and homes of people in the towns and cities our churches minister in are to pray for God's blessing to be upon the people we meet and upon the town we are lights to, that they will be receptive to God's Word. In general, that's the evangelistic attitude and intention of heart we as Christians are to foster!

We may have complaints about the people in the communities where we live; we may have beefs in terms of our cities' or town's government officials, but we must *always* have a burden for their salvation!

We may not always feel like blessing the people we come into contact with during the course of our day (and we may not always remember to). However, when we *do* remember to utter a prayer of blessing, our simple petition could possibly make an eternal difference to someone's life! We all have neighbours, co-workers, and loved ones who are hurting or seeking spiritually, and we can take some time to pray for them as God leads us. There's always time to pray for a burden to be lifted or carried and for a need to be filled all for the glory of God.

This will be the heart's intention of those Christians who have a revived and renewed hunger for personal evangelism, that is, to see the unconvinced and unbelieving people around them not only as neighbours, friends, or acquaintances but also as potential followers of Christ and contributors and difference makers for the Kingdom of God on earth. We might be out walking the dog in the evening, and yet we can look around at the homes and just bless our neighbours in prayer. Sure, it might be a challenge if we don't have a good rapport or relationship with our neighbours. However, such a spiritual exercise might actually change our relations with someone on our block!

I heard a story about a guy who said that every time he saw a certain man walk by his home he could tell the man was moving his mouth; the guy even felt "good vibrations." Though what the man experienced whenever the praying Christian walked by could be interpreted as being a little weird, perhaps, we should praise God for such incremental advancements of the gospel. We could do far worse to people with our spirituality!

However, what do we do when our neighbour plays his stereo so loud that we are thoroughly annoyed? We could just go and yell at him. Or, we could go and ask him nicely to turn the volume button down, but that doesn't always work. What about prayer? Perhaps we could just pray for our inconsiderate neighbour to be miraculously moved to turn the music down. When it comes to praying for people we're upset with, it's not always easy to ask God to bless them, right? It can seem as hard a thing to do as picking up a hammer and voluntarily banging our big toes with it!

How about when your neighbour doesn't take care of their lawn, and as a result things such as crabgrass maddeningly begins to move in on your nicely coiffed lawn? We might think, "Why should I bless them while they go about destroying the look of my property?" Whatever the case may be with those whom we live in close contact with, we are to ask God to bring His peace into their hearts and lives; souls, after all, are more important than grass, or even noise pollution!

We need to make prayer for our neighbours a priority in our spiritual lives; we never know when they might be going through a crisis and when we may be tilling the soil of their hearts just enough for them to accept Jesus at some point. I've seen how revival and spiritual renewal can capture the hearts and lives of Christians, how it can implant within God's people a prayerful preoccupation for the mission field around them and for God to "heal their land" (2 Chronicles 7:14).

Simply, if we desire to see people we love and care for alongside us in Heaven one day, the best way we can show that love is to *pray* for them. It may be all they allow us to do for them spiritually, but it's the *best* thing we could do for them just the same. It may seem like too tiny a spiritual seed we're sowing in their lives, but it's a seed they *really* need, nonetheless.

However, there's another step in us becoming beacons of ministry as a revived and renewed Church. In addition to our prayers, true evangelism always seeks to make relationships with people who are spiritually lost. If the door is open for us to pursue connecting with someone we've been praying for, we need to walk in, quick!

FORM RELATIONSHIPS WITH THE SPIRITUALLY LOST
When it comes to personal evangelism, building relationships with those who do not have a personal relationship *with* Jesus is *king!* The Lord was clear in that it wasn't the healthy that required a doctor but the sick. It is the lives of those who need Jesus whom we as the Church need to touch especially. This can only happen when Christians literally "cross the room" and ask to dance with the spiritual needs and dishevelled lives of those around them who are not a part of their comfortable and buffeting posse of Christian friends, those who are on the outside of their Sunday huddles and who remain on the periphery of an eternity without Christ.

Relationships are everything to most people. Even though Jesus did many great *things* for people, He also cared deeply about forming *relationships* with those around Him. These days, more often than not, you have to have a relationship with someone before they are going to permit you to advise them.

Can you imagine meeting somebody at a party or a coffee shop for the first time and asking them, "How's your marriage going? Any spats lately? Are there any problems you want to talk about? You can trust me!" Such a conversation will likely never happen. Our lives are just too personal a thing to share with just anybody (even with the well-intentioned child of God).

The same is also true with evangelism.

Spirituality is a very *personal* issue to most people. Who among the unsaved and even the "seeking" crowd would be naturally adept and uninhibited at sharing their spiritual views on a drop of a dime?

We may need a relationship with someone who knows they have secured our trust first before they may tacitly or even fully allow us to hear them out on such things as religion and spiritual beliefs. The principle saying that *people don't care about how much you know until they know how much you care* is very applicable in matters pertaining to personal evangelism.

Who will really want to hear about what we have to say and consider it if there's no real relationship between us? Too often God's people undercut grace when sharing about Christ and as a result end up overshooting the mark of people's hearts where the Holy Spirit aims to land in convicting fashion. Sometimes Christians can be so abrupt with the gospel that even we in the Church get offended!

In our zeal we have to be careful of trying to deliver the goods of the gospel a trifle too soon for spiritually lost people to be ready to buy it. When we look through the Gospels it's absolutely amazing how much time the Lord spent in cultivating relationships. It's obvious how much time He spent just eating and drinking with people and nothing more. In fact, Jesus did it so often that He afforded His enemies the opportunity for accusing Him of being a "glutton and a drunkard" (Matthew 11:19), saying in effect, "All this guy does is hang out with losers!"

Jesus, of course, wasn't a glutton, and neither was He a drunkard. So why did He hang with the perceived dregs of His society?

What was Jesus, then? If He wasn't a partier with a weakness for rubbing shoulders with the undesirables of His day, just how do we explain His willingness to be around down-and-outers and even people of questionable character? In the most basic terms, His ministry shows us that the Lord was an evangelist, that He was simply and yet profoundly a lover of souls!

Jesus loved *people!* The Lord longed to spend meaningful time with those He came into contact with. He may not have been around for a long time, but He desired to make that time one of quality. It was in the relationships He made with people that they saw His true shepherd's heart for them. The opposite is also true, then. If we lack a true concern for the spiritually lost, chances are it will keep us from connecting with them on a deeper level and consequently from communicating the love *God* has for them. Knowing the heart of God for the lost is seeing the unsaved as He sees them.

It is imperative as Christians that we learn how to connect with people who naturally struggle to relate with our biblical worldview. Getting a better hold on where the unchurched "are at" in terms of their values and level of religious understanding (or lack thereof) is paramount for God's people to be able to press the "start" button towards influencing them by our faith. We need relationships *with* such people in order to do this!

I like how one young and perceptively "radical" Anglican clergyman in small-town Nova Scotia sought to relate to young people where he took on a less than packed-out parish to minister in. The young rector accomplished this by recording a popular rap song with his own religious twist to it and posting the revamped tune on YouTube. That, in concert with involving the young people of his parish in doing various forms of community service, led to the upstart prelate transforming the culture and vitality of the ministry. Consequently, the small impressionable town and the church have never been the same since! Twenty or more young people now attend Sunday mass and see the rector as having breathed new life into how they view the Bible and spirituality.[73]

Revival and renewal in the Church may have many spiritual faces in terms of how it manifests within the Body of Christ, but its overarching purpose will always be to bring us closer to the missional and relational heart of God, something Jesus demonstrated so profoundly in His ministry. Our Lord will certainly judge in eternity those who will have ultimately rejected Him; until then, He will stop at nothing to lovingly befriend them! The ultra-convicting reality in all this is that Jesus chooses to use each of our beacons of personal ministry in which to do so.

A lot of people we converse with on a daily basis have some sort of pain within their lives. The Luke 10 passage clearly exhibits Jesus' desire that we pray for the healing of people's lives as a means of spiritual testimony to them.

SEEK TO HEAL THE PEOPLE GOD BRINGS INTO OUR LIVES
"When you enter a town…Heal the sick who are there and tell them, 'The kingdom of God is near you'" (Luke 10:8–9). What does it mean to "heal" people, really? Do we need to be a so-called "healer" in order to apply this part of the passage to our lives? Should we lay hands on people and expect healing pronto? Hardly! I've tried it, you've tried, but the reality is that it doesn't always work like that. Prayers for healing don't always function like surgery, where if we roll a sick person into the operating room of Heaven we can expect the person to be rolled out spiritually stitched up.

Jesus indeed demonstrated His supernatural powers through His disciples in order to produce miracles and healings. He did so to authenticate His coming Kingdom as the Son of God and Saviour of the world. Why we as Christians today are unable to miraculously heal physically impaired people in the same way the disciples were able to as a means of gaining a gospel hearing with them, I'm not sure.

Though we may very well at times be appointed by God to be channels of physical healing as we pray for people, we must realize that healing comes about in a variety of spiritual and physical ways and forms. For example, I could become a healing balm to people who distrust pastors by simply developing a trusting friendship with them; it may not cause them to come to Jesus, but they may get a step closer to that reality on account of the spiritual bridge I've built into their lives.

Hurting people usually like to talk about their struggles, and they'll start to open up about their teenager or about a loss they have experienced, about their job or their marriage. In this way we help to construct highways of healing into people's lives that God the Father can use to carry them to His Son (Jesus), the lover of their souls, so that they may experience their ultimate healing in Him.

Many people may not be going to church these days, but I'll bet that they wouldn't mind an answer or two from our prayers. They know which side the bread is spiritually buttered on! Sometimes, if it's uttered carefully and with genuineness, a simple statement from a Christian such as "I'll pray for you" can have a real impact on a needy and hurting unsaved person.

At the core of every life, when every other distraction and option is stripped away, there's a desire within each person to ascend to and to know their Creator (God). This is where we as believers in Christ with a revived vision for personal evangelism can tap into that spiritual reality.

Hudson Taylor went to China as a missionary in the 1800s. When he arrived, he didn't understand the language or the culture. He looked different, he ate different food, he talked different, and he could not win them over with the gospel. He simply trusted that God would use his English prayers for the Chinese people (as well as his efforts in personally evangelizing them) to supernaturally speak to the people about Himself.

What a tremendous privilege we have to carry the burdens we have for people to the merciful steps of God's throne in Heaven, even the burdens of a culture we can't always relate to or understand too well. God is able to relate to all peoples and all cultures, and our prayers on their behalf are received.

Sometimes it's difficult to articulate well in prayer the spiritual pressure-point and need of any given person's life, let alone those we are familiar with. Yet, as Hudson Taylor did, we can just lift them up to God; He knows all the rest, and He certainly knows how to help!

In Romans 2:4, Paul states that "God's kindness leads you toward repentance." People may be more open to receiving Jesus if they can somehow spot the heart of God in our concerns *(and prayers)* for them. God can certainly use the compassion of His own people to speak His longsuffering kindness into the lives of the unsaved. Becoming more the beacons of ministry Jesus calls us to be as His disciples allows us to see that even our tiny seeds of witness and service to the spiritually lost (praying for and with them, a card, a phone call) are all we really need to touch a life; it is God who makes our faithfulness fruitful!

All of our tested evangelistic theories and sound theological arguments may never touch someone's heart. The four-step road to salvation, even when expounded by sincere and mature believers, may still sound mechanically trite and too suspiciously easy for an unbelieving person to accept. Such efforts may not touch the hearts of people, *but prayer and a sensitive witness can, and will.*

What happens when God seems to open a door for us to share the gospel? What do we do when a person says, "I know you're a Christian; can you help me with something about God?" What do we do when someone who respects us and who regularly pours out his or her heart to us remains resistant spiritually? There's only so much coffee we can have with a person before we must challenge him or her by saying, "The greatest need in your life is to come to faith in Jesus."

The bottom line is that we must seek discernment to know when the waters are ripe for soul-fishing and when to put aside the pole and the bait. God's people must acutely sense when it's time to stall and wait when sharing the goods of the gospel with those they're evangelizing and when to go all out. Jesus came to go to the Cross for *everyone,* and so everyone is worth risking the gospel with. Jesus came to be a sacrifice for us and "to give his life as a ransom for many" (Matthew 20:28); that is where you and I who walk with the Saviour (who are His beacons of ministry) come in. The gospel really is simple. Is it profound? Yes! Is it as spiritually deep as it is wide? Yes! But *it is* simple, so simple, in fact, that even a child can accept it! Therefore we don't want to make it more complicated than it is but only remind people by our own lives that Jesus loves them. God never gives up on people and so we shouldn't either.

Amazing things happen whenever we as individual Christians visually imagine our names written between the lines of the Great Commission Jesus left us and begin to intentionally and consciously live a lifestyle of personal evangelism. To think that this can all start with a simple prayer-walk with the dog around our neighbourhood or with a heartfelt cry to God to remove our calloused cataract of indifference to the souls of the spiritually lost! How our culture chooses to respond, on the other hand, is another story altogether. Only let us be burdened enough to faithfully pray for spiritual revival to hit our communities and cities.

If our "commission" as Christ's Church was over, we wouldn't still be here on earth; for now, let us *stand out* amongst the crowd as we walk amongst and *stand in* the crowd.

CHAPTER 20

CATCHING THE CHURCH ACTING LIKE THEY'RE ALREADY IN HEAVEN
A Revived Longing for Our Heavenly Home

Perhaps the most mysterious destination the majority of humanity contemplates is one the Bible calls Heaven. Almost every unbeliever we talk to about the subject wonders if there is such a place as Heaven and what it might be like to go there. Even those we might not identify with the Church or with Christianity want to believe there's a better place beyond the complexities and cruelty of this present life.

The legendary musician and songwriter Eric Clapton tragically lost his five year old son, Conner, in 1995 as a result of an accident in which the young boy fell from the forty-fifth floor of an apartment building in Manhattan. That event sparked Clapton to pour out his heart's pain in lyrics that would become the song "Tears in Heaven." The lyrics in the song portray a grieving father's search for answers as to what Heaven would be like and what his relationship with his son might resemble if he saw him there.

People have always wondered what the realm beyond this present life may hold. In fact, throughout history pretty much all cultures have been concerned about the "afterlife." The Egyptians built the pyramids long before many other things were built upon the earth. In those massive triangular-shaped structures they buried their loved ones. Interestingly enough, they would bury them with an abundance of food and other valuables because they believed in life after death.

Though Scripture says Heaven is ours for the asking, it also tells us that not all people *will* go to Heaven. Despite this fact, we, as finite, created people, have an intrinsic desire within our souls to transcend the limitations of our present physical lives. We long to go on beyond the grave; *we'd rather not even die in the first place!*

God has given each of us the desire to make it to Heaven, and His Word is the only reliable source *about* Heaven. It gives us some indication of what an eternity in God's presence will be like. One of the areas in which it does is in the book of Revelation (21:1–22:5).

There, John, the author, in picturesque fashion, redirects our thoughts from being merely focused upon our grounded context of earth to the soaring eternal and the incredible reality of the realm of Heaven. In a vision he receives from Jesus, the aged disciple and Gospel writer sprinkles on our imaginations a glimpse of what eternity will be like for those who have trusted in God's Son–the Saviour of the world–in a place Christians call "Glory" (their home in Heaven).

The account of the Revelation 21 vision provides every believer in Christ with a vibrant expectant hope of what awaits them beyond this present physical life. It's a passage that has inspired paintings and various works of art as well as how ancient churches and cathedrals were designed. Stained glass windows in the fifth century were patterned after the images of precious stones and jewels as well as other pictures we find in John's description of Heaven in Revelation 21. The apostle's illustrative words concerning Heaven in the same passage also led to a plethora of writings from the early church fathers, perhaps the most well-known being St. Augustine's great work "City of God."

Although it's impossible to know everything we'd like to know about Heaven on this side of it, there's nothing wrong with us craving it! Many people at the moment of their deaths have felt the presence of God around them; some have even experienced visions of Heaven and eternity. I remember my mother-in-law, shortly before she passed away, telling my wife, Elaine, that she saw some angels swooping in and around the curtain of her hospital bed while she was reading Psalm 27!

The longer we live in this worn-down and darkening world, the more glorious the thought of arriving and being in a place like Heaven *for eternity* becomes. We often feel like we've had just about enough of all the trial, pain, and sorrow this merciless world keeps dishing out.

So often in life we sweat the "little" stuff. We may, for instance, be burdened with how our family is going to be able to get through another winter on the income we have to work with. Perhaps your simmering burden is why your children are saying words they shouldn't be saying since the start of the school year. We all know people who ask questions such as, "Why do I feel like I am always taking two steps back in my search for happiness in life?" The favourite burden in many a home is, "When will we ever be able to afford to buy a real car that doesn't keep breaking down?" See what I mean? The little stuff!

Right about now you're probably thinking, "Are you crazy? That's not exactly little stuff!" I would have to agree with you, on one condition: *it all depends on whose perspective you are looking at these kinds of challenges from!*

Humanly speaking, the aforementioned laments can be quite daunting to process and sift through mentally and emotionally. To our detriment, we are a people who have "PhD" credentials at creating a crisis before it's truly arrived! Jesus, however, cautioned us not to get too ahead of ourselves; "Each day has enough trouble of its own" (Matthew 6:34). The Lord stated the obvious because He knew the mind and heart of humanity; we tend to live by gathering into ourselves the troubles and cares of *tomorrow* that can only compound the one's we're already dealing with today. Each one of us, if we're not prayerful with our cares, can become "packrats" with our troubles. We're very good at playing the "What if" game with our lives, imagining outcomes and scenarios for them way too soon and before the time's due.

To borrow a spiritual image from Jesus in the Gospels, we often "strain out a gnat but swallow a camel" (Matthew 23:24) in terms of how we view and deal with the obstacles and hurdles life consistently throws at us. I know people who try to avoid the smallest of trials and mess-ups in life but seem unable, at the same time, to avoid the more consequential and obvious ones coming their way.

Then there are those concerns that are applicable to all of us universally. For instance, has there ever been a time in our world's history (perhaps outside of when the black plague hit) when there's been such a preoccupation with germs and the spread of disease? Whenever the fall season hits we are bombarded with reams of information reminding us to wash our hands, cough into our sleeves, get a flu shot, and to be diligent in eating properly and getting sufficient sleep at night. It's hard enough to just get through a single day sometimes with our sanity still glued together, let alone remember to take care of ourselves for our health's sake!

Media reports reveal there's an increase in so-called "super bugs" in the works. Apparently, new strands of bacteria are incubating that threaten to pounce on us and extinguish our lives in an instant, like Godzilla stamping on an ant-sized human being. Such findings can cause average humans to run with newfound anxiety, believing that the sky is now falling and they'll be the first ones it flattens! The struggles of this current life often become the stimulus for a longing of our heavenly home, where sickness and other human trials we experience on earth will *no longer* exist.

As Christians there are times when we not only ponder Heaven but acutely *ache* for it. Just think for a minute about all the moral depravity and human tragedy we lock ears and eyes with on almost a daily basis. Perhaps more perceptively than ever before we can surmise that our earth *is* right on schedule in its collision-course with the tribulation years and the Second Coming of Jesus Christ; a world in the rough shape the Bible said it would be at this late hour. "The end" as we know it *is* percolating at a biblically accurate pace.

It takes discipline as Christians to consistently view our present troubles on earth with the healing of Heaven as the backdrop. Herein lies the ever-present tension we face as a Heaven-aspiring people of God. Though we know "Glory" is ahead of us, it can seem farther away and more difficult to wait for when we're mired in the realities of heart-strangulating worldly battles and trial. God's Word purposes to give us a proper eternal perspective of our current earthly lives in light of the precious promises He makes us that include the certainty of a future home in Heaven.

Revival and renewal-needy Christians are more prone to observe the challenges and hardships of their lives as blurring and even distorting the greatness of their God to help them overcome. However, there's someone in the Bible who was exemplary in keeping his eyes heavenward as he faced concurrent and formidable trials and challenges in his life.

Most of us can recall the details of the account of David and Goliath in the Old Testament. I like stories about underdogs because perhaps like you, I too often feel like one. Before David was the king of Israel, he took a pretty impressive leap towards that throne by slaying the nine-foot Philistine monster Goliath, and with *authority!* With a stone and a slingshot, and with perhaps one stab at it, David would prevail! Israel's would-be king made his shot count!

What always sticks out to me about his victory is not how great it was in terms of the size-differential between him and Goliath; it's David's faith! The way his showdown with the overgrown Philistine was shaping up, things did not appear all that promising for David's survival. His scrap with Goliath was deemed a mismatch of historical proportions; it put him at a gross disadvantage size and leverage-wise. The militaristic, not to mention *physical* odds, were firmly set against David *and* Israel. If David missed and Goliath grabbed hold of him as his personal punching pillow, well, I'll spare you what the eventual gory outcome would have been for the brave youngster.

Any Israelite present at the scene of the battle that day must have cringed the moment David produced a resolved "I'm up to this!" look in his boyish eyes. No one in David's family or anyone else gathered around would have put money down on him to score a miraculous upset. When David refused to at least wear Saul's armour, all bets were off; all that awaited was the cleanup of what would be left of David.

However, we know how the event ends. David indeed did the absolute unthinkable. With raised hands and looking every bit the war-worthy gladiator he was, David triumphed, not over a wounded giant, but over a dead one! How could such an outcome be possible? The Bible's account of David's go-round with Goliath offers only one viable answer. David emerged victorious because he was the Lord's man. Period! David was able to face a mountain of trial and experience victory by the knowledge he had of God and by trusting in the faithful *promises* of his God.

How do we know that? In 1 Samuel 17:45–47, David, before pummeling Goliath, looks his gargantuan enemy square in the eyes and says, "I come against you in the name of the LORD…whom you have defied…Today…the whole world will know that there is a God in Israel. All those gathered here will know… that the LORD saves; for the battle is the LORD's." What incredibly confident words from David *prior to the outcome of his confrontation with the giant Philistine!* Goliath would receive a sermon before he ever received the mortal blow to his head! What enormous faith David had in the heat of a battle and while facing seemingly overpowering circumstances that could have left him obliterated, a mere footnote of folly in Israel's history.

We could use such a reminder as David's faith as we head towards an unstable future of the world. There should never be a time when the Church doubts that its presence in this world will survive, for "the gates of Hades will not overcome it" (Matthew 16:18). We can wait out the real tough stuff (as well as the little stuff) precisely because Heaven promises us something unfathomably blissful at the end of our earthly lives.

Concerning our ultimate future and eternal home as believers, Joni Eareckson Tada writes "Earth can't keep its promises, but aren't you glad Heaven does? And oh the joy of one day enjoying not only new glorified bodies, but hearts free of sin."[74]

David knew what he was facing in Goliath, but he also knew *how* to face him. Yet I think we can tend to be a bit parochial in how we apply the promises of God sometimes, whether it's the little stuff or the huge stuff we're grappling with in life. Marginalizing God's ability comes as easy for us at certain points as preventing physical pain! Our personal problems, granted, may be quite immense and very trying. Our mount Everest-like trials may tower over us and appear to be just as monstrous and un-scalable as the actual mountain itself. We can get to the point in life where we feel we'll never overcome our issues. Some of the challenges that stand before us in this world can seem like massive iron walls that will forever cast their ominous shadow of hopelessness back at us.

In these times we need to remember David's focus; his body may have been facing the perceptibly immovable and bone-crushing behemoth (Goliath), but his eyes were squarely on the ultimate Mover of all things that appear humanly immovable! If we don't believe God is presently moving mountains in our lives or in the world and think that all our striving for Him is for naught, the Bible challenges us to reconsider that perspective on theological grounds.

If even someone whom Jesus Himself acknowledged as "great" (John the Baptist) could fall into a life-and-death crisis of faith, wisdom tells us that we (the average Christian) can as well. John the Baptist, however, found out through his incarceration at the hands of King Herod that God is never at a loss for seeing His sovereign redemptive purposes advance, despite the temporal (earthly) welfare of His servants.

After John the Baptist was imprisoned and facing an uncertain future, John's disciples revealed that the Lord's first cousin was experiencing some doubts concerning who He (Jesus) really was. Who could blame the caged forerunner of Christ for feeling that way? John, after all, was the one on the inside looking out at those who appeared to have a better fate than him. Wasn't he supposed to be, as Jesus purported, "the greatest" man in Israel? Was it just a case of a great man of God having a faith-cramp? Was John sweating what was really the little stuff in light of eternity?

Something wasn't square in John's mind or heart, and he probably couldn't fathom his brutal luck. The proverbial "wrong end of the stick" was firmly in his possession, and it would only be taken from him by being pried from his cold, dead hands. Questions must have abounded for the baptizer as he sat hopelessly behind bars of injustice; *he knew he didn't belong there, and Jesus was nowhere!* Didn't he hear God Almighty affirm the divine identity of Jesus, the One the prophets foretold would come, the One whom the Spirit had descended on as a witness from Heaven? Why, then, did he suddenly find himself considering the rumour d'jour concerning Jesus? There was as much speculation about Jesus at the time as there were matzo balls cooking at Chez Jerusalem!

Jesus' response to the query of John's followers regarding his doubts made it sound like John just had to cool out. "Go back and report to John what you hear and see: The blind receive sight, the lame walk, those who have leprosy are cured, the deaf hear, the dead are raised, and the good news is preached to the poor. Blessed is the man who does not fall away on account of me" (Matthew 11:4–6).

Notice the peculiar vocabulary and grammar the Lord employed in this passage. It was spoken in the *present* tense. In other words, Jesus was saying that when all is seemingly going wrong around us and in the world and when Goliath-sized trials snarl at us, we're to remember not only what God has done *in history* but what He is *still* doing right now. Jesus was telling John the Baptist that God had not forgotten about him and his ministry role and accomplishments for the Kingdom of God. The Lord wanted John to be certain that His Father's redemptive agenda was right on schedule even though he was locked up.

Moment by moment, minute by minute, hour by hour, and day by day, God is working in the lives of people and working out His eternal purposes in the world; He "who works out everything in conformity with the purpose of his will" (Ephesians 1:11) "will not slumber" (Psalm 121:3).

We can be certain, then, that when things don't appear to be going our way or the Church's way, things are still going God's way, because He's sovereign. Our faithful God is still moving our "Goliaths" as if they were mere pylons; they are incrementally shifting their spiritual courses in our lives and in the world, even though we may not feel the gravitational pull heavenward. Just as our planet moves without our even noticing, so to does the unseen hand of God move in our circumstances. One day, the trials we presently face that now seem to span endlessly out in front of us on the road of life will seem tiny when compared to the vastness of eternity, where the enjoyment of our Saviour will be infinitely opened up to us.

Not one single tribulation we face now on earth will be able to prevent us from experiencing that reality. Therefore, like John the Baptist, we too must put our hope and confidence in that which is beyond and outside our present earthly circumstances: *Heaven.* We're not to allow our still unanswered questions for God to dictate the intensity of our faith or to pick-pocket the anticipation we have for our eternal home.

The difficulty arises whenever we get caught up in our expectations of God and when we desire for things to always make spiritual sense to us. In no way could John the Baptist have dreamed up that his head would eventually land on a platter; it wasn't exactly what he would have drafted as *his* vision of the power of Heaven at work in his life!

"When we all get to Heaven," as the classic hymn goes, the mysterious non-fitting pieces of our earthly lives will be fastened together; as for now, they are to remain an unfinished puzzle to us. As a wise old friend of mine often reminds me, we need "spiritual endurance" for the course of this life "far more than we need to shop!" Is this your perspective today, Christian soldier, as you face your battle? Or are you longing for a premature rapture, a sort of spiritual escapism and idealism that's never promised to God's people in Scripture on this side of eternity? Is it possible to live like a cost-counting disciple and yet have an attitude that insists on the best from God and even pines for the good life in this world? On the flipside, is it possible for us to wrap our arms around a sacrificial lifestyle and to willingly settle for fewer blessings while we're on earth as we wait to be ultimately satisfied in Heaven?

Sometimes Christians appear to be living like their trying to exit from the struggles of this earth as it applies to their spiritual journey and Kingdom role in it. Though as believers we're inwardly "groaning" (as is all creation) to realize our redemption, some of us are opting to live out the string of our faith as mere groupies of Jesus, crowding around Him on a Sunday, yet averse to the spiritual blessings of want and suffering while frolicking in a self-denial-free Christianity that expects all the heavenly trimmings and excess God can send our way.

We seem to be a Church, at times, who "wants it all" now. Away with the kind of spiritual growth that comes with a price! Granted, no one really wants a Goliath-sized trial in their life, and who can't live without the kind of lot John the Baptist had stretching their faith? Still, some Christians seem to be living like they believe they're entitled to have all their spiritual cake (here on earth) and eat it too (in Heaven). They view earth-bound challenges and trials as being inconvenient and incompatible with the Christian experience because such realities don't fit into their definition of an abundant "Rodeo Drive" type of spiritual life. They only get to ride around the sun so many times; only get to awake so many mornings. Utilizing the brake of *faith* is not nearly as appetizing or fulfilling as stepping on the gas towards whatever else that promises more for less spiritual work.

Joseph Stowell, in his book *Eternity*, writes,

> A heavenless Church seeks to satisfy longings and needs here, rather than serving and sacrificing here on earth—with a view to be satisfied

there. In a community that is not gripped by the reality of Heaven, even the gospel becomes increasingly therapeutic as a means to help feel forgiven…In fact, new adherents to the faith often expect great earth-side blessings as a result of finding Jesus as fulfiller, healer, helper and friend…which of course He is. But unless we focus our hopes on the ultimate healing…disillusionment sets in as the pilgrims experience seasons of hardship.[75]

Though the Lord did say that His Kingdom had come "near" (Matthew 10:7), He meant that term as *internally* (*within* His disciples), which naturally was to lead to *outward* societal change. That being said, Jesus never inferred to His would-be Church that they were to construct a concrete Heaven-on-earth. Rather, they were to help bring about a spiritual Kingdom of heavenly transformation to the world.

Imagine revived Christians all over the world, renewed in their expectancy of Heaven and curbing any tendencies to take earthly detours that can only dissatisfy. If our *first love* (our love for God above all else) drops to "third-wheel" status in its quality, we could end up wandering away from finding our true richest of joys *in Him;* worse, we may find ourselves snug in the arms of the world before we know it's happened, pursuing its cavity-laden candy store of deceptions.

The more we "love" the world, the more it will love us back. Getting too comfy with the attractive offerings of this world (even within Christian "culture") can put the child of God at risk of adopting the mindset that they can wait for Heaven and settle instead for a prematurely induced rapture of their own making.

By how some believers talk *and act,* you'd think they're out to create their own heaven-like culture club, the world be darned! Please realize that when I speak of a "premature rapture" I am not referring to a select, and perhaps *weird,* group of Christians who claim to have received information and instruction the rest of us believers didn't and are kumbaya-ing together until Jesus shuttles them to their "mansion" over the "hilltop." I'm referring to those believers whose presence in this world as a spiritual influence and righteous preservative can become, in a sense, hidden. If enough Christians around the globe removed themselves (in practice and in heart) from the necessities of cost-counting discipleship and evangelism, it could appear as though millions of us have actually been beamed through the cosmos (raptured) ahead of the appointed time! Some Christians may be quite unaware that they've been deceived into living with this kind of egregious spiritual shift in their heart. It's not so much that a premature rapture lifestyle of Christians would equal a lack of church attendance or participation in Christian culture as much as it would resist embracing the challenges to their faith that are *directly* related to their identification with Jesus in the world.

Ask the persecuted believers in China or Iran to live their lives of faith by that attitude, and they might just think that we as Western Christians have indeed been raptured and are now living in a Heaven of our own making. They would be right! If there's a trend in our Western Church culture today, it's that Christians are longing to become happier on earth, more healed here, more blessed here.

Our worship music is sounding more performance-based, "professional," and recordable than ever before. Our sermons are expected to be entertaining, yet deep; simple enough to stick, yet spilling over with spiritual treasure for the scooping. An increasing amount of church leaders are taking on the titles and authority of "executives" and "CEOs" like those of large corporations and business entities. As mentioned earlier, somehow our church experience today must do more for us than ever before. Give us the warm fuzzies*, or else!* With these sorts of misplaced desires and heightened expectations existing within the Body of Christ, it makes one wonder if we as Christians are truly longing for Heaven anymore.

The apostle Paul wrote that God's people are to "set" their "hearts" and "minds" "on things above, not on earthly things" (Colossians 3:1–2). Peter said we are "aliens and strangers" here on earth (1 Peter 2:11) and Paul said that our real "citizenship," our *real* home, "is in heaven" (Philippians 3:20). The author of Hebrews wrote, "We are looking forward to our city in heaven, which is yet to come" (Hebrews 13:14 NLT). The New Testament writers were talking about "the new Jerusalem" (Revelation 21:2), a heavenly city where the righteous of God will dwell forever in total peace and harmony with Him.

An idealized heaven on this fallen, yet-to-be-redeemed earth cannot be found anywhere (as good as our church experience can be). To enjoy our present earthly blessings is quite all right; to exalt them, however, is to depreciate our longing for the rewards we'll have bestowed on us in eternity. We can endure in falling short of God's ultimate for us on earth, knowing one day in Heaven we'll experience all that God has been planning for us in its entirety. Jesus is not only our Great Redeemer; He's our Great Rewarder as well!

It's okay to enjoy some of the best things our Christian community and culture has to offer. Such fare, as beneficial as it can be to us right now, only anticipates our ultimate spiritual reality and blessing: *Heaven.*

Some Christians sincerely believe they are not to possess sickness or disease and that any occurrence of such is clearly from the pit of Hell. (I guess these believers think they're immune from inheriting a fallen physical body too!) Then there's Christians who seem to take the "King's kid" mentality too far and expect the crème de la crème of this life to be thrown at their deserved feet. Yet Jesus said He came to give us an abundant *spiritual* life, not nearly a guaranteed abundant "material" life. As a Western Church, perhaps we have subscribed to our culture's credo of "He who has the most toys wins" and have applied it to the spiritual, resulting in a distorted, finite, and earthly view of the blessings of God rather than a truly biblical one.

We need to pray concertedly, as Western Christians living in a land of affluence, for God to help us accept what it means to be cost-counting disciples of Christ (the demands of our discipleship). If our attitude towards sanctification and spiritual maturation waylays the necessity for "blind" faith and self-denial, then we are out of touch with what it means to *be* a disciple; it amounts to an attempt to live outside the will of God for our lives.

We need God's vision for our lives, but they are lives, nonetheless, that must settle for something better than an earthly experience of Heaven. As God's people we must keep our spiritual feet grounded by seeking a revived and renewed perspective of our heavenly home as it relates to our experience as redeemed and yet sin-marred people who are still living on a cursed earth. Jonathan Edwards spoke quite often about eternity and the future heavenly home of God's people. The puritan preacher stated,

> It becomes us to spend this life only as a journey towards heaven, as it becomes us to make the seeking of our highest end and proper good, the whole work of our lives, to which we should subordinate all other concerns of life. Why should we labor for, or set our hearts on anything else, but that which is our proper end, and happiness?[76]

As Christians we should have a holy discontent for all that is plastic, brand-driven, and contrived within our church culture that gives us a false, shallow sense of spiritual security and contentment on earth. Instead, we're to hasten our Lord's return from our eternal home and "eagerly await a Savior from there"

(Philippians 3:20). We need prayerful quests for endurance to face the roads we still must tread and to not look for smoother, more levelled spiritual paths to walk down.

The Davids and John the Baptists of biblical history knew that despite the challenges to their faith and the occasional blips of doubt on the radar of their spiritual lives, there was a God in Israel who was still on the throne, a God who chooses to work out His redemptive plans for our lives by taking even our trials into account. *We* want to break speeding records in running as fast and as far as we can from heartache and hardship; God, however, is interested in crafting our character and spiritual maturity *through* them. *We* want God to spare us of a Christianity permanently stapled to sufferings, tests, and trials; God replies back, "You're not home yet (in Heaven)!"

Contrary to the kinds of theology some Christian leaders trumpet, we cannot (and were never meant to) live our "best" life, "now;" our best life, rather, will be lived *then,* when we're in eternity with the Lord. As for now, we live in a place where we lack, hurt, struggle, cry, and suffer. These realities will always be with us, but they won't *go* with us to Heaven. For now, we are to endure in a heavenless world.

CHAPTER 21

FINISHING THE DEVIL'S POWERFUL SERMON ON SUFFERING: THE BALLAD OF JOB

A Revived Apologetic for Human Suffering

Our world is a tragic place, a dimmed stage where the roles of darkness, heartbreak, and depression are acted out in human lives. Our world is also a physical, emotional, and spiritual playground where we live with the greatest bully of human existence: *suffering*. Suffering is a human reality that forces those *who* suffer to look outside themselves for hope. Oftentimes it's in the wake of tragedy and while mired in the pit of hardship that people begin to look to God for answers. I believe this is why most of the churches in lower Manhattan were packed out on Sunday, September 16, 2001, following the events of September 11.

We'll always have our questions about suffering; it's a reality as hard to hold back as the very wind itself. Suffering (whatever mode it may be) can be a mercilessly rude intruder who threatens to disfigure the home of our heart. Never invited and certainly never welcomed, human suffering always seems to barge in on our peaceful and contented lives like a deafening alarm clock waking us up from a deep sleep.

So often suffering sweeps into our lives from sources we'd least expect. In 2012, a student opened fire in a high school cafeteria in Ohio, fatally wounding three classmates and injuring four others before fleeing and eventually giving himself up. The small town of Chardon (near Cleveland) struggled to come to terms with being thrust into the media spotlight. The Chardon police chief, who was interviewed immediately following the shooting, stated the obvious: "This is sad news for all of us today." Sad and indeed senseless are such horrific events in life. We can only imagine what the families of the three students who lost their lives must have felt when they received the worst of all kinds of news: they'd lost a child, a brother, a sister, a niece or nephew, cousin or grandchild.

The cruel laceration of suffering slices right into our daily lives, regardless of our ethics, morals, or faith; none of us are ever safe from its steely, cold, and utterly indiscriminate presence and cut.

I often find myself entangled within the common petition that asks God why there has to be such enormous suffering in the world. We know we're living in a spiritually fallen realm, but, *really?* Is our depraved nature as human beings such that we're *so* deserving of it?

Every time we pick up a newspaper or flick on the news, we run a great risk of being run over by a Mack truck's worth of crushing human tragedy and suffering in our world. We may feel alone and isolated in our suffering when actually we're in great company. Someone once said that if a preacher preaches on suffering, he'll *always* have an audience! Who can't relate to messages coming from the pulpit that lift the covers of pain and hardship in our lives, exposing the raw and sensitive realities of them?

What *do* we do when a tragedy or extreme trial breaks down the door of our lives? For some, pain is dissolved in meditation (reading, relaxation therapy, yoga, prayer); for others, pain is drowned in social interaction or buried somewhere deep within one's life. We could respond to suffering in various ways. We could just give up; life's over. We could turn to a drug or alcohol. Even more hopeless (and yet nonetheless popular), we could blame God for our suffering. In fact, many have chosen to deal with their sufferings by doing that.

God is often the convenient scapegoat for the hardships we face because human rationality concedes that if anyone has the power to stay the hand of suffering from striking our lives, it's Him. As a result, human suffering is the most frequently raised objection to embracing the Christian faith.

SUFFERING AS AN OBJECTION TO THE CHRISTIAN FAITH

Many people, in and outside the Church, when observing the great sufferings in our world can't help but wonder, "Where is God in all of it?" More to the point, they ask, "How can we speak of a loving God who allows suffering to enter into the lives of people?" It may be a predictable question, but it's a great one all the same. The question of suffering is never more relevant, of course, than when we go through it ourselves. When our health or the welfare of our family is inflicted by the rabid bite of heartache and floundering in tribulations of many kinds, we are forced to have to own our faith; we come nose-to-nose with the question of how we will stand up to this unwanted robber of our peace and joy known as suffering.

When we think of suffering in the Bible, one of the first figures that may come to mind is Jesus Christ, the One who Isaiah prophesied would be "a man of sorrows, and familiar with suffering" (Isaiah 53:3). Perhaps our memory may carry us to another figure in biblical history, like the prophet Jeremiah or the apostle Paul, who, the New Testament tells us, suffered for his faith in Christ.

Yet when many of us hear the word *suffering*, we can't help but recall the biblical account of what happened to a man who lived in the land of Uz (likely east of the Jordan River). This man likely lived in the time of the patriarchs and knew all too well what it was like to receive abrupt and irreversible news of a personally devastating nature, a man who experienced the loss of not only his children and possessions of wealth but his health as well while hitting rock bottom spiritually, physically and emotionally—the man Job.

Much has been said and taught about Job, who has become a picture of what suffering looks like when it veers seemingly out of control and rams into the walls of someone's life. Job's suffering was so thorough and so bound up in the core of his being that he, in fact, despaired of the very day he was born.

When we read of Job we can't help but to mentally and visually wander down the ash heaps of grief that became his life. Incredibly, however, as we dig through the mound of mournful dust covering this extraordinary man's life, we can learn some valuable spiritual lessons from it that will not only give us a godly perspective of human suffering but a good theology of it.

Over the years *Time* magazine has featured their "Man of the Year." If *Time* was around in Job's day, he may very well have made the cover. His is as fascinating a story as it is a sad one—that is, before it got better. But just who was Job? Well, in his day, wealth was measured by livestock, something Job had the corner on! He owned 7,000 sheep, 3,000 camels, 500 teams of oxen, and 500 donkeys. But his wealth aside, the Bible tells us that Job was a man whom we might call squeaky clean—a godly man. "He was honest inside and out, a man of his word, who was totally devoted to God and hated evil with a passion" (Job 1:1 MSG).

By all accounts he was a faithful husband and a father who was mindful to make amends for any sins his children might have committed. Job was a righteous man; that much is crystal clear. It hits us like a cinder block whenever we see good people not just experience trials but have the most terrible of tragedies beset them. This is exactly what happened to Job.

All seemed to be going well and rather merrily for him. Job was enjoying life under the favour of God until one day when all the wheels fell off his cart of a godly and blessed existence. Then, like a sudden phone call delivering bad life-altering news, Job's world, as if out of nowhere, came crashing down around him; subsequently, he entered into the grossest of seasons of human suffering. The maelstrom of personal terror would leave its mark like an "act of God," as seen by the leftover rubble of his suddenly disastrous landscape of a life.

It all started when foreign invaders stole his oxen and donkeys. No big deal, right? However, a fire from the heavens swirled down and burned up his sheep as well as his workers. And if that was not nearly enough, a freak windstorm hit and killed all of his children. Wow! Topping off all of that grief and sorrow, Job would then be struck with painful boils all over his body, from head to foot. Even to this day, the excruciating totality of Job's suffering is off the human map and over the spiritual top of our fathoming!

One moment, life is grand, a lark, in fact. Then, boom, Job's reduced to a shell of the person he once was, mired in suffering and in a world of hurt. The death watch was on.

Even more intriguing for some who gazed upon Job's suffering was the question of how long it would take before miserable Job turned his back on God and threw in the towel of his faith. In the face of great suffering, would Job go from utterly blameless to faithless in an Old Testament minute?

What went on behind the scenes of Job's sudden and tragic misfortune? Was something or someone beyond his control pulling the strings of suffering over him?

WAS GOD RESPONSIBLE FOR JOB'S SUFFERING?

God is who He is, and He is always worthy of our praise and of being given glory—*even when we're suffering*. We're always astonished at the fact that Job agreed with such an attitude, even in the shape he was in! Job reacted to the news that he had literally lost it all by getting into the posture of worship. That might not have been our first response, yet it was Job's. The Bible says,

> *Job got up and tore his robe and shaved his head. Then he fell to the ground in worship and said: "Naked I came from my mother's womb, and naked I will depart. The LORD gave and the LORD has taken away; may the name of the LORD be praised." In all this, Job did not sin by charging God with wrongdoing* (Job 1:20–22).

Just think, Job had no idea why he was going through what he was going through. He knew nothing of the spiritual battle taking place over his life; he could only surmise that he was undeserving of anything that had happened to him. From a mere human vantage point, we'd think Job's snow-white quality of righteousness should have exempted him from experiencing the kind of suffering he had to endure. Wouldn't the glove of less suffering have fitted the hand of Job's life more appropriately?

Jesus gave His disciples a heads-up in terms of the realities of troubles in life and was clear in that even God's people would not get off scot-free from experiencing trials (John 16:33). Christians, then, should expect *and accept* that ever-lurking over their shoulders are the real possibilities of hard times and even intensely difficult seasons of life. Sometimes these come about as a direct result of one's faith in Jesus Christ meeting up with unfriendly opposition.

This was Job's reality, wasn't it? Due to his reputable faith in the Lord he became a target in the evil intentions of Satan to be oppressed and to ultimately be taken down. Any time the devil can discredit one of God's servants with a track record of exemplary living, he scores a bigger point with those who are already skeptical of religious people than if he took down a believer with less recognition. Job may have been nestled in his faith, but he was far from being home free in terms of suffering for it.

To be a disciple of Jesus, the New Testament tells us, is to be *prepared* to suffer for our faith in Him (see Philippians 1:29; 1 Peter 4:1). Who in their right mind could ever say Christianity is a safe religion? Rather, suffering for Christ is a gift from God, because it proves our faith as genuine; it humanizes the doctrine of the Church and personalizes its theology. If we believe in Jesus we must prove that trust by our willingness to endure hardship on account of our identification with His name. In truth, the Church has accomplished some amazing things of eternal consequence when it has, quite literally, had a gun against its head.

It's no coincidence that God is working mightily and unusually in areas of the world where Christians are the most attacked and abused for their faith. In light of this fact, perhaps we need more of a reviving joy from the Holy Spirit to enable us to endure in our intermittent yet growing struggles as Christians in secular culture here in the Western world. It's no wonder *why* God allows intense persecution to strike His people; it can serve to get them out of their complacency and indifference to mission.

It worked in Acts 8 to shake up the comfy-cozy Jerusalem church and get them off their couches of spiritual contentment in order to spread the gospel to the ends of the earth. It's as if the early believers didn't hear Jesus' starting gun (the coming of the Holy Spirit) and consequently forgot to run (into all the world with the gospel). The church was scattered so that the seeds of the good news would be scattered along with it.

GOD ALLOWS THE RIGHTEOUS TO SUFFER FOR HIS PURPOSES
Ultimately, God is responsible for the welfare of His suffering people, but was *He* responsible for Job's suffering? As we will see, God definitely made *provision* for the devil to strike His servant. Just as God allows the unrighteous to be blessed to a certain extent, He allows suffering, even intense suffering, to visit and even tent with the righteous. In His sovereignty over our lives, however, anything God permits to enter our lives (whether it's welcomed or not) He ultimately has a purpose for (as hard a truth that can be for us to grasp). Every trial and heartache is placed inside the "To make you more like Jesus" file in Heaven. The number one reason God allows suffering into our lives as His people is to conform us to the image of His Son (see Romans 8:28–29). It pains us to come to terms with the fact that God is more interested than we are in developing and chiselling our characters, even if it means allowing us to go through the refining fires of suffering and trial. Our ultimate spiritual growth and good is our God's first priority for us, not a suffering-free life (which the Fall renders impossible anyway).

God knows we are much more open to His invasive transformative work in our lives when we're on our knees than when we're on our self-sufficient feet. In the economy of God, our suffering is used of Him to advance our faith, not to subtract from it. What Satan *doesn't* want humanity to realize is that God is *not* vindictive, and neither is He reckless or malevolent in the exercising of His sovereign power. God doesn't flex His sovereign muscle because He can, but because He *cares*. We can't gauge the measure of God's love for us by how much or how little He allows pain and hardship into our lives. God loves all people equally, and He has one *plan* for all people: to introduce them to His Son Jesus and to have us know Him intimately as our Lord and Saviour. It's quite natural for a Christian to believe that to be righteous is to be in the place of *blessing*, not *hardship and pain*. Yet the Bible says that in the times of hardship and pain, we are blessed as well, in that we can come to know Jesus on a deeper level through suffering. Who can relate more to our suffering than He can?

All that Job's righteousness seemed to bring him was pain, not blessings. We read in chapter 2 of the book of Job that Satan was allowed to come before God, and though we are not absolutely sure *why* the devil was there, it would appear that Satan's motive was to seek permission to hurt Job. The profound truth of this matter, however, is that even what the devil does is permitted and used by God for good in the lives of His people. In Job's case, it is *God* who cuts to the chase by actually raising the name of His servant Job during a particular encounter with the devil. "Then the LORD said to Satan, 'Have you considered my servant Job? There is no one on earth like him…he is in your [Satan's] hands; but you must spare his life'" (Job 2:3–6).

Even knowing how it all works out in the end we still think, "God, this is the devil you're talking to. Isn't he *the* enemy? Why would You allow him to even remotely touch your righteous servant Job?" God didn't suddenly become someone here that the Bible says He is not. God's character can never change. In no way can He be goaded or tempted into doing something or allowing something to happen to us that's against His will. He's in perfect, unabated control; neither our circumstances nor the devil can override His sovereign plans. This is Theology 101! No trial in life is wasted on a surrendered and pliable child of God. God knows what He's doing, *all the time.*

SOMETIMES GOD ALLOWS EVEN THE DEVIL TO BE THE BRINGER OF SUFFERING

There may be points when we are infirm for a period of time and the origins are indeed the work of Satan. But there could be other reasons for our illness as well. We might just be in poor health; we might not be taking care of ourselves; we may have caught a "bug," and yet sometimes, it would seem from Job 2, the devil gets the "green light" to run us over in some way, even though he is limited in how fast and how far he can go. At times it can be difficult for our finite brains to wrap themselves around how suffering and other trials God allows in our lives (even those that come from the devil) could possibly work into His sovereign purposes for our lives.

That was Job's case to plead. "I'm a righteous man; I fear God; I serve God. Why me? What did I do? Where did I go wrong?" It's in those spiritually perplexing times when we feel we have a righteous leg to stand on, especially, that we desire to intensely quiz God for our misfortune. Does God somehow prune the spiritual quality of his faithful servants through their suffering? How much more righteous can the already righteous become?

We all want a reason for our suffering; without one, suffering is that much more abstract and cruel. If suffering can somehow be used for our spiritual gain, we want to be able to tangibly see that. We want heavenly answers to not only dilute but to also define our earthly pain.

That was the desire of Job's righteous heart. The entire Old Testament book of Job walks us through his transparent dialogue with the Lord. On the one hand, Job intermittently demonstrated an admirable stance of faith in God's nature and character, despite the fact that his suffering (to him) had no rhyme or reason; on the other hand, the book also reveals Job's profound regret of even being born and his longing to gain insight into his suffering from a hearing with God. It's a long and drawn-out story of Job's desire for God to be straight with him.

As we read along in the book of Job, we desperately want God to come quickly to His servant's rescue; instead we get God allowing his servant's pain to fester and Job having to endure spiritually, emotionally, and physically. It's too easy to view Job in the sympathetic light that he was wholly undeserving of what happened to him. Job's story seems to show us that his suffering had little to do with anything he might have done wrong; it had more to do with what he could learn from it (increased growth in righteousness). This is why the message of Job not only challenges us in our understanding of the reality of suffering but also helps us to view the devil's sermon on suffering for what it is: *half-baked!*

If we're living contrary to God's will by choosing to roll the dice with Scripture on a continual basis, perhaps we won't be surprised if something swoops down into our lives that causes us to suffer; we might even accept that we have it coming to us! But that's rarely the case when we *know* we're living for God; when we're in that camp, suffering is the last thing we think we'll have to go through.

Yet it is God's Holy prerogative to allow even the most righteous of His people to suffer for good reasons beyond their ability to comprehend. There are things Satan wants us to know, and then there's biblical reality and what *God* says is so!

Perhaps one of the most common perceptions as to why the righteous are allowed to suffer is so that their allegiance to God can be tested, strengthened, and even broadcasted for all to take notice. When the saints of God come through the refining fires of His trials, the world (and even the devil) must consider its spiritual significance. Satan thought Job would "curse" God and turn away from Him after what he was going to do to him. God, of course, knew better, and He trumped the devil by exploiting the evil one's own tactic to get Job to turn against Him.

Three amateur advisors popped up and formed a blarney sandwich around their beleaguered friend Job (their names, Bildad, Eliphaz, and Zophar, even sound like a counselling firm) in an attempt to help Job make sense of the tragedy that had struck his life. They issued insensitive findings that Job must have ruffled God something bad in order for him to be in the shape he was in. Another advisor, however, bypassed that strategy and pretty much tried to wheelbarrow him over the edge of his desperation.

Job's wife got the first crack at advising her husband before his three friends could drive him deeper into despair. To Mrs. Job, Mr. Job's "way out" was simple. "His wife said to him, 'Are you holding on to your integrity? Curse God and die!'" (Job 2:9). The response of Job's wife is interesting, for her pleading that Job should *"curse"* God matches exactly what Satan forecasted Job would end up doing in his desperate state. The devil is *not* all-knowing, and he couldn't have misjudged God's servant any more than he did.

It almost seems too natural a tendency for Christians and non-Christians alike to put God on trial, to lay charges against Him, and to even pronounce Him guilty of all our pain and suffering. This is precisely what the devil thought an out-of-answers and out-of-hope Job would do. It is the top-secret ploy of Satan to try to convince humanity that God is the only suspect in the crime of our suffering-induced pain. Our evil adversary knows how it goes with fallen human thinking—a good God wouldn't allow this—and so he appeals to us on that basis. Though Bible-believing Christians should be spiritually equipped enough to smell his deceptive schemes from a mile away and not give in, many people (including Christians) seem to have bought his counterfeit bill of goods concerning God's role in their suffering.

When we as God's people feel we've bottomed out and are mired in suffering, it's the attitude we carry to the throne of grace that most distinguishes us from the world: *trusting*.

Oftentimes we're tempted to blame ourselves for the trials we suffer; yet even in that state, the devil tries to put his foot in the door. Self-accusation is something the devil will keep shovelling into our psyche as long as we provide him with a handy shovel. It's crazy how we can go down our own "list of convictions" to justify why we may be suffering. Our friends may rush to tell us that we're suffering because God obviously has a "great plan" for us; a mentor may intimate that we perhaps have some hidden sin or secret motive that God isn't happy about. Sometimes it can seem that others can see ahead of us on the road of answers as to why we are experiencing troubles in life; God is speaking to them, but *not* to us.

When we gaze upon someone's suffering, sometimes the best thing to do in their presence is to say very little. It's best not to make promises for God when we're in the company of people who intensely suffer but to just let His Word speak for itself. Ultimately, when we're suffering as Christians we need to be reminded that not only is there temporary grace available to us but a day will dawn when we will never suffer again. Human suffering, the Bible says, is time-sensitive and time-limited. Charles Spurgeon, in response to the reality of human suffering, once said, "It is the very joy of this earthly life to think that it will come to an end."[77] What a profoundly biblical perspective to have on the subject of human suffering!

One blessed day there will cease to be suffering; crying, pain, death and goodbyes will be on permanent vacation. All the trials and sufferings of this life will disappear in a flash, like yesterday's leftover pizza. In Romans 8:18 Paul wrote words that help us to keep looking forward even while we're planted in our present tribulations: "I consider that our present sufferings are not worth comparing with the glory that will be revealed in us." What a wonderful verse of hope!

This is why we need a revived and spiritually renewed eternal perspective of suffering. We need to tell the devil that our *present* story (our current trials and suffering) is not the *end* of the story, because God is not *finished* writing the story of our lives; we'll read that book for an eternity in Heaven! As God's people we need to constantly remember that no matter how long and to what extent we're permitted to suffer in the here and now, every form of pain and suffering known to the human race will be vanquished at the presence of Jesus Christ at Heaven's front door.

A final thought about Job's life that helps us to finish the devil's half-baked sermon on human suffering is that *God always has the final say as to why we are allowed to suffer in this life.*

GOD HOLDS THE ULTIMATE REASON FOR AND BENEFIT OF OUR SUFFERING

We must look to not only the beginning of the book of Job but also the end of it in order to find what might be the best meaning and purpose for what happened to Job. First, we must take from Job's story that *suffering* (even extreme aspects of it) *is an incrementally faith-shaping part of the structure of our lives as God's people.* I particularly like what author Henry Ironside had to say about the role of God's sovereignty in our trials. "Nothing comes upon us that hasn't first passed through the filter of God's love; a God who is too good to be unkind, and too wise to err." We have to trust that God knows what He's doing when we're limping along in prolonged bouts of suffering and cannot see a way out. Ultimately, we must submit ourselves to the *peace* of God's wisdom whenever we're going through times of intense trial and prolonged forms of suffering (see Philippians 4:6–7).

When we suffer, we reach down into something, and our need is to take our knowledge of God's Word and push it down into our hearts. The believers who long for ongoing revivals of spiritual renewal in their lives grasp that they were made to crave a kind of endurance that's based on the promises of God during times of suffering that are tailor-made for God's trial-worn saints. There's a lot to be said of those Christians who bear up under much trial, who don't complain but rather find a contentment in the supernatural strength God's grants them to keep pressing on through! It's no wonder, then, that conversions to Christianity and spiritual growth are increasing in countries where there is so much human need and suffering.

Secondly, suffering in our lives calls us to a *greater surrender,* serves to *increase godly character,* and can lead to a *deeper kind of righteousness.* The Bible is clear in that Job was a "righteous" man whose quality of godliness most of us can only hope to reach in our lives. However, it would seem as though God, through His infinite wisdom and sovereign purposes, deemed Job's righteousness as lacking something that only suffering as he did could supply. A crisis in one's life can result in one's character being either sharpened or dulled by it. In the case of Job, his seemingly indomitable crisis definitely resulted in the former! In fact, while in the pit of despair Job's confounding trial was the means by which great spiritual lessons were imparted to him. "Teach a righteous man and he will add to his learning" (Proverbs 9:9).

At the end of the biblical account of Job's trials, we notice that he not only becomes a more humble man, but the horizon of his knowledge of God is broadened. In chapter 42, Job addressed God with words of resignation: "Surely I spoke of things I did not understand, things too wonderful for me to know… My ears had heard of you but now my eyes have seen you. Therefore I despise myself and repent in dust and ashes" (Job 42:3–6). God chooses to mature His people *through* trials, not in the absence of them. Our suffering, when placed in the hands of God, produces a heightened quality of character in us (Romans 5:3). It's the goal of God for our lives as well as Job's.

Lastly, the crowning comfort of the book of Job is that even though God may seem distant in our struggles and far off in our trials, *there is a point in our suffering when God comes near to us in our pain in a personal spiritual way.* From chapter 38 onward in the book of Job, we see that truth vividly unfold. In fact, throughout the Bible, its authors testify to God's heart and special concern for those who suffer. "The LORD is close to the broken-hearted and saves those who are crushed in spirit. A righteous man may have many troubles, but the LORD delivers him from them all" (Psalm 34:18–19). God will never allow the reality of suffering to mask His glory in the lives of those who are surrendered to Him and His sovereign purposes.

A first century martyr, a believer named Felicitus, was going to be thrown to the lions, but she was pregnant and the laws were such that a woman with child was not to be executed. This law pained Felicitus, for she wanted desperately to die alongside a group of other Christians whom she had befriended. As her story goes, she was prayed for "in a torrent of grief," for Felicitus still had a month to go in her pregnancy.

Amazingly, following the prayer on her behalf, she immediately went into intense labour pains and ended up having the baby (a girl). Before the birth, one of the Roman guards approached Felicitus and began to mock her. "You suffer so much now but what will you do when you are tossed to the beasts? Little did you think of them when you refused to sacrifice" (to Caesar). To this Felicitus responded, "What I am suffering now…I suffer by myself. But there's another who will suffer inside for me, just as I shall be suffering for Him."[78]

No one suffered like Jesus; He is the only One who is fully qualified to tell us, "I know how you feel." We worship not just an exalted Saviour but a God who knows our limitations and weaknesses as humans. Jesus is ever-present *to* us and ever powerful *in* us. Because of the Holy Spirit's presence in our lives, we have a relationship with Jesus that is not only personal but transformational as well. Aside from our Lord having the final say as to which trials and tribulations are allowed to encroach upon our lives, He also determines how our present sufferings will be used to make us into the perfect person, "like God," when we see Him in Heaven. (see 1 John 3).

The devil, for as long as he's been able to, has been manufacturing lies that counteract God's work in our lives and in the world. The evil one's half-baked sermon on human suffering is an example of that; it's an intentionally unfinished script that doesn't fully account for the truth (God's side of the story). It's a message that's powerfully believable because it plays not only on the most potent human trigger, *our emotions*, but on biblical ignorance as well.

Satan is very adept at twisting and warping both the interpretation and application of Scripture and even better at not making that fact evident. God's archenemy doesn't want people getting any idea that there's a bigger (eternal) picture to our suffering or having any biblical light shed on the subject. Rather, the devil desires to keep the world addicted to its God-angst, especially in terms of its idealistic expectations of Him within the reality of its suffering. But the Bible's timeless declaration is that God will never leave or forsake His people in their suffering, the silver underlining of the message of Job! This is His certain promise to me as well as His certain promise to you. In the spiritual light of this truth, then, "Let us hold unswervingly to the hope we profess, for he who promised is faithful" (Hebrews 10:23). We must hang on to our good God at all times, and in all circumstances, even if our suffering seemingly contains no apparent value, spiritual or otherwise, and even if we feel we don't deserve to suffer.

The great ship *Titanic* was supposed to be the "crown jewel" of all ocean liners. Whether the 1912 disaster was due primarily to human error, faulty building, or even arrogance (or all the above), over a thousand people lost their lives in the sub-zero waters of the Atlantic. What's my point? It's that we don't always suffer in this world because *we* have done something to warrant it; others may have done something that has inadvertently hurt us. We will suffer at times in life for the carelessness of others and for sinful actions and evil deeds that are not our own. Perhaps it's the hardest pill of reality we have to swallow in this life.

The world always notices how we, as God's people, respond to personal hardship, no matter where it comes from or what form it takes; it's a powerful "outreach" sermon! These are spiritual principles Job had to learn, and no doubt they're principles we must relearn throughout our spiritual lives.

The "saving grace" within our current earthly context of suffering is that Heaven holds the promise of solving and healing all that is wrong and unjust in this world. However, it's where we stand with Jesus Christ now that will determine how and where we will spend eternity. We don't *have* to suffer beyond this life!

CHAPTER 22

TERMINAL LIFERS AND THOSE ON THE EDGE OF ETERNITY

> Some people say all the world's a stage
> Where each one plays a part in life;
> While others proclaim that life is quite real,
> Its joys, its battles, its strife.
> Some say it's a joke, we should laugh it along,
> Should smile at the knocks and stings;
> Whatever is true just take this from me,
> There's a gate at the end of things.
> Don't try to kid yourself with the thought,
> You can do as you please all the while;
> Don't think you can kick the poor fellow who's down,
> While you climb to the top of the pile.
> Don't go back on your pal, just because he won't know,
> Oh, in his eyes you may be a king;
> Some day he will see you just as you are,
> At the gate at the end of things
> *Anonymous*

Many non-religious people either believe in or hope for the existence of Heaven. Though many believe in an eternal destiny after physical death, some are unwilling to attach a name to it; they only believe with "all their heart" that there is an "afterlife." This is a good thing!

It's hard to accept that there isn't another realm beyond this earthly one with all its inexplicable complexities. It seems too unintelligent a prospect to me that our human existence ends when our heart beats its very last. If plants get to grow back leaves and flowers and resurface into life and existence, why shouldn't human beings (the crown of God's creation) experience a new, resurrected life?

Perhaps what's even harder to fathom, looking at this life through the lens of a biblical worldview, is how some people can live this life without a regard for the one that is to come. People arrogantly postulate that there is "nothing" after we die and that we will simply "cease to exist"; anything to the contrary, they say, is the stuff of pixie dust and fairy tales!

Thankfully, we cross paths with people who hold to a vastly different view of death and the afterlife (eternity). Such people have inspired me by their readiness to embrace death and dying simply because they know whom they've entrusted their souls to, whom they've believed in, and as a result know where they're going after they pass (see 2 Timothy 1:12).

As a pastor I've made a good number of visits over the years to people suffering from terminal diseases. They can be the most heart-wrenching of visits as much as they can be the easiest. One elderly fellow from my first church was dying of cancer, and everyone knew it. All the physical signs pointed to the fact that he needed a modern-day miracle if he was to remain with us much longer. The gentleman, at that point, was in some discomfort and was lying in a borrowed hospital bed in his living room. When it came time to pray over him, he asked me to not pray for healing but rather to petition the Lord and simply ask that His will be done.

Being new to the pastoral role at the time, I found myself more uptight and anxious than the frail man I was ministering to! In fact, I was blown away that afternoon at the obvious peace that cradled this man and the shining confidence he exuded at the prospect of his eternal destiny and the ultimate healing that awaited him there. This faithful saint had decided long before, to follow Jesus, and it was a decision that was soon going to pay off for him in eternity. Although he was terminally ill, he was also eternally saved, by his faith in Christ, making him a terminal "lifer." Although he was dying, he was ready to die! The man, though wasting away, was headed towards the fullness of his reward for trusting Jesus, when God would breathe the breath of Heaven into him upon his arrival at the gates of glory. My elderly friend would live again, very soon; this time, it would be forever! When his eyes would shut in this life for good, they'd open for good in the one to come.

Encounters like these tend to do more for the minister than they do for the one being ministered *to*. It's a profound joy to see how believers' faith in the Saviour can pay spiritual dividends for them when they're within hours of realizing their own mortality. The presence of faith and the confidence we have in the Object of our faith (Jesus Christ) can speak volumes to people around us, even if many of them do not personally hold to a religious belief.

Even manufacturers of technology acknowledge the reality of religious faith and worship in the lives of people today. By now most of us are familiar with Bible programs on computers and with hearing sermons delivered from an iPad! We now even have a software application available to us entitled "40 Days: Lent Observance Tracker," which is designed to help Christians monitor their progress in the spiritual disciplines during the season of Lent (from Ash Wednesday to Easter).

While various strands of the Church give the impression they're leaving cultural relevance in their thick traditional dust, our increasingly computerized world has not left worshippers behind! As advancements in technology are made, it is still accepted that people in the new millennium are connected to a belief in God and to the practice of that belief.

Scripture indeed speaks of a connection between God and His people in terms of a spiritual contract threaded from the beginnings of biblical history to the present day, known as a covenant. It was God's promise to one man, Abraham, that would bring about the establishment of a great people (the Israelites) from whom the saving Messiah of God's people, the Christ of the Church, would come. It was God's plan that through Abraham "all peoples on earth" would be "blessed" (Genesis 12:1–3).

God then made a promise to the people (Israel) He formed out of His servant Abraham in the form of another covenant. In scholarly circles, this covenant has been called the three-part, or "tripartite," formula of promise: *"I* will be your God, you will be My people, and I shall dwell in the midst of you." The ceremonial manner in which a covenant was sealed in Old Testament times in the Near Eastern world was to "cut" a covenant. This involved taking an animal, sacrificing it by cutting it in half, and then separating the two halves so as to make an aisle in the middle. The parties of the covenant would then walk between the pieces. They would be saying in effect, "If I fail to obey this agreement I am making, may what happened to these animals happen to me!"

In Genesis 15, God asked Abraham to prepare a sacrifice for Him. The patriarch in the making was to set up the animals for a covenant-cutting ceremony in order to "seal the deal" God had made with him. However, two interesting things happened.

First, with the sun setting Abraham went into a deep sleep and was surrounded with a "dreadful darkness." Why would this happen? God was ready to put His name on the dotted line of the covenant contract, and Abraham was snoring! The patriarch settled in for a good old-fashioned desert-style siesta, seemingly unaware of what the Lord was up to.

Secondly, only God, as a torch, is mentioned as moving through the aisle between the sacrificed animals. What brought about this turn of events? Why would God not follow the cultural custom set up for covenant making where all parties involved in the making of a covenant were to go through the aisle?

The message is this: by the Lord alone going through the aisle, He was obligating Himself *only* in the keeping of the covenant; *Abraham was off the hook!* We can see it this way: when Israel was enslaved in Egypt and helpless to ditch Pharaoh, it was God who raised Moses up to lead them out; by doing so, the Lord, exclusively preserved the covenant He made with His people. "God heard their groaning and he remembered his covenant" (Exodus 2:24). The Hebrew word for "remember," *zekar*, means "to call to mind and to act." In the Old Testament, the Lord's memory equaled His actions. So when God remembered His promises (His covenant He made with His people), He acted in some way to keep it and preserve it.

As a nation, Israel's survival depended on the Lord's sovereign might to come through for them in the clutch. This really is a picture of our need for Jesus and what He did for us on the Cross at Calvary. When we were still dead in our sins and powerless to have them forgiven, God sent His one and only Son. God remembered our fallen state and acted on our behalf, through Jesus Christ, to save our souls. Before we were even born, Jesus remembered us on the Cross and willingly endured the horror of crucifixion for each one of us as if we were the only sinful person who had ever lived.

However, we who are disciples of Christ must now *remember* what He did for us! Jesus, at the "Last Supper" (the Passover meal), instructed His original followers as He broke bread and took of the cup, "Do this in remembrance of me" (Luke 22:19). As the Body of Christ, we are to call to mind what Jesus did for us at Calvary and respond by righteous living.

Our penchant for sinning is way too powerful a spiritual monster for us to contain without God's grace and mercy. We needed Jesus to act on the Cross for us, and He did. And as we pray for the spiritual power and strength we need to live as God would have us, He will give us that too! We will possess an indescribable peace that will never leave us. It may meet up with hardship and battle with our sense of unworthiness, but it will never escape us. Jesus made it possible for us to become not only a peace-filled people but *terminal lifers,* people who are saved for eternity and saved to become *like* Him and to live *for* Him in this present life. This is precisely why in the Greek-speaking world of the first century the gospel was referred to as the *evangelion,* "good news."

The early believers could see the difference between those who were living for the world (for the bidding of Rome) and those who lived for the Saviour. With God, it's all about grace, not merit. As Israel could do nothing to salvage themselves from Egypt, so we too can do nothing to gain salvation and eternal life without faith in the One who sacrificially died for our sin. In short, salvation is a gracious gift given to us by our Father in Heaven, but its acceptance comes through our faith in Christ and Him alone (see Ephesians 2:8–9).

Only God went through the aisle between the sacrificed animals in order to show Abraham (and us today, as Abraham's "seed") that He alone is the true covenant-keeper, which is also true of the new covenant He's made with us through our faith in His Son, Jesus. He will not forsake it! It's a unilateral covenant in that it is not reliant upon what *we* do to keep our end of the deal; God obligates Himself solely (see 2 Timothy 2:13). In our current sin-marred state, we are spiritually incapable of being 100 percent faithful to God; we slip up, mess up, blow up, and sometimes we even fall away. At the same time, if we have placed our faith in Christ as our Saviour, we are saved once for all; we cannot lose our inheritance of Heaven that is given to us through the Holy Spirit's indwelling of our lives (see Ephesians 1:13–14).

The Bible's teaching of the believers' eternal security is one of the most underappreciated and under-preached doctrines in Christian theology. Just as salvation cannot be *taken* from us once it's been bestowed upon us, we cannot "earn" it either. We cannot achieve something (salvation) that only God can achieve on our behalf.

Someone wise once said, "Confidence is the feeling you have just before you understand the situation." For the apostle Paul, confidence was definitely the feeling he had just before he knew the situation about his life and why he needed Jesus. Paul realized that one cannot mix or confuse the merit of man with the gift of God (salvation). When writing to the church in Philippi Paul admitted that he had reason for putting confidence in his "flesh" and listed his spiritual resume as a Pharisee, which once in his eyes would have automatically recommended him to God (see Philippians 3:4–6). Paul thought the righteous portfolio of his spiritual life was pretty impressive—that is, until it got tipped over, emptied out, and trampled underfoot on a Damascan highway, where it was eventually relegated to "rubbish" status (see Philippians 3:8).

If we learn anything from Paul's "Saul" days, it's that we can think we're on the right spiritual road, with the right spiritual credentials in tow, and be sincerely mistaken. Like Paul found out, we must cease from trying to credit our own way into acceptance from God, a useless exercise on the level of trying to walk on spiritual waters without the faith needed to stay afloat. It'll never work. Our good works, achievements, and "high ideals" cannot bring us into a saving relationship with Christ or pay for our sin. They'll be tipped over, emptied out, and trampled underfoot by Jesus on the day of judgment. Only by a sincere faith in the worthy and wonderful Lamb of God, Jesus Christ, whose righteousness will cover us on judgment day, can we seal the spiritual deal of gaining everlasting life!

God already acted in history on our behalf. God's Son walked through the "aisle" all the way to the Cross, and now all we have to do is remember this, accept it as being done for us, and act accordingly (ask Christ into our lives). The spiritual transaction that took place on Calvary's Cross, where Jesus secured our forgiveness as well as our entrance into heavenly eternity, is activated in our lives when we individually, by faith, choose to live in the light of that event. "And he died for all, that those who live should no longer live for themselves but for him who died for them and was raised again" (2 Corinthians 5:15).

We read a passage like this and struggle to apply it to those who were responsible for putting the life-snuffing spikes into our Lord's hands and feet. How could anyone at Golgotha on the day of the Crucifixion possibly end up living for Jesus, who hung before everyone, so seemingly defeated and utterly dead?

This is where the Cross changes everything! The Gospels show that even those who were at the base of Jesus' crossbeam were affected by *how* He died, not by the fact *that* He died. One of them was a Roman centurion, who likely drove a nail into God's flesh yet ended up admitting that Jesus was indeed "the Son of God" (Matthew 27:54). Who knows if the contrite and awestruck Roman official who gazed upon our expired Lord eventually ended up worshipping Him? Was he one of the five hundred in the Gospels who saw Jesus after He was resurrected, the One who now is seated at the Father's right hand and who intercedes for His Church?

Jesus not only continues to minister to His disciples; He continues to pursue the spiritually lost. He seeks the unlikely as well as the ungodly. He reveals Himself to unbelief and sheds light on the darkness of doubt, just as He did at Calvary's cross. The humbled centurion who laid the Saviour on His Cross possibly went from being a dead man (prior to Jesus' crucifixion) to being a terminal lifer (after our Lord's last breath). The Cross changes everything, *especially lives!*

Jesus, at present, is going to places that the Church often won't and is impressing hearts that the Church often overlooks or gives up on. Perhaps He's speaking to yours right now.

If you haven't already, why not go ahead and ask Jesus into your heart and life today as your Lord and personal Saviour? When we come to Jesus by faith, we are asking Him to take over the ship of our life and to take it into a safe harbour, where all the aimlessness of life that's kept us spiritually tossed about is calmed. Don't waste another day of the covenant God cut a long time ago, and start enjoying the redeemed life Jesus died to give you! Don't nurse your own cross of objection, like one of the criminals on crosses beside Jesus did who mocked our Lord's suffering and refused to believe in Him.

Not one religious or spiritual teacher in history has ever had the ability to cross the gulf between us and holy God: Buddha couldn't (nor did he claim to); Confucius couldn't either. Not one religious leader today, no matter how godly and dynamic he or she may appear, can cross the great chasm that exists between us and God either. However, God made that bridge, *Jesus Christ,* and each one of us will be held eternally accountable for the decision we make about Him prior to our physical deaths.

Candy Chang, a New Orleans-based artist, started a public art project in February 2011 that became somewhat of a phenomenon for how it caught fire worldwide. Chang painted the side of a derelict home in her community with the unfinished sentence "Before I die I want to ___" "Anonymous people wrote down their hopes and secrets. They were funny, sad and poignant."[79]

We could finish Candy Chang's cliff-hanger statement with any manner of wording, though the Bible says the best way anyone could round out such a sentence would be by expressing their commitment to Christ "before" they die! The Bible doesn't guarantee any of us "tomorrow," only the opportunity today to repent of our sin and to choose Christ. Before we die (and it could be tomorrow), we need a Saviour, Jesus Christ.

It doesn't matter what we've done in life, for better or for worse; what matters is what Jesus has already done for you and me: *He paid the debt we owed God for our sin, in full!* When Jesus looked at the Cross He saw all the heartache of centuries upon centuries as well as millennia of destructive sin, meaning He also looked through that Cross and saw you and me! Someone doubting what the Bible says about the deity of the historical Jesus doesn't change one iota of its truth. Remember, the truth of God's Word doesn't depend on my believing it; it won't fall if I don't think it's true, but I cannot be saved unless I believe it is true.

All we have to solve in our hearts (and that, with God's help) is the question "Is Jesus alive today?" "Of course He's alive," God's people cry. Jesus Christ was born over two thousand years ago, and His death and resurrection remain history's most important events. Great men and women have come along in this world, but as great as they were, after their deaths they have never been heard from. They're gone!

Jesus, however, after His resurrection was physically seen, touched, and heard from; the Scriptures speak of that reality. Jesus is not only great, and He not only came back from the dead; the Bible tells us that He will also return to this earth. We may have grown up in the Church and attended Sunday school; we may have been baptized and have sung in a church choir. But guess what? Without spiritual regeneration (that is, without our becoming spiritually alive, born again) through faith in Christ, all our history with the Church amounts to is just *religious activity.*

Still, our largely unchurched and increasingly secularized society retains its yearning to reach for the eternal. Blaise Pascal, the sixteenth century French mathematician and Catholic philosopher, rightly said, "There is a God shaped vacuum in the heart of every man which cannot be filled by any created thing, but only by God, the Creator, made known through Jesus." The Bible puts it another way, in that God "has also set eternity in the hearts of men" (Ecclesiastes 3:11). This is why we will never be totally satisfied with the things we have in this world.

I once heard a very successful and award-decorated professional athlete confess during an interview that there had to be "more to this life" than what he had already experienced and accomplished. If you feel empty in your heart today, if you feel you have everything but nothing brings you joy and something's missing; if you long for peace, meaning, and hope, not only in this life but beyond this life, then congratulations: you are experiencing what most of the book of Ecclesiastes in the Old Testament talks about. You have something in common with King Solomon, who, the Bible says, was the wisest man ever to live!

Solomon knew there was more to this life than simply living well, more to it than dining from fine china, sleeping on satin sheets, and enjoying all the success, fame, and material things of life. The king discovered that ultimately only a life that is genuinely centred upon God can give the kind of meaning, purpose, and satisfaction our hearts covet. With God, being satisfied in this lifetime, no matter who we are, is immensely possible. We can have both piety and pleasure; we can serve God and enjoy Him now and reign forever with Him later.

This is what God has been getting at through His Son Jesus Christ for over two thousand years. Jesus, as He entered Jerusalem to die, knew that many people were going to miss the spiritual rescue that was placed right before their very eyes through His ministry and the Kingdom He was offering them. Scripture says the people "did not recognize the time of God's coming" (Luke 19:44). Many today remain blind to what God is doing in the world through Jesus and persist in that way. As fallen human beings, we can't measure our goodness or worthiness for Heaven by what we do or don't do, by what we resist or by whatever positive impact we may have on others. Yes, we are far worse off as sinners than we may have thought. We inherited a terminal spiritual sickness at the point of birth called a *sin nature;* we didn't know it, didn't ask for it, don't really want it, but we've got it for life.

Despite humans' best intentions, they cannot appease that part of them that is privately dark and inwardly crooked. There's a lack of assurance that chronic failures and mistakes (sin) have been absolved. People try to do "good" and the "right" things because the image of God is imprinted within each of us. Yet as hard as we try, we'll never be spiritually fit enough to punch our own tickets to Heaven, and we'll never have true peace unless we accept Christ's sacrifice for us.

Sadly, many people think they're ultimately in control of their own destinies, like in William Henley's poem "Invictus," which says he is the master of his fate, the captain of his soul. Every one of us, if left to our own spiritual devices without the saving ministry of Jesus Christ regenerating us, would be hopelessly doomed for an eternity without God. We were not born wise; we were born fallen and made to look to God for guidance *and* salvation. Someone once asked Socrates why there was such unhappiness in the world. The philosopher responded, "The problem with man is that he takes himself wherever he goes."

Therefore, it is the height of human wisdom to trust in Christ as our Saviour. And if it is God's wisdom for us to accept His Son Jesus, then it is clearly the height of human folly to reject Him. We all have our life stories, many of which are laden with pain and even sad and tragic events. Perhaps the final chapters of our lives are not looking too promising either. Whatever the case, the "greatest story ever told," which tells of the greatest Life ever lived, has the power to edit the final chapter of our lives by ensuring a secure and glorious new beginning in eternity.

When Jesus was arrested and falsely accused, a criminal was also sentenced to die. In his final moments he asked for mercy. Had he asked it from the people, it would have been denied. Had he asked it of his victims, they would have laughed in his face. But he didn't turn to them to seek grace. He turned instead to the bloodied One who hung on a cross next to his and pleaded, "Jesus, remember me when you come into your kingdom." The remorseful criminal was assured by the Lord, "Today you will be with me in paradise" (Luke 23:42–43).

The Bible says God loves us more than we could ever imagine; the Cross proves it, the Spirit witnesses to it, and Jesus died to demonstrate it. If only those of us who are Christians and who make up the Church of Jesus Christ could live more in the light of that truth and communicate it with more clarity in these darkening times!

It's a crazy, hair-pulling life of faith we're called to as Christians. We live in a world where success is often interpreted in terms of one's income, friendships, or status and influence in life. The child of God, on the other hand, is called to a life of faith, service, and prayer, with often no outwardly measurable benefits for the unbeliever to see. Indeed, "worldly" people can make us believers feel as though we have our heavenly heads in the clouds and need to get with reality.

Why does the world so often seem to be happier and more prosperous than us in the Church? No wonder Jesus said that the wide road in life that leads away from God (the highway to Hell) is so packed with human traffic! (See Matthew 7:13–14.) In some ways, it's far easier to live life on that freeway. If we feel that this life is all there is and we have no fear of divine accountability or eternal judgment after our physical deaths, what have we got to lose? This I do know: everything I'm not (for my eternal sake) and everything I am (for His glory) Jesus accomplished in my life, and if He can do it in my life, He can do it in yours!

Only God knows for certain where the spiritual temperature, effectiveness, and fervency of His Church is in terms of its witness to the world in these endtimes and last days. That being said, the state of the Church of Jesus Christ around the world today is undeniably wobbly and hurting and in dire need of being revived and renewed. Lukewarm churches don't sit well with Jesus; they actually turn His stomach (see Revelation 3:16).

Yet God sustains His Church throughout all generations; He remembers His covenant with us and acts on our behalf. He spiritually resuscitates His people so that they may rise up yet again and carry out the purpose of their existence on this earth. There's a necessary righteousness at hand: a continuously revived and renewed Church! We're still entirely necessary as Christians in the world today!

We're on the edge of eternity, and God's people must awaken anew to their capacity to transform the hemispheres, instead of wasting precious servant time in the Saharas of their complacency. An end-time world is dying for the Church to be revived from its spiritual swoon.

I end with the cry of Paul's pastor heart as he addressed the Christians in Rome. "The hour has come for you to wake up from your slumber, because our salvation is nearer now than when we first believed" (Romans 13:11).

Endnotes

1. John Stott, quoted in Chip Ingram, R12 video series, Living on the Edge: Dare to Experience True Spirituality, 2011 Video series/11:09–11:57/session one: God's Dream for Your Life.
2. "Revival in the Church," Biblical Discernment Ministries, paraphrased or excerpted directly from three 1991 issues of *The Trinity Review*, May/June, July/August, and September/October, "Ought the Church to Pray for Revival?" and "The Great Revival of Religion, 1740–1745" (Pts. 1 & 2), http://www.rapidnet.com/~jbeard/bdm/Psychology/revival.htm.
3. Oliver Price, *Revival Insights,* vol. 3, no. 4.
4. Leon M. Lederman and Dick Teresi, *The God Particle: If the Universe is the Answer, What is the Question?* (Houghton Mifflin Company, 1993), 22.
5. D. Goodmanson, "The Future Dying Church," Goodmanson, http://www.goodmanson.com/church/the-future-dying-church.
6. "One in Seven (14%) Global Citizens Believe End of the World is Coming in Their Lifetime," Ipsos, May 1, 2012, http://www.ipsos-na.com/news-polls/pressrelease.aspx?id=5610.
7. Michelle Boorstein, "One in Five Americans Reports No Religious Affiliation, Study Says," *The Washington Post*, Oct. 9, 2012, http://articles.washingtonpost.com/2012-10-09/local/35500483_1_politics-affiliation-protestants.
8. Goodmanson, "The Future Dying Church."
9. "6 Reasons Young People Leave Church" (adapted from a list by David Kinnaman in *You Lost Me: Why Young Christians are Leaving Church…and Rethinking Faith*), *Leadership Journal* (Winter) 2012: 11.

10. Leonard Sweet, *The Gospel According to Starbucks: Living with a Grande Passion* (Random House, 2008).
11. Sweet, *The Gospel,* back cover.
12. "Americans Say Serving the Needy Is Christianity's Biggest Contribution to Society," Barna Group, October 25, 2010, www.barna.org/faith-spirituality/440-americans-describe-christianity-contributions.
13. David Jeremiah, *I Never Thought I'd See the Day* (FaithWords, 2011), 201.
14. John Algeo and Adele Algeo, "Among the New Words," *American Speech* 63 (4), 1988: 235–236.
15. Gordon MacDonald, "To Serve and Protect," *Leadership Journal* (fall 2012): 37.
16. "Barna Group's Biblical Literacy Survey: We Have Work to Do," Churchmouse Campanologist, churchmousec.wordpress.com/2010/04/14/barna-groups-biblical-literacy-survey.
17. Ibid.
18. Ibid.
19. Ibid.
20. David Jeremiah, *Turning Point Magazine & Devotional*, Sept. 22, 2011, 33.
21. Steven J. Lawson, "Preach the Word," *Tabletalk Magazine*, 01/01/2010, http://www.ligonier.org/learn/articles/preach-word/.
22. Chuck Swindoll, *Hand Me Another Brick: How Effective Leaders Motivate Themselves And Others* (Nashville: W. Publishing Group), 106.
23. Lawson, "Preach the Word."
24. Charles Spurgeon, in Lawson, "Preach the Word."
25. Pewforum.org, wgcl-tv.
26. F.L. Cross and E.A. Livingstone, eds., *Dictionary of the Christian Church* (Peabody Massachusetts: Hendrickson Publishers, 2007), 1394.
27. Martyn Lloyd-Jones, quoted in "Revival in the Church."
28. "The Red Bull Gospel," *Leadership Journal* (Spring 2011): 34, quoted in David Kinnaman, *UnChristian: What a New Generation Really Thinks about Christianity…and Why It Matters* (Grand Rapids, MI: Baker Books, 2007).
29. Elias J. Bickerman, "The Name of Christians," *The Harvard Theological Review* 42 (April 1949) (2): 145, 147.
30. Oswald J. Smith, *The Revival We Need* (Fairfax, Va.: Xulon Press, 2003), 15.
31. Buckskin Brady, *Stories and Sermons* (Toronto: William Briggs, 1905), quoted in Dr. David Jeremiah, *Turning Point Magazine*, January 2012.
32. Lorna Dueck, "Liberia Proves the Power of Prayer," *The Globe & Mail*, May 30, 2012.

33. John Stott, *Commentary—Sermon on the Mount* (Downers Grove, Illinois: IVP, 1978), 143–144.
34. John F. Devries, *Why Pray? Forty Days from Words to Relationship*, (Mission India, 2005), 54–55.
35. Marshall Shelley, "Spiritual War Vets," *Leadership Journal*, 5.
36. Athanasius, *The Life of St. Antony* trans. Robert T. Meyer (New York: Newman Press), 22.
37. Devries, *Why Pray?*, 54.
38. Stephen Chapman (2007), "Broken," on *This Moment* (CD), Sparrow Records/Peach Hill Songs, 2007/2008.
39. *Dictionary of the Christian Church* (Cross & Livingstone), 889.
40. Phillip Yancey, *Reaching for the Invisible God: What Can We Expect to Find?* (Grand Rapids, Michigan: Zondervan, 2000), 19.
41. Ronald J. Sider, "The Scandal of the Evangelical Church," Christianity Today (2005), http://www3.dbu.edu/jeanhumphreys/SocialPsych/evangelicalmind.htm.
42. Dietrich Bonhoeffer, Common Quote, *http://commonquote.com/quote/157446/erwin-w-lutzer/when-god-calls-a-man-he-bids-him-come-and-die-wrote-dietrich-bonhoeffer-during-the-dark-days-whe*.
43. Os Guinness, *The Call: Finding and Fulfilling the Central Purpose Of Your Life* (Nashville, Tenn.: W Publishing Group, 2003).
44. "Humility," *Our Daily Bread*, http://www.sermonillustrations.com/a-z/h/humility.htm.
45. "Humility," *Today in the Word*, August 5, 1993, *www.sermonillustrations.com/a-z/h/humility.htm*.
46. Dave Harvey, quoted in "The Glory Drive," *Leadership Journal* (Fall 2010), 22, 23.
47. David Gibbons, NewSong Church.
48. Andrew Murray, *The Wisdom of Andrew Murray*, vol. 1 (Radford, VA: Wilder Publications, 2008), 30.
49. Dave Jackson and Neta Jackson, *Hero Tales—A Family Treasure of True Stories From the Lives of Christian Heroes* (Bethany House), 42.
50. Craig Groeschel, "Human Hands, God's Fingerprints," *Leadership Journal* (Spring 2011), 39.
51. Owen Strachen and Douglas Sweeney, *Jonathan Edwards on the Good Life*, The Essential Edwards Collection (Chicago: Moody Publications, 2010), 34, 35.

52. Charles Stanley, *The Blessings of Brokenness: Why God Allows Us to Go Through Hard Times* (Zondervan), 34, 35.
53. J. D. Considine, review of *Wrecking Ball*, *Globe and Mail*, Saturday, March 10, 2012.
54. Pat Buchanan, *Suicide of a Superpower* (New York: St. Martin's Press, 2011), back cover.
55. Gretta Vosper, quoted in Brian Bethune, "The Jesus Problem," *Maclean's* 121, no. 12, Mar 31, 2008.
56. Steve Turner, *The Gospel According to the Beatles* (Louisville, Kent: Westminster John Knox Press, 2006), 178.
57. Ibid.
58. Ibid.
59. James Fuller, quoted in Charles Colson, *Life Sentence*, 33.
60. Alain de Botton, quoted in John Allemang, "An Atheist's Defence of Religion," *Globe and Mail*, March 3, 2012.
61. D. Martyn Lloyd-Jones, *Studies in the Sermon on the Mount* (Grand Rapids, Michigan: Eerdmans, 1959–60), 28.
62. Heather Mallick, "A Snapshot of Modern Screaming Times," *Toronto Star*, Feb. 22, 2012.
63. Lisa I. Iezzoni, Sowmya R. Rao, Catherine M. DesRoches, Christine Vogeli, and Eric G. Campbell, "Survey Shows That at Least Some Physicians Are Not Always Open or Honest with Patients," *Health Affairs Journal* 31, no. 2 (Feb 2012), 383–391.
64. Paul Tuns, "MP Urges Parliamentary Debate on Status of Unborn," *The Interim: Canada's Life and Family Newspaper* 29, no. 12, Feb. 2012, 3.
65. Guiseppe Valiante, "Religion Course to Remain Mandatory in Quebec," *Toronto Sun*, Feb 17, 2012.
66. "Bishop Condemns Gay Marriage in Speech to US Bishops," AFP, March 9, 2012.
67. Michael Spencer, "The Coming Evangelical Collapse," *Christian Science Monitor*, March 10, 2009.
68. (Stephen Adams, "Pope's Good Friday Message Warns of a Drift into a 'Desert of Godlessness'" *Telegraph*, April 10/09.
69. "How Many North Americans Attend Religious Services (and How Many Lie about Going)?" Ontario Consultants on Religious Tolerance, http://www.religioustolerance.org/rel_rate.htm.

70. Jennifer A. Marshall and Sarah Torre, "Why Do Feminists Ignore Gendercide?" The Heritage Foundation, January 18, 2012, http://www.heritage.org/research/commentary/2012/01/why-do-feminists-ignore-gendercide.
71. Billy Graham, *Just As I Am: The Autobiography of Billy Graham* (Harper Collins, 1997), 399.
72. Devries, *Why Pray?*, 106–107.
73. Amy Dempsey, "This Young Rapping Priest Is 'Fightin' the Beast,'" *Toronto Star*, July 22, 2011.
74. Joni Eareckson Tada, quoted in Randy Alcorn, *Heaven*.
75. Joseph Stowell, *Eternity* (Chicago: Moody Press, 1995), 58–59.
76. Jonathan Edwards, "The Christian Pilgrim," Bible Bulletin Board's Jonathan Edwards Collection, http://www.biblebb.com/files/edwards/pilgrim.htm.
77. Charles Spurgeon, "Quotes—Suffering and Joy," http://www.suffering.net/suffjoy.htm.
78. The Martyrdom of Saints Perpetua and Felicitas," in Herbert Musurillo, ed., *The Acts of the Christian Martyrs* (Oxford: Clarendon, 1972).
79. Katie Daubs, "'Before I Die' Wall Coming to Toronto This Summer," *Toronto Star*, May 24, 2012.

MY FANATICAL, Regrettable TOUR OF MINISTRY

*Memoirs of a Zealous Leader
who Trips Landmines in the Church*

Ron Mahler

Also by Ron Mahler

My Fanatical, Regrettable Tour of Ministry:
Memoirs of a Zealous Leader who Trips Landmines in the Church
www.myfanaticalbook.wordpress.com

ISBN: 9781770693050

All Ron Mahler really aspired to be in life was an artist. The stars seemed to be aligned that way. However, after struggling to come to faith in Christ, God threw a heavenly curveball his way and issued him a swift call to the ministry. That's when his struggles really began. Not only were the first four churches he served in loaded with trials of many kinds, but he ended up leaving three of them consecutively, under duress. It was a long road back, each of the three ministries having had their own unique brand of disaster written all over them. Ron's greatest challenge went deeper than his need to forgive those who had hurt him; he also had to forgive himself.

Consequently, Ron became a man caught between the ministry he was absolutely enamoured with and the tribulations inherent in church life. In addition, he experienced numerous onslaughts from the enemy of his soul, as Hell's devilish schemes sought to weaken his spiritual resolve and put an end to his ministry. Through all the twists and turns, second-guessing, and painful learning curves, you are invited to take a ride on his fanatical, regrettable tour of ministry. Although the final destination is unknown, its path has led to some surprising—even rewarding—events and discoveries!

"Ron Mahler's sensitive heart and appropriate vulnerability are compelling. He is a pastor who has been through the battle and lived to tell about it. Good reminders for all of us who are striving to remain faithful as we march forward in a tour of duty for the Kingdom of God."

~ Rev. Laird Crump

About the Author

Ron Mahler is a multifaceted person, as seen by his roles and abilities as a pastor, author, educator, and visual artist. Before his entrance into pastoral ministry, Ron worked for seven years as a graphic artist in various commercial advertising businesses and agencies. He came to know Christ as his Saviour when he was in his mid-twenties and has since served in various churches throughout central and southern Ontario in the areas of youth ministry and senior pastoral ministry. He is ordained in the Associated Gospel Churches of Canada and is currently pastoring Highland Lakes Community Church in Minden, Ontario, a position he's held since 2007.

Some of his volunteer positions include stints as a board member with the Haliburton Pregnancy Crisis Centre, as an outreach worker with Youth Unlimited (formerly Youth for Christ), and as a pastoral-team minister to seniors. Ron continues to enjoy the tender aspects of shepherding God's people, growing the Church as well as hobnobbing with those distant from Christ. He has a passion to learn God's Word and to present it in a clear and effective fashion.

As a budding author (this being his second published book), Ron enjoys creating pictorial vignettes with his words and sees his writing as a natural extension of his overall ministry and life as a grateful but "in process" follower of Jesus Christ.

Aside from ministry, Ron is an avid reader of biographies, world history, and politics, enjoys drawing as a relaxing pastime and watching sports, and has a deep affinity for music.